Instructor's Manual

to accompany Bade and Parkin

FOUNDATIONS *of* MICROECONOMICS

Carol Dole
State University of West Georgia

Mark Rush
University of Florida

Addison
Wesley

Boston San Francisco New York
London Toronto Sydney Tokyo Singapore Madrid
Mexico City Munich Paris Cape Town Hong Kong Montreal

Instructor's Manual to accompany Bade and Parkin,
Foundations of Microeconomics

Copyright © 2002 Pearson Education, Inc.

ISBN: 0-201-74603-4
1 2 3 4 5 6 7 8 9 10-VG-0504030201

Table of Contents

IV

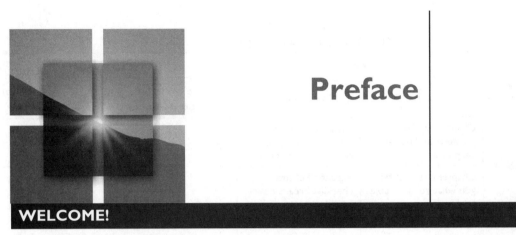

WELCOME!

■ Using Your Teaching Resources

Our teaching resources are the most comprehensive, carefully developed, and accurate materials ever made available. We recognize and respect the desire of every instructor to use a text and package that contains no nasty surprises—that is safe. This text and package are safe! Foundations Interactive, the Study Guide, the Web site, and the Test Banks all key off the Checkpoints in the textbook. The entire package has a tight integrity. We are the authors of Foundations Interactive and the Web site and we've played a key role in reviewing and revising the Study Guide, Instructor's Manual, and Test Banks to ensure that every element of the package achieves the level of coherence that students and teachers need.

Your *Foundations of Microeconomics* teaching package consists of:
- Textbook
- Instructor's Manual
- Three Test Banks
- PowerPoint Resources
- Instructor's Resource Disk with Computerized Test Banks
- eFoundations

And eFoundations consists of the same tools that your students have:
- eText—the complete text online with animated figures and audio
- eStudy Guide—the complete Study Guide online, with links to the textbook
- Foundations Interactive—Java tutorial and quiz software (also available on CD)
- Web quiz—Multiple choice and true or false questions with instant feedback and links to rect page in eText

plus
- PowerPoint lecture notes
- Classroom experiments resources
- Online "Consult the Authors"

The grid on the next page shows you how the students tools interact to provide them , learning environment.

Your Students' Learning Tools at a Glance

Activity	Print		eFoundations	
	Textbook	**Study Guide**	**eText and eStudy Guide**	**Foundations Interactive**
Getting into a chapter	Chapter opener—previews and places chapter in context	Chapter in perspective—a short summary of the core material		
	Chapter checklist tells you what you'll be able to do when you've completed the chapter	Expanded chapter checklist breaks down your tasks into detailed bite-size pieces		
Learning the material	Explanations; matched tables and figures; figures with numbered captions		eText has exactly the same content as the print textbook plus: dynamic figures and audio explanations	Fast track summarizes each topic. Textbook figures are interactive in Action and animated in Demo
	Key terms defined in text and in margin	Key terms list for review	Key terms with hyperlinks to definitions, examples, and related terms in both tools	
	Chapter checkpoint • Key points • Key terms list			
Practice makes perfect	Checkpoints • Practice problem • Exercise • Solution to practice problem	Checkpoints • Practice problem • Additional practice problem • Expanded solution to practice problem	eText practice problems, exercises and solutions; eStudy Guide additional practice problems and expanded solutions	Interactive Quiz with explanations. Five question types: • Fill in the blanks • True or False • Multiple Choice • Numeric • Complete the graph
	Chapter checkpoint exercises		Chapter checkpoint exercises with links to external sites	
Self Test		Self Test: • Fill in the blanks • True or False • Multiple Choice • Complete the graph • Short Answers and Numeric	eStudy Guide has the same content as the print Study Guide. Online quizzes with hyperlinks to eText for further review: • True or False • Multiple Choice	Self Test version of Interactive Quiz: • Fill in the blanks • True or False • Multiple Choice • Numeric • Complete the graph
Enrichment, Critical Thinking, and Applications	Eye On ... • The U.S. economy • The global economy • The past		Spreadsheets with data for most of the data graphs in the textbook	
	Economics in the News		Economics in the News hyperlinks to news article and related sites	

■ Checklist and Checkpoints: The Glue that Holds Your Tools Together

Each chapter of the textbook opens with a Chapter Checklist that tells your students what they'll be able to do when they've completed the chapter. The number of tasks varies from two to five and most often is three or four. Each part of a chapter, in the textbook, Study Guide, and eFoundations is linked directly to a Checklist item to enable your students to know exactly what they're studying and how it will enable them to accomplish their learning objective. Each part of a chapter in the textbook ends with a Checkpoint—a page that offers a Practice Problem to test understanding of the key ideas of the part, a worked and illustrated solution to the Practice Problem, and a further (parallel) Exercise.

Our Checkpoints enable students to review material when it's fresh in their minds. We suggest that you encourage your students to work the Checkpoints and if possible, devote some class time to working sample problems with them. The Test Banks are organized by Checkpoints so that you can match your tests and exam papers closely to the parts of each chapter that you've emphasized most.

■ Three Test Banks

Three separate Test Banks, with more than 11,000 questions, provide multiple-choice, true-false, numerical, fill-in-the-blank, short-answer, and essay questions. Mark Rush reviewed and edited questions from six dedicated principles instructors to form one of the most comprehensive testing systems on the market. Our questions authors are Seemi Ahmad (Dutchess Community College), Susan Bartlett (University of South Florida), Jack Chambless (Valencia Community College), Paul Harris (Camden County Community College), William Mosher (Assumption College), and Terry Sutton (Southeast Missouri State University). The same questions authors also wrote questions for the Study Guide and Web site to ensure consistency across the entire package.

■ PowerPoint Resources

Working closely with Charles Pflanz (Scottsdale Community College), we have played a large role in creating the PowerPoint tools. Every figure and table—every single one, even those used in Checkpoint questions and solutions—is included in the PowerPoint lecture notes, many of them animated so that you can build them gradually in the classroom. We have created these figures and determined the optimal build sequence for those that are animated. They are all produced with the same degree of clarity and precision as the figures in the text.

For instructors who prefer to make up their own PowerPoint notes and who want larger versions of the figures, we've also provided a set of full-screen figures that can be used alone or be cut and pasted into the instructor's own PowerPoint presentations. We've also provided special PowerPoint shows on the Economics in the News features of each chapter. These materials might be used to motivate students when starting a new topic, or used as a wrap-up and summary.

■ eFoundations

You have all of the same resources as the students, but with the addition of PowerPoint lecture notes, classroom experiments resources, and an online "Consult the Authors" feature — ask your questions and make your suggestions via e-mail, and one of us will answer you within 24 hours!

■ Overhead Transparencies

Full-color overhead transparencies of *all* figures from the text will improve the clarity of your lectures. They are available to qualified adopters of the text (contact your Addison-Wesley sales representative).

■ Instructor's Resource Disk with Computerized Test Banks

This CD-ROM contains Computerized Test Bank files, Instructor's Manual and Test Bank files in Microsoft Word, and PowerPoint files. All three Test Banks are available in Test Generator Software (TestGen-EQ with QuizMaster-EQ). Fully networkable, it is available for Windows and Macintosh. TestGenEQ's graphical interface enables instructors to view, edit, and add questions; transfer questions to tests; and print different forms of tests. Tests can be formatted by varying fonts and styles, margins, and headers and footers, as in any word-processing document. Search and sort features let the instructor quickly locate questions and arrange them in a preferred order. QuizMaster-EQ, working with your school's computer network, automatically grades the exams, stores the results on disk, and allows the instructor to view or print a variety of reports.

■ FastFax Testing

FastFax Testing is designed for instructors who do not have access to a computer or an assistant who can help prepare tests for students. Simply choose from a large pool of questions in the print testbank and include custom headers, if you like. Fill out the test information sheet that lists instructor-selected questions and test preferences that describe how the test should be generated. You may even request multiple forms of a test and receive answer keys for each one.

Turnaround time is usually 48 hours or less and test pages can be mailed or faxed back to you by the date the test is needed. FastFax Testing is fast, reliable, and free to qualified adopters of this text.

■ CourseCompass

CourseCompass is a dynamic, interactive online course management tool powered by BlackBoard. CourseCompass provides flexible tools and rich content resources that enable instructors to easily and effectively customize online course materials to suit their needs. Now instructors can track and analyze student performance on an array of Internet activities. Please contact your Addison-Wesley representative for more details.

■ Instructor's Tell us What Works for *You*

Please tell us the tools that you find most helpful. And tell us what you think we can improve. You can email us at robin@econ100.com or michael.parkin@uwo.ca, or use "Consult the Authors" on your Foundations Web site.

Robin Bade
Michael Parkin
Ontario, Canada
June, 2001

HOW TO USE YOUR INSTRUCTOR'S MANUAL

Robin and Michael just presented an overview of the tools available to help you with your course. I, personally, think that the existence of these tools is incredibly good timing because at no time in history has teaching your students the principles of economics been either more challenging or more important. Similar to all the resources available to qualified adopters of *Foundations of Microeconomics*, this Instructor's Manual is designed to assist you in your teaching, so I want to spend some time discussing it in more detail. You might be teaching principles for the first time or you might be an experienced teacher. In either case, I hope that you will find material of value in this manual.

■ Chapter Outline

Leading off is a brief outline of the chapter. This section is designed to help you as you rush off to class and need one last glance to discover whether a certain topic is covered in the chapter. The outline is brief, highlighting the major headings in the book. The extended lecture outline, presented later in this Instructor's Manual, is a more complete outline.

■ Chapter Roadmap

The Chapter Roadmap has three concise sections that let you see how the current chapter fits into the flow of the material. One section covers "Where We Are;" another, "Where We've Been;" and the third, "Where We're Going." This section also is designed as a lecture helper, so if you need to determine how the chapter fits into the scheme of things, turn here for an overview.

■ Class Time Needed

This short section can be extremely valuable, particularly if during the term, you run out of time before you run out of material! The Class Time Needed section presents a careful estimate of how many 50-minute lectures are usually needed to cover a particular chapter. These times are just estimates, but they are the results of consideration by several experienced instructors. There is *nothing* wrong with using more time or less time, depending on your interests and the class's participation. But, if you wonder how other instructors allocate the material in the text between their lectures, these estimates can be useful.

■ Extended Lecture Outline

The Extended Lecture Outline is a detailed outline of the chapter. It has been carefully aligned with the textbook so that the order of presentation is the same as the in textbook and all the topics in the chapter are included in this outline. Terms in bold face indicate glossary terms from the textbook, which are newly introduced to the students in the chapter. This section is designed to help you prepare your lecture notes, but you might also use it as your lecture notes when you don't have time to put together your own notes. This section might well be the most valuable section in the Instructor's Manual when you are pressed for time and need to gather notes for your lecture!

■ Lecture Launchers

We know how fascinating and relevant economics is. But nowadays, with so many other events competing for our students' attention, it is much too easy to lose out to the latest craze. This section helps overcome this problem by presenting class-tested methods devised by award-winning teachers that will stimulate your students' interests. As you glance through this section, you will see a variety of suggestions that cover a wide range of teaching styles. Select those that work best for your style. And if you have suggestions for other lecture launchers, please drop me a note at the e-mail address at the end of this preface—I am collecting additional suggestions for the next edition.

■ Landmines

As instructors, we know that certain topics are difficult for students. Determining the best way to present difficult material can be a hard and tricky task. This section is designed to ease this problem by using the insights of talented and experienced instructors. The Landmines section identifies areas that students have found difficult to grasp and then presents suggestions about how to overcome these problems. In my career, I have taught over 30,000 students but I have found this section to be incredibly valuable and, even as I worked on this Instructors' Manual, I adopted the suggestions into my class. So check out the suggestions and, once again, if you have further tips please e-mail me.

■ Answers to Checkpoint Exercises

One of the remarkable pedagogical tools of the textbook is its use of Checkpoints to divide the material into smaller, coherent chunks. At the end of each major section of the textbook, a Checkpoint presents a Practice Problem and solution (with a more complete solution available in the Study Guide). Also the Checkpoint includes an additional, unanswered parallel Exercise. If you assign these Exercises to help encourage your students to try active learning, you will especially appreciate the next section of the Instructor's Manual. It has complete answers to these Exercises. You can use these answers to help you in grading assigned Exercises or you can copy the answers and distribute them to your students.

■ Answers to Chapter Checkpoint Exercises

The Chapter Checkpoint in the textbook includes Exercises that you can assign to help ensure that your students grasp the material in the chapter. The answers to these Exercises are in the next section of the Instructor's Manual. Similar to the answers to the Checkpoint Exercises above, you can either use the answers in the Instructor's Manual to help you grade your students' work or copy them and distribute them to your students.

■ Additional Exercises for Assignment

The next section of the Instructor's Manual presents some additional discussion questions. Some of these questions are suitable for essay exams; others, more open-ended, are probably best used for classroom discussion. All of them are designed to make your students think and use the material you have been teaching them. In addition, the Instructor's Manual has suggested answers. Use these answers as help when grading your students' work or copy them and distribute them to your students.

■ Answers to Economics in the News

To help your students truly understand the role that economics plays in shaping the world in which we live, each chapter of the textbook has an "Economics in the News" item. This section highlights a news story and then poses several questions for the students to answer. This section of the Instructor's Manual presents answers that you might find helpful. Use them yourself or hand them out to your students; it's your choice! But keep this section of the textbook in mind because it truly is a valuable addition to help you illustrate the usefulness of economics.

■ "Eyes On"

A wonderful feature of the textbook is the material presented in each chapter called "Eyes on." "Eye on the U.S. Economy" describes the U.S. economy today or in the recent past. "Eye on the Global Economy" and "Eye on the Past" help the student to place current and recent U.S. experience in a global and historical perspective. This material is fascinating and lends itself to further discussion or assignments. This last section in the Instructor's Manual presents suggestions about how you can use these "Eyes on" for either class discussion or assignments. In either case, check out our suggestions because they can deeply enrich your course!

ACKNOWLEDGMENTS

In a very real sense, teaching the principles of economics is "work in progress." As new insights are uncovered, as new knowledge is developed, the principles of economics is always changing and evolving. You can be assured that Bade-Parkin's *Foundations of Microeconomics* will likewise always change and evolve to remain the best book available for you and your students' use. So it is with a great deal of pleasure that we acknowledge people who have helped create this Instructor's Manual.

First, Carol Dole of State University of West Georgia is the author of the Instructor's Manual. Aside from formatting, correcting typos, writing this introduction, and trying to take more credit for this book than I deserve, my contribution was meager. Carol's e-mails with her chapters were always eagerly anticipated because I know she would have some joke or comment as well as a chapter of exceptionally high quality.

I know that Carol and I both want to thank Meredith Gertz at Addison Wesley. I don't think Carol needed it as much as I, but Meredith sure kept me on track! She was invariably chipper and constantly checking to be sure that we had everything we needed. She also made sure that I was well aware of the schedule!

Addison Wesley assembled a talented team of instructors who checked the accuracy of the entire set of supplements. Although some did not look explicitly at the Instructor's Manual, often comments they made on the Study Guide or Test Banks, helped improve the Instructor's Manual. So I want to thank all of them:

- Carol Conrad, Cerro Coso Community College
- Marie Duggan, Keene State University
- Steven Hickerson, Mankato State University
- Douglas Kinnear, Colorado State University

- Tony Lima, California State University, at Hayward (Tony, I believe you were one of my instructors when I was an undergraduate—thanks for helping excite me about economics!)
- Michael Milligan, Front Range Community College
- Barbara Ross-Pfeiffer, Kapiolani Community College

I admit that at first I had my doubts about how many people were involved, but the number of errors they found and the improvements they created are beyond count. I soon learned that without their help, this Instructors' Manual would be a much inferior product.

Equally valuable are Kevin Beckwith and Sheryl Nelson. Both Kevin and Sheryl proofread, copy-edited, corrected, and made improvements throughout the process of writing the Instructors' Manual. I constantly and consistently learned from them, not only about my errors but also about writing. Thanks to both of you. I will use what I learned from you and your comments forever.

Even with all this help, it is undoubtedly the case that there remains substantial room for improvement in this Instructor's Manual. Indeed, any corrections, suggestions, or comments that you might have would be greatly appreciated. Moreover, it is extremely easy for you to bring these to my attention. You can either write me, at the address below, or e-mail me at rush@dale.cba.ufl.edu. Either way, I would greatly appreciate hearing from you. In a better world, there would be some compensation offered for suggestions, corrections, and comments you might make. Unfortunately, this is not that better world! But I can promise that I'll acknowledge your help in future editions of this book.

Mark Rush
Economics Department
University of Florida
Gainesville, Florida 32611
June, 2001

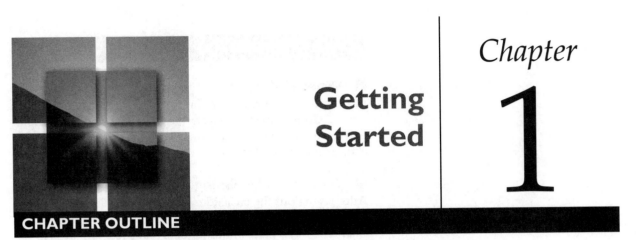

Getting Started

Chapter 1

CHAPTER ROADMAP

■ Where We Are

In Chapter 1, we review definitions and address questions that economics helps answer. We also discuss how people make rational choices and preview the fact that these are the choices that individuals and firms make everyday.

■ Where We're Going

After laying out the basic ideas of economics in this chapter, and some basic facts about the economy in the next, in Chapter 3 we'll start building tools and models that help us understand how the economy works. These tools and models, such as the production possibilities frontier and the supply and demand framework, provide valuable insight into how the economy that we operate in each day works.

IN THE CLASSROOM

■ Class Time Needed

You can complete this chapter in one session. As simple as the ideas might seem to you, covering the definitions and questions are important to your students, especially in the context of current events and topics. Thus do not shortchange this chapter.

An estimate of the time per checkpoint is:

- 1.1 Definitions and Questions—15 to 20 minutes
- 1.2 Economics: A Social Science—15 to minutes
- 1.3 The Economic Way of Thinking—15 to 20 minutes
- 1.4 Explain Why Economics Is Worth Studying—5 to 10 minutes

■ Extended Lecture Outline

1.1 Definitions and Questions

A. The study of economics occurs as a result of unlimited human wants and limited productive resources.
  1. **Scarcity** is the inability to satisfy all our wants.
     a. Rich and poor individuals, as well as societies face scarcity.
     b. Scarcity forces us to choose among various alternatives.
  2. **Economics** is a social science that studies the choices made by individuals, firms, governments, and societies as they cope with scarcity.

B. **Microeconomics**

Microeconomics is one of the two main branches of economics. It focuses on the choices individual firms and people make, how the choices interact with each other, and the influence the government exerts on these choices.

C. **Macroeconomics**

The other branch of economic study focuses on the aggregate effects of how people, firms, and the government interact and participate in the national and global arenas.

D. Microeconomic Questions

   1. Microeconomic decisions answer three questions.

      a. *What* goods and services get produced and in what quantity?

      b. *How* are goods and services produced?

      c. *For whom* are goods and services produced?

1.2 Economics: A Social Science

A. Economics (like all sciences) takes a scientific approach in examining the choices that people and societies make and how the economic world works.

   1. Economists must distinguish between two kinds of statements.

      a. *Positive statements* assert what is. These statements can be proven true or false.

      b. *Normative statements* suggest what ought to be. These statements are value judgments or opinions and hence cannot be tested.

B. Observing and Measuring

   1. Economists collect data to help in model building and forming theories.

C. Model Building

   1. After collecting data, economists build **economic models** that describe the economic world.

      a. Models simplify the real world and focus on the pertinent economic questions.

D. Testing

   1. Models are repeatedly tested and those that produce results that agree with reality are the basis for economic theories. An **economic theory** is a generalization that summarizes what we understand about economic choices and the economic performance of industries and nations.

E. Unscrambling Cause and Effect

   1. Finding answers to economic questions can be difficult because it is difficult to disentangle cause and effect.

      a. *Ceteris paribus* is a Latin phrase meaning "other things held equal." To effectively test economic models, economists isolate the factor of interest and allow it to change, holding constant all other factors.

      b. Actually being able to hold economic factors constant is easier said than done. To deal with this problem, economists test models in three ways.

      c. Natural experiments occur in the ordinary course of economic affairs.

      d. Statistical investigations look for **correlations,** when two variables move in a predictable and related way. But, the *post hoc fallacy,* assuming (in error) that just because one event occurs before another event that the first event causes the second event, may occur.

      e. **Economic experiments** use real people in decision-making situations in order to conduct experiments to test economic models.

1.3 The Economic Way of Thinking

A. Rational Choice

A **rational choice** occurs when a person uses the available resources to most effectively satisfy the wants of the person making the choice. A rational choice compares costs and benefits.

B. Cost: What You Must Give Up

The **cost** of a choice is measured by what must be given up. The best alternative that must be forgone when making a choice is the **opportunity cost** of that choice.

1. A **sunk cost** is a previously incurred cost and is irrelevant in making a choice.

C. Benefit: Gain Measured By What You Are Willing To Give Up

The **benefit** of a choice is the pleasure the choice brings and is measured by what is willing to be given up.

D. On the Margin

When making a choice, a person makes the decision on the **margin** by comparing the relevant alternatives systematically and incrementally.

1. The **marginal cost** is the cost of a one-unit increase in activity. It measures the cost of what you must give up to get one additional unit of something.
2. The **marginal benefit** is the benefit gained when you get one additional unit of something.
3. When making a **rational choice,** the decision maker compares the marginal cost of the choice to the marginal benefit of the choice. If the marginal benefit is greater than the marginal cost, the choice is made. If the marginal cost is greater than the marginal benefit, the choice is not made.

E. Responding to Incentives

People are motivated by **incentives** to take a particular action. The incentive, or inducement, can be a benefit or a cost.

1.4 Why Economics Is Worth Studying

A. Understanding

By studying economics you can understand the economic ideas that are pervasive in your life.

B. Expanded Career Opportunities

People that excel at identifying and solving problems earn high incomes. Studying economics encourages you to engage in these activities and to learn useful economic concepts.

C. The Costs of Studying Economics

The costs of studying economics include the forgone knowledge that could be gained by taking another class or enjoying leisure time.

D. Benefits Versus Costs

Deciding whether you should study economics means you must compare *your* costs and benefits of taking an economics course.

 **Lecture Launchers**

1. You can take a low-tech or high-tech approach to launch your students into the economic world. Collect newspaper headlines and make copies or overhead transparencies or produce video clips of current economic events such as a collection of a firm's decision to hire or layoff workers or change output levels; mergers of energy, airlines, telecom or financial firms; the deregulation of the energy industry; consumers booking low-price trip tickets

over the Internet, and so forth. If you've got video capabilities, you can spend a few days taping news reports and editing salient headlines. In either case, highlight how each of these stories is "microeconomics in action" and explicitly point out to the students that what they will study this semester will give them insight into how these decisions are made.

2. Remind students that, whether they realize it or not, they have been using economics since they were very young. Some students enter the class thinking that economics will all be new, confusing material. But you can tell them otherwise! Robert Siegler, a professor of psychology at Carnegie-Mellon University in a recent issue of *Click Magazine*, said that studies show that children between the ages of three to five understand that buyers must pay sellers money and that having money is a good thing. They also understand that as demand for a good increases, sales and prices increase. By ages seven to nine, children begin to understand that sellers try to make as much money as possible. (You can always joke that Bill Gates was shown to exhibit this knowledge at age two!) At this age, a child also understands that competition among firms reduces their ability to set higher prices (again, you can joke about Bill Gates or your favorite monopolist).

■ Land Mines

1. There are not many difficult points to cover in the first chapter. The biggest mistake you can make is *not* conveying to your students that economics is easy to understand and can be fun to learn and use. You can even do an example of the Prisoner's Dilemma the first day in class. Use the situation of prisoners being interrogated rather than duopolists attempting to collude because students already have the tools to understand the prisoners' choices, but are unaware of the implications for cartels and collusion. Once you grab their attention with this example, tell them that soon enough they will use some of the same sort of reasoning to understand some important antitrust issues. Let them know that you've got a semester's worth of the same stuff up your sleeve!

ANSWERS TO CHECKPOINT EXERCISES

■ CHECKPOINT 1.1: Definitions and Questions

1. The only way to avoid making choices is to either limit our wants or conjure up unlimited resources. Because neither is possible, we will always face choices.

2. The answer to this question will depend on what was in the news during recent days in your community.

3. The answer to this question will depend on what your local paper(s) have put in their headlines in recent days.

■ CHECKPOINT 1.2: Economics: A Social Science

1a. Positive statement.

1b. Positive and normative. We can collect data on how free trade affects developing countries, but what "harm" is depends on a person's values.

1c. Normative statement.

2. The only totally positive statement is the first, so it is the one that the students should describe how to test. In order to test whether more scholarships for poor people reduces poverty, we can collect data over a period of years. The series of data would be the amount of money provided to students from impoverished homes. Another series of data would show the poverty level over the same years. We could test whether an increase in the amount of scholarship money led to a decrease in the poverty level.

■ CHECKPOINT 1.3: The Economic Way of Thinking

1. Even though Bill Gates is very rich, he still experiences scarcity. For example, he might prefer to spend time with his family, but his job requires him to attend a business meeting. He must choose one or the other way to spend time.

   As long as Gates compares the benefits and costs of his donations and made the best decision he could, his donations are the result of rational decisions.

   Gates perhaps responded to incentives when making these donations. For example, by making these donations, he reduced his taxable income. And, by making these donations, he gained favorable publicity that might have carried over to his battle against the Justice Department.

2. Steve Fossett's opportunity cost of the adventure was whatever was the next best alternative forgone by going on the trip. Fossett received benefits from making the trip, because otherwise he would not have taken it. The benefits could have been the satisfaction of meeting the challenge or the knowledge he gained.

   Anheuser-Busch, like any decision maker, considers the benefits and costs when making a decision. By deciding to offer a $1 million prize, the company must believe that the benefits, likely in the form of favorable publicity, outweigh the costs.

3. The costs of Tony's choice of any extra course might include the extra tuition as well as less time available for studying for other courses, for work, or for leisure. The benefits include increased knowledge of history. An incentive to taking the course might be the promise of a better job or perhaps the fact that he is required to take a history class as a general education requirement in order to graduate.

■ CHECKPOINT 1.4: Why Economics Is Worth Studying

4. Mick Jagger quit his economic course because the opportunity cost of attending was greater than the benefit of attending class. Some of the benefits would have been the knowledge gained from lectures or meeting other people interested in economics.

ANSWERS TO CHAPTER CHECKPOINT EXERCISES

1a. The news item is a (positive) microeconomic issue.

1b. The news item is a (normative) microeconomic issue.

1c. The news item is a (positive) macroeconomic issue.

1d. The news item is a (positive) microeconomic issue.

2a. Stores using computers for inventory records today answers the "How" question.

2b. Deciding whether to produce a cleaner environment or more space exploration answers the "What" question.

2c. Deciding whether a better public transit system gets built answers a "What" question. Using a higher gas tax (versus issuing bonds) to finance the system answers the "How" question.

3a. This news item is a normative statement.

3b. This news item is a positive statement.

3c. This news item is a positive statement.

4. Economists unscramble cause and effect by building economic models that isolate the influence of one factor at a time. In the real world, it is impossible to do this. Economists can use three approaches to address the problem of simultaneously occurring events: natural experiments, statistical investigations and economic experiments.

   Economists use the *ceteris paribus* assumption in order to show the cause and effect relationship among various factors. By changing only one factor at a time, economists get a clearer picture of how that factor impacts others.

5. Correlation is the tendency for the values of two variables to move in a predictable pattern. Economists can investigate correlations using three approaches:

   Natural experiments. These are naturally occurring situations in the course of economic events. They produce one factor of interest that is different and other things that are similar and therefore provide a "natural" setting for testing cause and effect.

   Statistical investigations. Economists collect data to see whether two events are related.

   Economic experiments. Economists study people and the decisions they make while facing real-life situations.

6. The *post hoc* fallacy is the mistake that the timing of events determines cause and effect. By assuming that an event that occurs first causes a subsequent event solely because one occurs prior to the other, you commit the *post hoc* fallacy. Though your students' examples will differ, a *post hoc* fallacy occurs when students assume that you presented an economics lecture because a group of them gathered together in the room. Another *post hoc* fallacy occurs when a student claims that it rained today simply because he or she forget his or her umbrella.

7. Pam, Pru and Pat's decision to go to Hawaii is rational. All three of them considered the cost and benefit of various New Year's plans. All three were at least willing to go to Hawaii while Pam and Pat were unwilling to go skiing and Pru was unwilling to go on a cruise. The opportunity cost of the trip for Pam is a cruise; for Pru, it is skiing; and for Pat, it is a cruise. The benefit each receives is the pleasure, the relaxation, excitement, or knowledge gained from the trip.

8. The school should consider the costs and benefits of enrolling more students. The costs might include crowded classrooms, more classrooms needed, traffic congestion, or more dormitory space. The benefits might include increasing revenues, meeting the region's educational needs, or recruiting better students. In order to use scarce resources efficiently and make a rational choice, the school will make its decision at the margin.

9a. We assume both kinds of vineyards are making rational decisions. Each vineyard looks at the cost of using workers versus using machines. Additionally, each vineyard considers the benefits of using workers versus machines. Some vineyards use more machines because they conclude that the benefits outweigh the costs. These vineyards might be relatively flat, making it simple and inexpensive to use machines. Other vineyards, with different benefits and costs, choose to use more workers because the benefits of using workers outweigh the costs. These vineyards might be quite mountainous, making it difficult and very expensive to use machines.

9b. Vineyards, in order to make a rational decision, look at the margin when choosing how to pick grapes. Vineyards probably look at incentives when answering the "How" question. An incentive might be a tax credit for developing new technology or a tax credit for hiring additional workers. In addition, an important incentive will be the cost of the machine(s) versus the cost of the workers.

ADDITIONAL EXERCISES FOR ASSIGNMENT

■ Questions

1. Propose three variables for which it is important to hold one of them constant in order to investigate the cause and effect relationship between the other two.

2. Survey your classmates (or, a selected group of your classmates) regarding the opportunity cost of attending class. If you get different answers (which you will!), explain how these differences affect choices.

■ Answers

1. One potential answer is diet, weight, and exercise. If you are interested in how changing your diet affects your weight, you must hold exercise constant. Otherwise you cannot determine whether changes in your diet or changes in how much you exercise affect your weight. If you are interested

in how the amount of exercise affects your weight, you should hold your caloric intake the same.

2. You will get a variety of answers. This fact shows that everyone faces different opportunity costs and, subsequently, people make different choices. Indeed, students for whom the (perceived) opportunity cost is too high simply were not present to participate in your survey! And, even though people have different opportunity costs, nonetheless, their choices remain rational.

USING EYE ON THE PAST

■ Adam Smith and the Birth of Economics as a Modern Social Science

Adam Smith used the example of pin making in his opus, *The Wealth of Nations*, to explain an elementary but profound point. It was an example to which people of his time could easily relate. Before introducing Smith's work, you might want to consider asking students how productive one worker could be if he or she were the only one on duty at a local McDonald's restaurant at noon time. The likely response is not very productive. The person would have to cook the burgers, fry the french fries, prepare the drinks, ring up the orders, and clean the dining area. Students will not find it difficult to accept that few customers will be served at this restaurant under these conditions! Next, ask how productivity would change if a second worker were asked to help out at this same restaurant and at the same time. Students will answer that the restaurant will be able to serve more customers. You can point out the gains from division of labor and specialization that are likely to be enjoyed by hiring the second worker. Explain that we owe this simple logic to the founding father of modern day economics, Adam Smith.

Appendix:
Making and
Using Graphs

Chapter

1

APPENDIX ROADMAP

■ Where We Are

The appendix to Chapter 1 is a thorough review of the mathematics and geometry used in the text. There are no economic concepts introduced in it, only mathematical concepts.

■ Where We've Been

Chapter 1 introduced economics and presented information about important topics in the course.

■ Where We're Going

Chapter 2 continues presenting background economic material. Chapter 2 uses none of the mathematical concepts covered in this appendix. However, starting in Chapter 3, which presents the production possibilities frontier, most of the remaining chapters use various parts of the review in this appendix.

IN THE CLASSROOM

■ Class Time Needed

Depending on your class's mathematical sophistication, you might decide to make this appendix optional. If you cover it in class, you should spend no more than one class session on it. The topics most likely to need review are the different types of relationships (positive and negative), covered in the second section, and slope, covered in the third section. Ideally, you will present these sections together and spend no more than 30 minutes on them.

■ Extended Lecture Outline

A.1 Making and Using Graphs

  A. Basic Idea

    A graph presents a quantity as a distance. The vertical axis is the *y*-axis and horizontal axis is the *x*-axis.

  B. Interpreting Data Graphs

    1. **Scatter Diagram** graphs the value of one variable against the value of another variable.

    2. **Time-Series Graph** measures time along the *x*-axis and the variable of interest along the *y*-axis.

      a. A time-series graph shows whether a variable has a **trend,** the general tendency for the variable to rise or fall.

    3. **Cross-Section Graph** shows the values of an economic variable for different groups in a population at a point in time.

  C. Interpreting Graphs Used in Economic Models

    1. When two variables move in the same direction, they have a **positive,** or **direct relationship,** as illustrated in Figure A1.1.

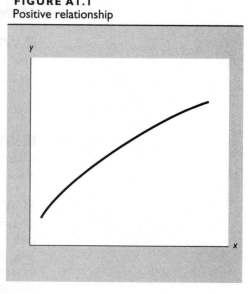

FIGURE A1.1
Positive relationship

2. When two variables move in opposite directions, they have a **negative,** or **inverse relationship,** as illustrated in Figure A1.2.
3. Some variables have a relationship in which there is a maximum or a minimum point.
4. When two variables are independent of each other, their graph is either a vertical or a horizontal line.

D. The Slope of a Relationship

The **slope** of a relationship equals the change in the value of the variable measured on the y-axis divided by the change in the variable measured on the x-axis or, in terms of a formula, the slope equals $\Delta x / \Delta y$.

1. The slope of a straight line is the same at any point on the line.
2. The slope of a curved line at a point equals the slope of a straight line drawn so that it touches the curved line at only that point. In Figure A1.3, the slope of the curve at point A equals the slope of the straight line that is touching the curve at only point A.

E. Relationships Among More Than Two Variables

To graph a relationship among more than two variables, we must use the *ceteris paribus* assumption.

1. *Ceteris paribus* is the Latin phrase meaning "other things remaining the same."
2. To graph a relationship between more than two variables, select the two of interest and then draw the relationship between the two, assuming that none of the other variables changes (that is, use the *ceteris paribus* assumption). When one of the other variables changes, the entire graphed relationship shifts.

FIGURE A1.2
Negative relationship

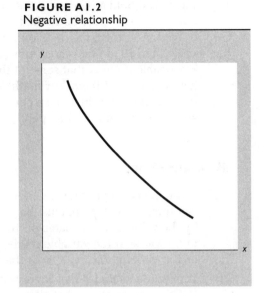

FIGURE A1.3
Slope of a curved line

■ Lecture Launchers

1. An unfortunate number of students are "afraid" of mathematics. Do your best to convince them that math is a tool for them to use and, as such, it is their friend. Start by telling the students that you are aware of the fact that many of them might have a fear of math, a math phobia. Then tell them that you do not understand why they would have this fear because math is just a tool and no one should have a phobia about a tool. Point out that a pen is a tool and that no one you know has a pen phobia. Take a pen and ask your students what it would be like to have a pen phobia. Start your hand shak-

ing as you hold a pen and point out all the ways that pens can scare people: Some of them must be clicked to work, while others must have a cap removed. And then, the decision must be made as to which end of the pen to use! All in all, a pen is a *lot* more complicated than a pencil (?!) and so it is reasonable to think that some of the students will be deathly afraid of pens, just like some of them fear math! Then conclude by explaining to your students that math is just like a pen: It's a tool to use and there is no more reason to fear it than to fear a pen!

■ Land Mines

1. Slope is a concept that sometimes confuses students. In particular, students can think that slope equals the value of the variable on the y-axis divided by the value of the variable on the x-axis, that is, y/x, rather than the *change* in the value of the variable on the y-axis divided by the *change* in the value of the variable on the x-axis, that is, $\Delta y/\Delta x$. Be sure to clearly explain to your students that slopes involve changes.

    One way to stress that slopes are computed using changes is to present the slope as equal to the "rise over the run," a saying common among carpenters (and, I presume, others). By expressing the slope as rise over the run, the students are reminded that they must calculate the "rise," that is, the change in the value of the variable measured on the y-axis, as well as the "run," the change in the value of the variable measured on the x-axis.

ANSWERS TO APPENDIX CHECKPOINT EXERCISES

1. Figure A1.4 illustrates the relationship of the data from the spreadsheet between expenditure on recorded music and expenditure on Internet services. The relationship is positive, especially in the last six observations, which are those farthest to the right.

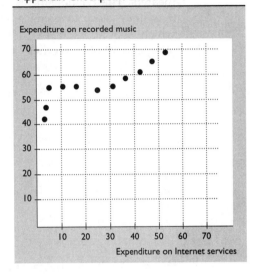

FIGURE A1.4
Appendix Checkpoint Exercise 1

2. Figure A1.5 illustrates the relationship of the data from the spreadsheet between expenditure on Internet services and expenditure on movies in theaters. The relationship is weakly positive, but it is quite close to being a vertical relationship, which would indicate that the variables are independent of each other.

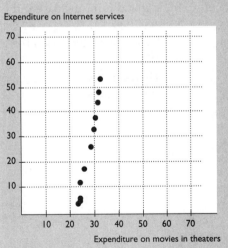

FIGURE A1.5
Appendix Checkpoint Exercise 2

3. Figure A1.6 illustrates the relationship of the data from the spreadsheet between expenditure on recorded music and expenditure on movies in theaters. The relationship is weakly positive, but it is quite close to being a vertical relationship, which would indicate that the variables are independent of each other.

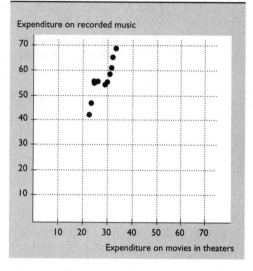

FIGURE A1.6
Appendix Checkpoint Exercise 3

4. Figure A1.7 illustrates the time series of expenditure on Internet services using the data from the spreadsheet.
4a. Expenditure was the highest in 2002.
4b. Expenditure was the lowest in 1992.
4c. Expenditure increased the most between 1996 and 1997.
4d. Expenditure increased the least between 1992 and 1993.

There is a definite upward trend in the expenditures.

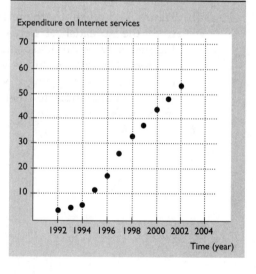

FIGURE A1.7
Appendix Checkpoint Exercise 4

5. Figure A1.8 illustrates the time series of expenditure on recorded music using the data from the spreadsheet.

5a. Expenditure was the highest in 2002.

5b. Expenditure was the lowest in 1992.

5c. Expenditure increased the most between 1993 and 1994.

5d. Expenditure increased the least between 1996 and 1997 when it decreased.

    There is a general upward trend in the expenditures

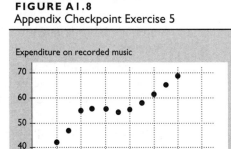

FIGURE A1.8
Appendix Checkpoint Exercise 5

6. Figure A1.9 illustrates the relationship between x and y.

6a. The relationship is positive: When x increases, y also increases.

6b. The slope of the relationship equals the change in y divided by the change in x. When x equals 2, y equals 4 and when x equals 4, y equals 16. Thus the change in y equals 12 and the change in x equals 2, so the slope equals $12/2 = 6$.

6c. The slope of the relationship increases as x increases.

6d. An economic relationship that might have this shape could be the number of computers a small shop produces in an hour and the total cost of producing the computers. The number of computers would be measured along the x-axis and the cost along the y-axis. Your students' answers, however, will differ from the one given and you must be the judge of their correctness.

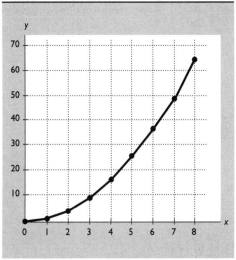

FIGURE A1.9
Appendix Checkpoint Exercise 6

7. Figure A1.10 illustrates the relationship between x and y.

7a. The relationship is negative: When x increases, y decreases.

7b. The slope of the relationship equals the change in y divided by the change in x. When x equals 2, y equals 39 and when x equals 4, y equals 22. Thus the change in y equals -17 and the change in x equals 2, so the slope equals $-17/2 = -8.5$.

7c. The slope of the relationship decreases in magnitude (the relationship becomes less steep) as x increases.

7d. An economic relationship that might have this shape could be the number of computers a small business would buy in a year. The x-axis would measure the number of computers purchased and the y-axis would be the price. Your students' answers, however, will differ from the one given and you must be the judge of their correctness.

8a. Figure A1.11 illustrates the relationship between the price and the number of rides holding constant the temperature. Note that there are three relationships, one for each temperature.

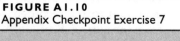

FIGURE A1.10
Appendix Checkpoint Exercise 7

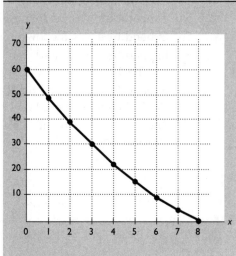

FIGURE A1.11
Appendix Checkpoint Exercise 8a

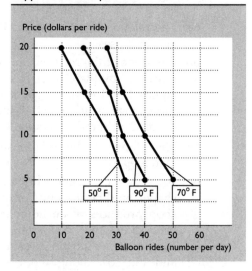

8b. Figure A1.12 illustrates the relationship between the number of rides and the temperature, holding constant the price. Note that there are four relationships, one for each price.

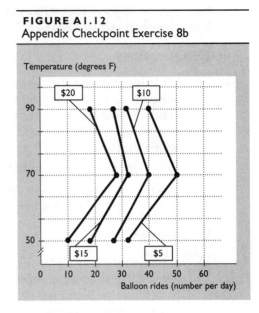

FIGURE A1.12
Appendix Checkpoint Exercise 8b

8c. Figure A1.13 illustrates the relationship between the temperature and the price, holding constant the number of rides. Note that there are six relationships, one for each number of rides.

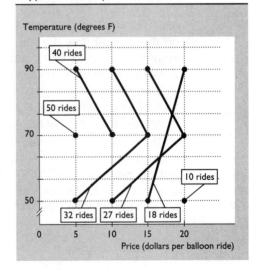

FIGURE A1.13
Appendix Checkpoint Exercise 8c

ADDITIONAL EXERCISES FOR ASSIGNMENT

■ Questions

1. What is the difference between a time-series graph and a scatter diagram? Suppose you have data on the unemployment rate and the inflation rate between 1970 and 2000. To determine if there is a relationship between the two variables, which is the better diagram to use, a time-series graph or a scatter diagram?

2. How is the slope of a straight line calculated? The slope of a curved line?

3a. Draw a curve with a positive and decreasing slope.

3b. Draw a curve with a positive and increasing slope.

■ Answers

1. A time-series graph plots time along the horizontal axis and the values of the variable(s) under examination along the vertical axis. A scatter diagram plots the value of one variable along the horizontal axis and the value of the other variable along the vertical axis. To determine if there is a relationship between any two variables, a scatter diagram is the better diagram to use because a scatter diagram essentially is designed to reveal the relationship, or lack thereof, between two variables.

2. Slope is defined as the change in the value of the variable on the vertical axis divided by the change in the value of the variable on the horizontal axis. The slope of a straight line is constant; that is, between any two points on the straight line, the slope is the same. Thus to calculate the slope of a straight line, select two points on it. Then, measure the amount by which the variable on the vertical axis changes and the amount by which the variable on the horizontal axis changes. Divide the change in the value of the variable on the vertical axis by the change in the value of the variable on the horizontal axis, and the resulting quotient is the slope.

   The slope along a curved line is *not* constant; it generally changes at each point on the line. Thus to compute the slope of a curved line, you must select the point at which the slope will be calculated. Then draw a straight line that touches the curved line at only that point. Calculate the slope of the straight line. The slope of the curved line at that point equals the slope of the straight line.

3a. A curve with a positive and decreasing slope is illustrated in Figure A1.14.

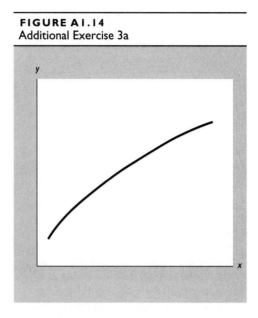

FIGURE A1.14
Additional Exercise 3a

3b. A curve with a positive and increasing slope is illustrated in Figure A1.15.

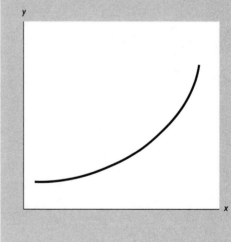

FIGURE A1.15
Additional Exercise 3b

22

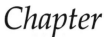 *Chapter*

The U.S. Economy

2

CHAPTER ROADMAP

■ Where We Are

In Chapter 2, we describe what, how, and for whom goods and services are produced in the United States. We use the circular flow model to provide a picture of how households and firms interact. We also describe the economic activities of governments in the United States.

■ Where We've Been

In the previous chapter, we covered the definition of economics and distinguished between microeconomics and macroeconomics. We described what economists do and some of the problems they encounter. In addition, we explored the four core ideas that define the way economists think about macroeconomic questions. Finally, we explained why economics is worth studying.

■ Where We're Going

In the next chapter, we develop the production possibilities frontier model. We put the model through its paces, thereby illustrating some of the concepts developed in Chapters 1 and 2, such as the "what" question, the "how" question, and opportunity cost.

IN THE CLASSROOM

■ Class Time Needed

The material in this chapter should be covered in no more than one class session.

An estimate of the time per checklist topic is:

- 2.1 What Goods and Services Are Produced?—5 to 10 minutes
- 2.2 How Are Goods and Services Produced?—5 to 10 minutes
- 2.3 For Whom Are Goods and Services Produced?—5 to 10 minutes
- 2.4 Circular Flows—25 minutes

■ Extended Lecture Outline

2.1 What Goods and Services are Produced?
A. What We Consume
   1. In the United States, medical care is the single largest consumption category.
   2. Over time, incomes in the United States have increased and our spending on necessities has fallen as a percentage of income while spending on services has risen as a percentage of income.
B. What We Produce

   Most of what we consume is produced in the United States, and most of what we produce is services.
   1. As a percent of total production, real estate services represents the largest item produced.
C. What We Buy From the Rest of World

   We sell goods to other countries and also buy goods, such as oil, produced in other countries.

2.2 How Are Goods and Services Produced?

A. We use productive resources to produce the goods and services we buy. These resources fit into one of four categories and are called **factors of production**.

B. Land

Land includes all the "gifts of nature," the natural resources including land, minerals, energy, water, air, animals and plants.

C. Labor

Labor includes the work time and effort people provide to produce goods and services.

1. As the population increases or if a larger percentage of the population works, labor increases.

2. **Human capital** is the knowledge and skill that people acquire from education, on-the-job-training and work experience.

3. As human capital increases, the quality of labor increases.

D. Capital

Capital includes machines, buildings, and equipment such as tools.

1. Financial capital, like stocks, bonds, and money, are not productive resources and hence are not considered capital in an economic sense.

2. The total amount of capital increases over time.

E. Entrepreneurship

Entrepreneurship is the human resource that organizes labor, land, and capital.

2.3 For Whom Are Goods Produced?

A. Incomes determine who gets the goods and services produced. People earn incomes by selling the services of their factors of production.

1. **Rent** is paid for the use of land.

2. **Wages** compensate people for providing labor.

3. **Interest** is paid for the use of capital.

4. Entrepreneurs earn a **profit (or loss)** from running a business.

B. The **functional distribution of income** is the percentage distribution of income among the factors of production. In the United States, labor earns about 70 percent of the total.

C. The **personal distribution of income** shows how income is distributed across segments of the population. Incomes are not equally distributed across these segments.

1. In the United States, the richest 20 percent of the population earn about 50 percent of the income.

2. In the United States, the poorest 20 percent of the population earn 4 percent of the income.

2.4 Circular Flows

A. The **circular flow model** shows the circular flows of expenditures and incomes that result from decision makers' choices.

B. Households and Firms

1. **Households** are the individuals or groups of people who live together as decision-making units and own the factors of production (land, labor, capital, and entrepreneurship).

2. **Firms** are the institutions that organize the production of goods and services.

C. Markets

Markets are any arrangement that brings buyers and sellers together and enables them to get information and do business with each other.

1. **Goods markets** are the markets in which goods and services are bought and sold.

2. **Factor markets** are the markets in which factors of production are bought and sold.

C. Real Flows and Money Flows

The real flows are the goods and services and the factors of production. The money flows go in the opposite direction to the real flows.

D. The Government Sector

1. Federal Government

   a. The federal government has three major expenditures: provide public goods and services, make social security and welfare payments, and make transfers to state and local governments.

   b. The federal government collects three main taxes: personal income taxes, corporate taxes, and social security taxes.

2. State and Local Government

   a. The state and local governments have two major expenditures: provide local public goods and services, and make welfare payments.

   b. The state and local governments collect three main taxes: sales taxes, property taxes, and state income taxes.

E. Government in the Circular Flow

The government sector provides goods and services to both households and firms. Households and firms pay taxes to and receive transfers from governments.

F. Federal Government Expenditures and Revenues

1. The largest expenditure categories are social security (22 percent of expenditures), other transfer benefits (20 percent), national defense (18 percent), interest on the national debt (15 percent), and transfers to state and local governments (13 percent).

2. The largest sources of revenue are personal income taxes (48 percent of revenue), social security taxes (35 percent), and corporate income taxes (12 percent).

G. State and Local Government Expenditures and Revenue

1. The three largest expenditure categories are education (40 percent of expenditures), public welfare (20 percent), and highways (8 percent).

2. The largest sources of revenue are sales taxes (25 percent of revenue), transfers from the federal government (23 percent), property taxes (21 percent), and personal income taxes (15 percent).

■ Lecture Launchers

1. Part of this chapter implicitly focuses on the standard of living that we enjoy. As an icebreaker you might want to poll students by asking them what they believe are some of the most important achievements of the twentieth century. Ask them to concentrate on achievements that have helped raise the standard of living for Americans and other people around the world. You could give students two minutes in class to compose a list of about ten items. Make sure to tell them that there really are no "right" or "wrong" answers. The only requirements are that the items were introduced (not necessarily invented) in the twentieth century and had some impact on our standard of living. When time is up, have students share with you their items and merge them with a list of your own. As an aid, here is a short list that might prove useful:

   a. Electricity
   b. Automobile

  c. Airplane
  d. Radio
  e. Television
  f. Telephone
  g. Air conditioning
  h. Computer
  i. Highways
  j. Spacecraft
  k. Internet
  l. Refrigeration
  m. Laser and fiber optics
  n. Nuclear power

  Discussion of this list could center around a number of issues. First, the discussion will allow you the opportunity to get students to question the mainstream view that an increase in the standard of living depends only on the quantities of goods and services produced and the number of people among whom those goods and services are shared. Point out that official measurements of standard of living around the world focus on average income earned per day. As a standard benchmark, these data are extremely useful, but they do hide some very important information, namely the quality of goods and services. You could pick any number of items on this list and ask students what kinds of advancements have occurred that make the good or service better. The automobile will likely be a favorite. Here is a short list of some of the advancements of the modern automobile: airbags, 5 m.p.h. bumpers, fuel injection (instead of carburetors), safety glass, seat belts, window defrosters, global positioning systems (mostly on luxury cars), radio, television, compact disc players, climate control systems, four-wheel drive, anti-lock braking systems, power (steering, brakes, seats, locks etc.) daytime running lights, side crash severity sensors, cruise control, etc. You could add even more to this list and have fun with some of the others. Students will probably have a ball talking about all that has changed with the personal computer.

2. Students are often bombarded by news of rising costs and rising prices. A good respite from this sea of pessimism is to take stock of many of the goods and services that's costs and prices have fallen because of changes in technology. Here is a short list to warm up the discussion: telecommuting, laproscopic surgery, and smart structures.

  a. Telecommuting (the ability to work productively at home). Thanks to the spread of personal computers, e-mail, fax machines and the like, telecommuting has increased in magnitude. Studies have shown that telecommuting saves businesses roughly $10,000 annually for a worker earning $44,000. This gain is the result of saving in lost work time and employee retention costs, plus gains in worker productivity.

  b. Laproscopic surgery (minimally invasive surgery). With the use of a digital camera, fiber optic cables, and a video monitor, surgeons can perform gall bladder operations, procedures involving the stomach, appendix, esophagus, and other organs with three or four 1/3 inch incisions. Typically, patients can resume normal activities in a week as compared to six weeks with older procedures. The procedure results in less down time for patients and costs less in physician and hospital fees.

c. Smart structures (structures with advanced technology built in). Maintaining the integrity and safety of structures like highways, roads, bridges and dams can be very expensive. The current process involves drilling holes into these structures to obtain core samples. This procedure is a highly labor intensive process. By equipping these structures with fiber optic cables, the structure itself can provide local and state authorities with important up-to-date information on structure strain, temperature, vibration, magnetic fields, cracks, road-salt corrosion, and penetration. Application of this type of technology to the rest of the nation's infrastructure could result in further cost savings.

All of these examples are from the *Annual Report*, Federal Reserve Bank of Dallas, 1999, page 12.

■ Land Mines

1. When you write the four economic resources on the board (land, labor, capital, and entrepreneurship) the greatest challenge is to get students to think "out of the box." Students often take each of the terms too literally.

   For instance, when economists use the term land, it is important to emphasize that this term encapsulates *all* natural resources, not just the obvious area of land in terms of acres or plots. "Land" also includes water, oil and other important and strategic minerals.

   Labor refers to human labor. However, there is a natural tendency for students to think of the entire population and the labor force as synonymous. Take care to mention that the labor force includes not only people who are working but also people who are unemployed and actively seeking work. In addition, it is worth mentioning that the size of the labor force can change from increases in population and also from changes in demographics. This point could give rise to a short discussion of the instability of the social security system. Because many polls indicate that young people do not expect to draw from the system, you could argue that these feelings are rooted in some measure of truth.

   Capital is usually not a concept that is difficult for students to grasp. However, it is sometimes confused with financial capital. Point out that unless economists specifically say "financial capital," they are invariably referring to physical capital such as factories, machines, and equipment. Inform them that financial capital is a term that is used in business to refer to cash, loans, stocks, and bonds.

   Lastly is the term entrepreneurship. While the obvious icon here is that of a business person who is responsible for bringing together all the other factors of production, it is worth noting that the most important characteristic of an entrepreneur is that of being a risk taker. Explain that risk taking is a trait that is quite scarce in supply. If students ask for proof, merely ask them what most people do for a living. The answer is that they work for someone else. The very act of being an employee involves a certain implicit preference of risk aversion.

ANSWERS TO CHECKPOINT EXERCISES

■ CHECKPOINT 2.1 What Goods and Services Are Produced?

1. The United States produces services such as real estate services, retail and wholesale trade, health services, and education. The United States also produces goods including construction and electrical equipment, food, and industrial equipment. From other countries we import many goods and services, such as oil, clothing, office equipment, TVs, VCRs, toys and sporting goods.

2. Today businesses in the United States produce more services than goods, with the largest production of a service being real estate services. Earlier in the 20th century, the production of goods dominated the U.S. economy. In terms of imports, the United States buys clothing, TVs, and oil. Prior to the 1960s, the United States produced many of these goods itself.

■ CHECKPOINT 2.2 How Are Goods and Services Produced?

1. Over the last few decades, the size of the labor force has increased. The composition also has changed, because the percentage of women in the labor force has increased from 42 percent (45 million/106 million) to 47 percent (66 million/141 million). In terms of human capital, 25 percent of the population have a college degree today versus fewer than 3 percent in 1910. This increase in education has contributed to our nation's human capital.

2. In the world, there are enough reserves of coal, natural gas, and oil to last about 79 years, 40 years and 27 years, respectively. The amount of these resources held in the United States will last about 77 years (coal) and 7 years (oil and gas). As these nonrenewable resources are used, we will find new sources and discover more fuel-efficient technology.

3a. The arch in St. Louis a factor of production. It is a piece of capital involved in producing scenic vistas as people ride to the top of the arch.

3b. Niagara Falls is a factor of production. Electricity is generated from it and because it is a gift of nature, it is classified as a land resource.

3c. U.S. senators are a factor of production involved in producing government services. They are people, so they are classified as labor.

3d. The NASA rocket launcher is a factor of production, frequently involved in producing a variety of space-based services. They are built by people and hence are classified as capital.

3e. A U.S. government bond is not a factor of production.

3f. A ski run at Aspen is a factor of production producing skiing services. It is classified as capital.

■ CHECKPOINT 2.3 For Whom Are Goods Produced?

1. If everyone were to consume an equal quantity of goods and services, there would be a redistribution of 29 percent of income from the top 20 percent of income earners. The second richest 20 percent would have to transfer 3 percent.

■ CHECKPOINT 2.4 Circular Flows

1. Households choose the quantities of land, labor, capital, and entrepreneurship to provide to firms. Firms choose the quantities of services of the factors of production to hire and the quantities of goods and services to produce. Households decide what to buy in the goods markets. These simultaneous decisions play major roles in determining the answers to the "what," "how," and "for whom" questions.

2. Governments modify the answers to the "what," "how," and "for whom" questions by their interactions with firms and households. In the goods market, governments decide what goods to buy, thereby affecting the "what" question. Governments also tax firms and households and give firms and households transfer payments. These directly effect the "for whom" question because taxes decrease the payer's ability to buy goods and services while transfers enhance the recipient's buying power. The taxes and transfer payments also affect households' and firms' decisions about what factors of production to provide and what factors to buy. Hence the taxes and transfer payments also affect the "how" question.

ANSWERS TO CHAPTER CHECKPOINT EXERCISES

1a. Factor of production. The van is a piece of capital equipment that is used to help produce bread.

1b. Not a factor of production. The 100 shares of Amazon.com stock can be considered financial capital, but they are not a productive resource used produce goods or services.

1c. Not a factor of production. The oil will become a factor when it is discovered and used.

1d. Factor of production. The garbage truck is a piece of capital equipment used to help collect the garbage and thereby provide a sanitation service.

1e. Not a factor of production. The stick of bubble gum is not a factor of production because it is not used to help produce goods or services.

1f. Factor of production. The President of the United States is a worker who helps provide government services.

1g. Factor of production. Disneyland is capital that helps provide the service of amusement and entertainment.

2a. During the next decade we can expect jobs in the medical care field to increase. This increase is a result of our spending on health care and expectations that as our population ages, we will spend even more. Given that we also spend a large portion of our incomes on housing and real estate services, we can expect more jobs in this segment of the economy.

2b. In the next 50 years as technology advances, we will see more jobs that require a highly skilled labor force. In addition, we will probably see more and more people providing services instead of producing goods.

2c. The quantity of human capital will continue to grow as technology expands and as the delivery of education changes (i.e. more distance-based learning that provide more people greater access to education).

2d. This answer allows for a normative statement, but in most cases we would not expect all jobs to disappear. Even if all jobs are performed by robots, we will still need someone to develop, manage, and repair the robots.

3a. If agricultural land continues to disappear at the same rate it did between 1982 to 1997, which was about 2.7 million acres per year (40 million acres/15 years), agricultural land will be gone in about 340 years (930 million acres remaining/ 2.7 million acres per year).

3b. The trend will probably continue as long as technology allows more agricultural output to be produced from ever decreasing amounts of land. At some point though, we might expect this trend to taper off and the loss of agricultural land to slow.

4a. Given that there are only known oil reserves to last 27 years, we would expect oil to be the nonrenewable resource that is used up first.

4b. If the United States uses up its nonrenewable resources before other countries do, we would expect that the United States will develop more fuel-efficient technologies and also will buy these resources from other countries.

5. Income is unequally distributed because resources are unequally distributed. People have different levels of human capital and entrepreneurial skills and so they earn different incomes. Other resources (capital and land) produce incomes that also are unequally distributed. Whether the inequality of income distribution "matters" depends on how you interpret the word "matters." If you are thinking in terms of fairness, you might say that the inequality matters only if people have unfairly obtained the resources. If people have fairly obtained the resources without harming other people, then you might say that the inequality does not matter. If, on the other hand, you think about the word "matters" in terms of economic growth, it is probably true that the economy has a greater chance of economic growth if the lower segments of the population gained more skills and knowledge, which would allow them to earn greater incomes.

6. This question requires a normative statement. Some students will reply that government is too big and others will explain why they think government is too small.

7. The government receives a small part of its tax receipts from businesses because the government wants to give business the incentives to produce output without a large disincentive to pay taxes on the profit earned by this production. In addition, the government ultimately earns the tax receipts

from individuals who are paid incomes from the firms and from capital gains taxes paid by stockholders.

The next question will be answered using a normative statement. Students will explain why or why not businesses should pay more taxes. One point to keep in mind is that the circular flow diagram shows that anything that affects firms will also have an effect on households.

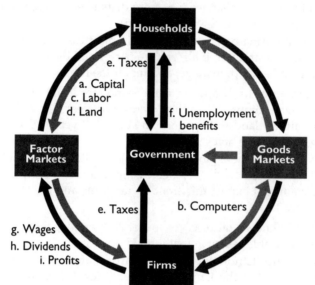

8. The flows are labeled in the figure above.

ADDITIONAL EXERCISES FOR ASSIGNMENT

■ Questions

1. In the goods market, households and firms both have a role to play. In the factor markets these roles are reversed. Why does the reversal occur?

2. Identify the payments that are made to each of the four factors of production.

■ Answers

1. Households are the buyers in the goods market and firms are the sellers. In this market, households pay firms money in exchange for goods and services. In the factor markets, the roles are reversed. Households are the sellers of labor, land, capital, and entrepreneurship and firms are the buyers. In this market, firms pay households money in exchange for the factors of production.

2. Wages are paid to labor, rent to land, interest to capital, and profits (or losses) to the entrepreneur.

USING EYE ON THE PAST

■ The Changing Size of the Federal Government

Class discussion of the size of government invariably focuses on absolute dollar amounts. Point out that although these figures are accurate and insightful, they might overlook some information. In particular, as the population of a country, state or city grows, it is natural that the absolute dollar amount of expenditures by government would increase. Simply put, more people require greater services, roads, bridges, highways, courthouses, etc.

What is likely to raise eyebrows is the percentage of national income that is devoted to government spending. Undeniably this figure has risen at a rapid rate until the mid-1980s. Here we might be tempted to conclude that our elected representatives were simply "spending like a bunch of drunkards." However, upon closer inspection, a very large part of federal outlays that has grown significantly since World War II is the result not of more expenditure upon goods and services but rather increases in transfer payments. Here it is instructive to point out the difference between two things: government purchases of goods and services and government transfers. The former involves the actual command over resources, as when the government expends money to build a highway or a courthouse or pay a sailor's salary. The latter involves a transfer of tax revenue from one party to another. It does not involve a direct command over resources. Total government outlays is the sum of these two components.

USING EYE ON THE U.S. ECONOMY

■ How We Produce in the New Economy

After presenting students with the graph demonstrating job changes, you might want to ask them what fundamental changes in the economy have been underway in the United States. The likely response is that the goods and services that we produce today and will produce tomorrow are different than in decades past. This answer is basically correct. In the 1970s, manufacturing was a more dominant part of the economy. Today, many goods and services require the processing of information or the creation of intellectual property. A quick look at the companies that made the top ten in terms of stock market capitalization in 1970 and the top ten in 1999 will demonstrate this point vividly.

1970 Top Ten
IBM, AT&T, General Motors, Standard Oil, Sears, Eastman Kodak, Texaco, General Electric, Xerox, Gulf, DuPont, and Ford

1999 Top Ten
Microsoft, General Electric, Cisco Systems, Exxon Mobil, Wal-Mart, Lucent Technologies, Intel, IBM, SBC Communications, AT&T, Citigroup, and America Online
(*Annual Report*, Federal Reserve Bank of Dallas, 1999, page 11.)

Explain to students that this list is provisional. Recent mergers over the last year might have caused a reshuffling of some of the major players and stock market changes might raise the market capitalization of some companies while lowering others (For instance, in 2000 Lucent dropped like a stone from the top ten, while Pfizer joined it.) However, the salient point is not lost. Energy and manufacturing were the big boys of the 1970s. They have given way to the knowledge sectors of high tech, telecommunications, and health care.

The Economic Problem

Chapter

3

CHAPTER OUTLINE

1. Use the production frontier to illustrate the economic problem.
   A. Production Possibilities Frontier
   B. Attainable and Unattainable Combinations
   C. Full Employment and Unemployment
   D. Tradeoffs and Free Lunches

2. Calculate opportunity cost.
   A. The Opportunity Cost of a Bottle of Water
   B. The Opportunity Cost of a CD
   C. Opportunity Cost is a Ratio
   D. Increasing Opportunity Cost
   E. Increasing Opportunity Costs Are Everywhere

3. Define efficiency and describe an efficient use of resources.
   A. Two Conditions for Efficiency
      1. Production Efficiency
      2. Allocative Efficiency
   B. Marginal Benefit
   C. Marginal Benefit Schedule and Curve
   D. Marginal Cost
   E. Efficient Use of Resources
   F. Efficiency in the U.S. Economy

4. Explain how specialization and trade expand production possibilities.
   A. Comparative Advantage
   B. Achieving the Gains from Trade
   C. Absolute Advantage

CHAPTER ROADMAP

■ Where We Are

In Chapter 3, we use the production possibilities frontier to illustrate the economic problem and calculate opportunity cost. We illustrate the effect of unemployed resources using the production possibilities frontier model. In addition, we use the production possibilities frontier to explore efficiency and introduce the concepts of production efficiency and allocative efficiency. Lastly we explain how specialization and trade expand production possibilities.

■ Where We've Been

In Chapter 2, we described what, how, and for whom goods and services are produced in the United States, thereby motivating the production possibilities frontier model developed in this chapter. In Chapter 2 we used the circular flow model to provide a picture of how households and firms interact. We described the economic activities of governments in the United States. Finally, we described the macroeconomic performance of the United States, including the standard of living, cost of living, and economic fluctuations.

■ Where We're Going

The next chapter introduces the supply and demand model. We will distinguish between quantity demanded and demand, and explain what determines demand. Likewise we will distinguish between quantity supplied and supply, and explain what determines supply. We will explore how demand and supply determine price and quantity in a market, and explain the effects of changes in demand and supply.

IN THE CLASSROOM

■ Class Time Needed

The material in this chapter can be covered in two to three class sessions.

An estimate of the time per checklist topic is:

- 3.1 Production Possibilities—45 to 60 minutes
- 3.2 Opportunity Cost—20 to 40 minutes
- 3.3 Using Resources Efficiently—30 to 45 minutes
- 3.4 Specialization and Exchange—25 to 40 minutes

■ Extended Lecture Outline

3.1 Production Possibilities

A. Production Possibilities Frontier

The **production possibilities frontier,** or *PPF,* is the boundary between the combinations of goods and services that can be produced and the combinations that cannot be produced, given the available factors of production, land, labor, capital, and entrepreneurship, and the state of technology.

B. Attainable and Unattainable Combinations

Production combinations that are on or inside the *PPF* are attainable. Combinations that are beyond the *PPF* are unattainable.

C. Full Employment and Unemployment

1. Full employment occurs when all the available factors of production are being used.

a. At full employment, the economy is producing at a production point on the *PPF*.

2. Unemployment occurs whenever any of the factors of production are not being fully utilized, that is, there is unemployed labor, idle land or idle capital.

a. When there are unemployed resources, the economy is producing at a production point within the *PPF*.

D. Tradeoffs and Free Lunches

1. A **tradeoff** is a limit that forces an exchange, or a substitution, of one thing for something else.

a. Changes in production from one point on the *PPF* to another involve a tradeoff, as some of one good must be forgone in order to gain more of another good.

2. A free lunch is the absence of a tradeoff, when it is possible to take an action and not forgo something else.

a. Production points within the *PPF* offer a free lunch because it is possible to get more of some goods and services without giving up anything else.

3.2 Opportunity Cost

A. The Opportunity Cost of a Bottle of Water

The opportunity cost of a bottle of water is the decrease in the quantity of CDs divided by the increase in the number of bottles of water as we move (down) along a *PPF*, such as that illustrated in Figure 3.1.

B. The Opportunity Cost of a CD

The opportunity cost of a CD is the decrease in the quantity of bottles of water divided by the increase in the quantity of CDs as we move (up) along the *PPF* illustrated in Figure 3.1.

C. Opportunity Cost is a Ratio

1. The opportunity cost equals the change in the quantity of the good forgone divided by the change in the quantity of the good that is gained.

D. Increasing Opportunity Cost

As more of a product is produced, its opportunity cost increases. In Figure 3.1, moving from point A to point B to point C and so on, the opportunity cost of the additional bottles of water increases.

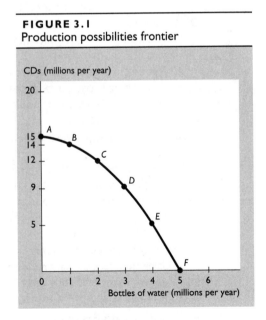

FIGURE 3.1
Production possibilities frontier

1. Increasing opportunity cost is reflected in the shape of the *PPF*, specifically the bowed out shape of the *PPF*.

2. Opportunity costs increase because resources are not equally productive in all activities.

E. Increasing Opportunity Costs are Everywhere
1. Virtually every activity is one with an increasing opportunity cost.

3.3 Using Resources Efficiently

A. Two Conditions for Efficiency

Efficiency occurs when we produce the amount of goods and services that are most highly valued.

1. **Production efficiency** occurs when we cannot produce more of one good or service without producing less of some other good or service.
   a. Production efficiency occurs when an economy is producing *on* its *PPF*.
   b. Producing *inside* the *PPF* is inefficient because some resources are unemployed.
2. **Allocative efficiency** occurs when we produce the quantities of goods and services that are more highly valued.
   a. While all points on the *PPF* are production efficient, only one of those points is allocatively efficient.

B. Marginal Benefit
1. The marginal benefit of a good or service is measured by what a person is willing to give up to get one more unit of it.
2. The principle of decreasing marginal benefit is reflected in the fact that additional units of a good provide ever-smaller additional benefits.

C. Marginal Benefit Schedule and Curve
1. The marginal benefit schedule shows, in tabular form, the amount of one good that a person is willing to forgo to get one more unit of another good.
2. The marginal benefit curve is a graph of the marginal benefit schedule. It is downward sloping.

D. Marginal Cost
1. To ensure allocative efficiency, the marginal benefit of a good must be compared to the marginal cost of that good.
2. A good's marginal cost equals the opportunity cost of producing one more unit of that good.
3. The marginal cost curve slopes upward and reflects the fact the marginal cost (and the opportunity cost) of producing additional units of a good increases as more of the good is produced.

E. Efficient Use of Resources
1. By comparing marginal benefit and marginal cost we can determine an efficient use of resources.
2. If the marginal benefit of a unit of a good *is greater than* the marginal cost of that unit, more of that good should be produced. If the marginal benefit of a good *is less than* the marginal cost of that good, less of that good should be produced.
3. When the marginal benefit of a unit of a good equals the marginal cost of that unit, allocative efficiency is achieved.

F. Efficiency in the U.S. Economy
1. Using the ideas of marginal cost and marginal benefit, future chapters will address whether the United States efficiently uses its resources to produce energy, mass transportation, education, health care, and other goods and services.

3.4 Specialization and Exchange

A. Comparative Advantage

A person has a **comparative advantage** in an activity if that person can perform the activity at a lower opportunity cost than someone else. Because opportunity cost is the ratio of how much of one good must be given up to produce an additional unit of another good, every person and nation has a comparative advantage at producing some good or service

B. Achieving the Gains from Trade

1. Individuals can gain by specialization according to comparative advantage and then trade with other people.

2. The gains from trade allow individuals to get outside their individual production possibilities frontiers.

C. Absolute Advantage

Absolute advantage is when one person is more productive than another person in several or even all activities.

1. Possessing an absolute advantage does not imply that the person or nation possesses a comparative advantage.

2. It is *not* possible for anyone to have a comparative advantage in everything even though they might have an absolute advantage in everything.

3. Even though someone might have an absolute advantage in everything, both that person and the trading partner gain by producing according to their comparative advantage.

■ Lecture Launchers

1. Many students almost instinctively relate costs to monetary costs. In order to help them grasp the idea of opportunity cost while moving along the *PPF*, it is important to get students to realize very early on that thinking only of monetary costs is a narrow view and that it ignores the most important cost of all—opportunity cost.

    Demonstrate the fact that that opportunity cost does not necessarily involve money by launching your lecture with an example that hits close to home. Ask your students to take a minute to write down a list of things that qualify as the opportunity cost to them of attending your economics class. Expect a fairly wide range of answers from the downright silly to the very thoughtful. Stress that the true opportunity cost of any endeavor is only the one next best alternative forgone. The reason is because you can only perform one other activity in place of whatever it is you are doing at present. In other words, you will need to convince your students that even though they have come up with a fairly long list of items, the opportunity cost of attending your economics class can only be one of them. This one is the one that will rank above the others as the next best available alternative. Here might be some possible answers: by taking economics your students cannot take biology, physics or chemistry; they might have to give up overtime at work (if they are taking a night class); or the cost could be the forgone extra sleep they could have enjoyed if they are taking an 8:00 a.m. class!

2. As the text points out quite clearly, specialization involves interdependence. If each individual or nation specializes in what he or she has a comparative advantage in, trade must take place with others to obtain the goods and services not being produced by the person or nation but desired by the person or nation. Sometimes students will point to the trade as a sign of weakness. They might say that being interdependent means that people or nations cannot be self-sufficient and will argue that self-sufficiency is a source of strength. This assertion is an opportunity to turn the tables by

asking each student what would be required of them if indeed they were to maintain a life of self-sufficiency. The answer is quite enlightening. Below is a short list:

Grow our own food; make our own clothes; provide our own water supply; find our own sources of energy; provide medical care; and many more.

■ Land Mines

1. Perhaps the concepts that give students the most trouble in this chapter are absolute advantage and comparative advantage. It flies in the face of intuition to say that even though someone has the ability to produce something using fewer resources than someone else, nonetheless, it still pays for the two to trade. It is an especially difficult concept to grasp when you up the ante by saying that the same would still be true even if that person enjoyed an absolute advantage in everything over their trading partner! This might be a good opportunity to use a very concrete example that students should be able to compute right in the classroom. Lay out the following scenario: Assume Suzie, a computer consultant, is very good at repairing computers and also happens to be a very good house painter. In fact, she is so good that it turns out she is more productive at both things than her neighbor, Bob, who happens to paint houses for a living. To the right is a table that shows the amount of time it takes for Suzie and Bob to perform

	Time it takes Suzie	Time it takes Bob
Repair a computer	2 hours	24 hours
Paint a house	30 hours	48 hours

each of the two activities. In addition, let's assume that Suzie (and Bob) earns $100 per computer she repairs and Bob (and Suzie) earns $960 per house painted. Ask the students to compute the opportunity cost for Suzie and Bob repairing a computer and painting a house.

The new table to the right contains the opportunity costs. (To calculate these numbers, take Suzie's opportunity cost of painting a house. In the 30 hours it

	Opportunity cost for Suzie	Opportunity cost for Bob
Repair a computer	$64	$480
Paint a house	$1,500	$200

takes her to paint a house, she could have repaired 15 computers, so the opportunity cost is 15 computers times $100 each.) It reveals that Suzie has the lower opportunity cost of repairing computers and Bob has the lower opportunity cost in painting houses. What this example demonstrates so powerfully is that a person can have an absolute disadvantage in everything, as is the case for Bob, but still manage to have a comparative advantage in an activity. Point out to students that this logic applies between individuals and also across cities, states, and even nations.

ANSWERS TO CHECKPOINT EXERCISES

■ CHECKPOINT 3.1 Production Possibilities

1. Crusoe's production possibilities frontier in the winter is given in the table to the right. The production possibilities frontier also is illustrated in Figure 3.2.

2i. Attainable

2ii. Not attainable. After spending 4 hours producing 10 fish, Crusoe has only one hour left to devote to picking fruit, which will only yield him 6 fruit, not 13.

2iii. Attainable

3i. The combination uses all Crusoe's available 5 hours a day.

3ii. The combination uses all Crusoe's available 5 hours a day.

3iii. The combination does not use all of Crusoe's time.

4i. This combination provides him with a tradeoff. If he increases his fish by a pound, he must decrease his fruit.

4ii. This combination gives Crusoe a free lunch. It does not use all of his time and so he could increase his fish by a pound without giving up any fruit.

Possibility	Fish (pounds)		Fruit (pounds)
A	0	and	28
B	4	and	24
C	7	and	19
D	9	and	13
E	10	and	7
F	11	and	0

FIGURE 3.2
Checkpoint 3.1 Exercise 1

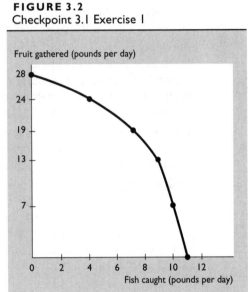

■ CHECKPOINT 3.2 Opportunity Cost

1. Crusoe's opportunity cost of a pound of fruit is the fish he forgoes. To calculate the opportunity cost, start by computing the increase in fruit picked as he increases the time he devotes to picking fruit. Calculate also the decrease in the fish he catches. Then, divide the

Move from	Increase in fruit picked (pounds)	Decrease in fish caught (pounds)	Opportunity cost of fruit (pounds of fish)
F to E	7.0	1.0	0.14
E to D	6.0	1.0	0.17
D to C	6.0	2.0	0.33
C to B	5.0	3.0	0.60
B to A	4.0	4.0	1.00

decrease in fish by the increase in fruit to get the opportunity cost per pound of fruit. The table has these data, that is, the increases in fruit picked, the decreases in fish caught, and the opportunity costs for the different movements along the production possibilities frontier.

2. His opportunity cost of a pound of fruit and a pound of fish are both zero. The reason is that he is operating inside his production possibilities frontier. Presently he could pick 6 more fruit without giving up any fish or alternatively catch 2 more fish without giving up any fruit. Thus Crusoe is in a position to reap a free lunch.

3. If the extra 2 pounds of fish imposes an opportunity cost of 6 pounds of fruit then that is the equivalent of saying that 1 pound of fish has an opportunity cost of 3 pounds of fruit.

4. Crusoe's opportunity cost of a pound of fruit increases as he spends more time picking fruit. This result is demonstrated in the table above. As Crusoe spends more time picking fruit, so that he moves from spending no time at point F to 1 hour at point E to 2 hours at point D and so on, his opportunity cost of a pound of fruit rises from 0.14 pounds of fish to 0.17 pounds of fish to 0.33 pounds of fish, and so forth.

■ CHECKPOINT 3.3 Using Resources Efficiently

1. Any production combination of yogurt and ice cream that is on the *PPF* meets the conditions for production efficiency. To determine which of those combinations meets the condition for allocative efficiency, we must use the marginal benefit and marginal cost curves.

   To calculate the marginal cost schedule, take the movement from 150 cartons of yogurt to 140 as an example. For this change, 10 ice cream cones are gained. The opportunity cost is 10 cartons of yogurt. Hence the opportunity cost for 1 ice cream cone is (10 cartons of yogurts)/(10 ice cream cones) = 1 carton of yogurt for an ice cream cone. Because this marginal cost is calculated between 0 ice cream cones and 10 ice cream cones, to what quantity does it apply? Use the midpoint of 5 ice cream cones. Thus the marginal cost of 1 carton of yogurt per ice cream cone is at 5 ice cream cones. The rest of the marginal cost schedule is given in the table.

Quantity (cones)	Marginal cost of a yogurt (cartons per cone)
5	1
15	2
25	3
35	4
45	5

   The marginal cost curve intersects the marginal benefit curve when 25 ice cream cones are produced. The production of 25 cones is the allocatively efficient amount.

■ CHECKPOINT 3.4 Specialization and Exchange

1a. If Sara devotes all of her resources to producing boards, she will produce 15 boards. If she devotes all of her resources to producing sails, she will produce 10 sails. For each board Sara makes, she forgoes 2/3 of a sail, so the opportunity cost of 1 board is 2/3 of a sail.

1b. If Sid devotes all of his resources to producing boards, he will produce 10 boards. If he devotes all of his resources to producing sails, he will produce 15 sails. For each board Sid makes, he forgoes 1 1/2 sails, so the opportunity cost of 1 board is 1 1/2 sails.

1c. Sara has the comparative advantage in producing boards because her opportunity cost of a board, 2/3 of a sail, is less than Sid's opportunity cost of a board, 1 1/2 sails.

1d. Sid has the comparative advantage in producing sails. His opportunity cost of a sail is 2/3 of a board, while Sara's opportunity cost of a sail is 1 1/2 boards. Hence Sid's opportunity cost of a sail is less than Sara's opportunity cost of a sail.

1e. If they specialize and trade, Sara will produce boards and Sid will produce sails. Sara will devote all of her time to boards, and so she will produce 15 boards. Sid will devote all of his time to sails, and so he will produce 15 sails.

2a. If Sid installs a machine that doubles his production of both sails and boards, his opportunity costs remain the same. In particular, the opportunity cost of a sail is 2/3 of a board and his opportunity cost of a board is

1 1/2 sails. Hence the comparative advantage remains as before, with Sara having the comparative advantage in producing boards.

2b. Yes, there are gains for Sara and Sid if they specialize and trade. As before, Sara should produce boards, because she can produce boards at a lower (opportunity) cost than Sid. And Sid should produce sails because he can produce sails at a lower opportunity cost than Sara. It costs Sid more to produce a board than it does to get one from Sara, so he is going to gain from trade. And it costs Sara more to produce a sail than it does to get one from Sid, so she, too, is going to gain from trade.

ANSWERS TO CHAPTER CHECKPOINT EXERCISES

1a. Because of Napster and other Web sites devoted to music, the production possibilities frontier for recorded music and other goods and services has changed. The maximum amount of music has increased, and so the *PPF* frontier has rotated outward. (Note that the maximum amount of the other goods and services has not changed.)

1b. For conventional music, that is, CDs and tapes, the opportunity cost remains unchanged, in particular, the goods and services forgone by producing another CD or audio tape. For music obtained from a "free" site on the Web, the direct opportunity cost is the bandwidth and computer time that is used to download the music. Presumably there is some cost of electricity and wear on hard drives, but these costs are negligible. A more profound opportunity cost could come in forgone new music as artists and companies opt to engage in endeavors other than music creation and production because their property rights to their work cannot be protected as consumers download from "free" Web sites..

2a. The spread of AIDS has had a profound effect on African economies. In some of these nations, upwards of 35 percent of the population is infected with either HIV or AIDS. In these nations in particular, the production possibilities frontier has shifted inward as their population—and hence their labor force—has decreased because of deaths.

2b. The spread of AIDS has increased the opportunity cost of health care because more health care services are being produced than was previously the case. Presuming that these countries are producing on their *PPFs*, as more health care services are produced, the opportunity cost of health care increases. And, as fewer other goods and services are produced, the opportunity cost of these other items decreases. For instance, because of the population decline, likely fewer houses are being built and so the opportunity cost of a house might have decreased.

3a. The production possibilities frontier is illustrated in Figure 3.3.

3b. Producing 50 units of good food and 50 units of entertainment is attainable. However, at this production point, Survivor Island's resources are not fully employed. The opportunity cost of an additional unit of entertainment is zero.

3c. Producing 40 units of entertainment and 60 units of good food is attainable. There is a tradeoff because the island is operating on its production possibilities frontier. The opportunity cost of one unit of entertainment is 1/2 unit of good food. The reason that the opportunity cost is 1/2 unit of good food is because in this range, in order for the island to produce 20 more units of entertainment it would have to give up 10 units of good food. Hence the opportunity cost of another unit of entertainment equals the units of good food forgone, 10, divided by the units of entertainment obtained, 20, or 10/20. Thus each unit of entertainment has an opportunity cost of 1/2 unit of good food.

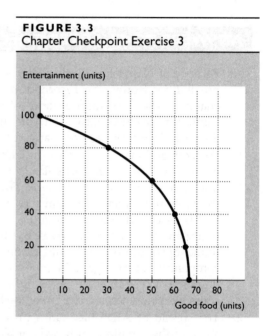

FIGURE 3.3
Chapter Checkpoint Exercise 3

3d. The opportunity cost of each unit of good food rises as Survivor Island allocates more resources to producing good food.

3e. The marginal cost of a unit of entertainment is 15 units of food. When moving from 60 to 80 units of entertainment, you must give up 20 units of food. When moving from 40 to 60 units of entertainment, you must give up 10 units of food. Therefore, at 60 units of entertainment, Survivor Island faces a marginal cost of 15 units of food.

3f. If 40 units of entertainment represents allocative efficiency, then the marginal cost of entertainment must equal the marginal benefit at this point. At 40 units of entertainment, the marginal cost (and hence the marginal benefit) of entertainment is 7.5 units of food.

4a. If Alpha increases its production of robots from 0 per year to 1 per year, Alpha must give up 100 units (2,000 units – 1,900 units) of other goods and services. The opportunity cost of the robot is 100 units of other goods and services.

4b. If Alpha increases its production of robots from 0 per year to 2 per year, Alpha must give up 300 units (2,000 units – 1,700 units) of other goods and services. On average, the opportunity cost of each robot is 150 units of other goods and services, with the (actual) opportunity cost of the first robot equaling 100 units of other goods and services and the (actual) opportunity cost of the second robot equaling 200 units of other goods and services.

5a. If Willy uses all of his time to produce pizzas, he produces 20 pizzas. If he devotes all of his time to sundaes, he produces 50 sundaes. Thus for Willy to produce 50 sundaes, the opportunity cost is 20 pizzas, so the opportunity cost for 1 sundae equals 20 pizzas/50 sundaes = 2/5 pizza per sundae.

5b. If Wendy uses all of her time to produce pizzas, she produces 50 pizzas. If she devotes all of her time to sundaes, she produces 20 sundaes. Thus for Wendy to produce 20 sundaes, the opportunity cost is 50 pizzas, so the opportunity cost for 1 sundae equals 50 pizzas/20 sundaes = 5/2 = 2 1/2 pizzas per sundae.

5c. Calculating the opportunity cost of a pizza similarly to how the opportunity cost for a sundae was calculated in parts (a) and (b) reveals that Willy's opportunity cost of a pizza is 2 1/2 sundaes per pizza and Wendy's opportunity cost of a pizza is 2/5 sundae per pizza. Wendy's opportunity cost of a pizza is lower than Willy's, so Wendy has the comparative advantage in producing pizza.

5d. If Willy and Wendy specialize, Willy will produce (only) sundaes and Wendy will produce (only) pizza. Hence 50 sundaes will be produced (by Willy) and 50 pizzas will be produced (by Wendy).

6a. The comparative advantage belongs to the producer with the lower opportunity cost of producing a kite. Hence we need to calculate Tom's opportunity cost and Tessa's opportunity cost.

For Tom to switch from producing 3 kites to 5 kites requires him to decrease his production of jigsaw puzzles from 4 puzzles to 3 puzzles. Hence to gain 2 kites has an opportunity cost of 1 jigsaw puzzle, so the opportunity cost of 1 kite equals 1/2 jigsaw puzzle per kite.

And, for Tessa to switch from producing 2 kites to 6 kites requires her to decrease her production of jigsaw puzzles from 5 puzzles to 2 puzzles. Hence to gain 4 kites has an opportunity cost of 3 jigsaw puzzles, so the opportunity cost of 1 kite equals 3/4 jigsaw puzzle per kite.

Tom's opportunity cost of producing a kite is lower than Tessa's opportunity cost, so Tom has the comparative advantage in producing kites.

6b. Tom has the comparative advantage in producing kites, so Tom specializes in producing more kites. Calculations similar to the above show that Tessa has the comparative advantage in jigsaws and so Tessa specializes in producing more jigsaw puzzles.

6c. Tom and Tessa will gain from specializing in production and trading with each other. The reason is that Tom can produce kites at a lower opportunity cost than can Tessa and Tessa can produce jigsaw puzzles at a lower opportunity cost than can Tom.

ADDITIONAL EXERCISES FOR ASSIGNMENT

■ Questions

1. If you were seeking out a trading partner, would you choose someone whose tastes are similar to yours or different? Explain your answer.

2. Bob is a lawyer with a large law firm. He is very good at preparing briefs and as it turns out very good at typing. Let's assume that Bob's legal assistant Tom can prepare one brief in two hours which turns out to be twice as long as it takes Bob. In fact, to add insult to injury Bob can not only prepare briefs twice as fast as Tom but can also type faster. In one hour Tom can type 6 pages and Bob can type 9. Identify which person has the absolute advantage in preparing briefs and which in typing. In addition, determine which person has the comparative advantage in preparing briefs and which in typing.

■ Answers

1. Though there is no hard and fast answer, most likely you would want a trading partner with different tastes. If a trading partner with similar tastes were to show up to trade with you, it seems unlikely that you would find anything appealing in what the other has to offer. That is to say, the other trading partner would no doubt show up to trade with the same goods you do not want and hence offer to trade and want in exchange the same goods you want. By contrast, someone with different tastes is likely to offer you things for sale that you would find appealing and vice versa. While this discussion does not prove that trade could not exist between parties with similar tastes, it does suggest that the advantages to trade are heightened when the two parties have different tastes.

2. Bob has an absolute advantage in doing both things. The reason is that he is using fewer resources than Tom to do both things. Evaluating comparative advantage is a different matter. If Bob prepares a brief in one hour his opportunity cost is the 9 pages of documents that he gives up by doing so. If Tom prepares a brief in two hours his opportunity cost is 12 pages of documents. Bob has the comparative advantage in preparing briefs. With regard to typing the opportunity costs are reversed. If Bob spends one hour typing he gives up one brief that he could have prepared. By contrast, Tom only gives up 1/2 of a brief if he spends one hour typing. Thus Tom has the comparative advantage in typing.

ANSWERS TO ECONOMICS IN THE NEWS

■ Pre-sliced Apples Going to Market

1. It is hard to put a quantitative value on "large." Probably the opportunity cost is not huge, because the machinery, storage, transportation, and so forth necessary to create and market sliced apples is not huge. But, the opportunity cost is not zero, either. However, the answer to the second part of the question is more straightforward, specifically the opportunity cost likely will increase as more sliced apples are produced. As more sliced apples are produced, poorer quality apples must be used and it seems likely that the slices would need to be sorted so that the ones with half a worm in them are discarded.

2. The *PPF* is in Figure 3.4. The *PPF* is in accord with the previous answer because its bowed outward shape indicates that the opportunity cost of an apple slice increases as more apple slices are produced.

3. The benefits seem mainly to be in terms of convenience. For instance, one benefit is in the time that is saved. If someone wants sliced apples (say, kids) then there is less time involved in serving sliced apples. Another benefit is in serving sizes. If someone wants 2 slices of an apples (again, say a kid) the person can get precisely 2 slices.

4. The efficient quantity is determined as the quantity at which the marginal cost equals the marginal benefit.

FIGURE 3.4
Economics in the News

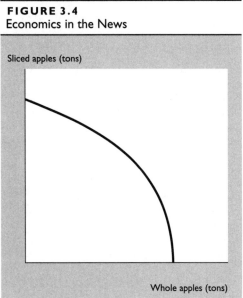

Sliced apples (tons)

Whole apples (tons)

50

Chapter 4

Demand and Supply

3. Explain how demand and supply determine price and quantity in a market and explain the effects of changes in demand and supply.

    A. Market Equilibrium

    B. Price: A Market's Automatic Regulator

    C. Effects of Changes in Demand

    D. Effects of Changes in Supply

    E. Changes in both Supply and Demand

       1. Increase in Demand and Increase in Supply

       2. Decrease in Demand and Decrease in Supply

       3. Increase in Demand and Decrease in Supply

       4. Decrease in Demand and Increase in Supply

CHAPTER ROADMAP

■ Where We Are

In Chapter 4, we create a tool (the supply-demand diagram) to use in examining how a market operates. The chapter explains how to derive demand and supply curves. By combining the supply and demand curves, we see how the market determines market equilibrium. We also see how a change in supply, a change in demand, or a change in both affects the price and quantity in the market equilibrium.

■ Where We've Been

We've explored how scarcity and opportunity costs require us to make choices. We've also looked at the U.S. and global economies.

■ Where We're Going

Now that we've created a tool to examine how market prices and quantities are determined, we use it to see how market equilibrium responds to changes in prices. This responsiveness, or elasticity, plays a role in how taxes affect the market and the efficiency and fairness of government influences.

IN THE CLASSROOM

■ Class Time Needed

You might try to cover these topics in three sessions, though if you have a lot of examples, or participation and questions from the class, the time could lengthen to four entire classes.

Take as much time as possible on the differences between movements along the supply and demand curves versus shifts in the curves. Go over the reasons for the shifts and give several examples. Try to use current event examples to explain movements in price and quantity.

An estimate of the time per checkpoint is:

- 4.1 Demand—45 to 60 minutes
- 4.2 Supply—45 to 60 minutes
- 4.3 Market Equilibrium—45 to 70 minutes

■ Extended Lecture Outline

4.1 Demand

A. Competitive Markets

Markets are arrangements that bring buyers and sellers together. We study a competitive market with so many buyers and sellers that no one can influence the price.

B. Quantity Demanded

The **quantity demanded** of a good is the amount that people are willing and able to buy during a specified period at a specified price. The quantity demanded refers to only one price.

C. The Law of Demand

1. The law of demand states that, other things remaining the same, if the price of a good rises, the quantity demanded of that good decreases, and if the price of a good falls, the quantity demanded of that good increases.
2. The law of demand applies because people have a limited income and try to get the best deals they can find.

D. Demand Schedule and Demand Curve

1. **Demand** is the relationship between the quantity demanded and the price of the good when all other influences on buying plans remain the same. The demand tells the quantity demanded at all prices.
2. The **demand schedule** is a list of the quantities demanded at each different price when all other influences on buying plans remain the same.
3. The **demand curve** is a graph of the relationship between the quantity demanded and the price when all other influences on buying plans remain the same. Demand curves are downward sloping.

E. Individual Demand and Market Demand

1. The **market demand** is the sum of the demands of all buyers in a market.
   a. The market demand curve is the horizontal summation of all the individual demand curves.

F. Changes in Demand

1. When the price of the good changes, there is a **change in the quantity demanded,** which is illustrated by a movement along the demand curve.
2. When any other influence on buying plans changes, there is a **change in demand,** which is illustrated by a shift in the demand curve. Factors that change demand are:
   a. Prices of related goods. The demand for a good increases if the price of a substitute rises, and the demand for a good decreases if the price of a substitute falls. The demand for a good decreases if the price of a complement rises, and the demand for a good increases if the price of a complement falls.

     b. Income. An increase in income increases the demand for a normal good. An increase in income decreases the demand for an inferior good.

     c. Expectations

     d. Number of buyers

     e. Preferences

3. When demand increases, the demand curve shifts rightward; when demand decreases, the demand curve shifts leftward.

4.2 Supply

A. Quantity Supplied

The **quantity supplied** of a good is the amount that people are willing and able to sell during a specified period at a specified price. The quantity supplied refers to only one price.

B. The Law of Supply

1. The law of supply states that other things remaining the same, if the price of a good rises, the quantity supplied of that good increases, and if the price of a good falls, the quantity supplied of that good decreases.

2. The law of supply results because sellers use their resources in a way that brings them the greatest reward, that is, the greatest profit.

C. Supply Schedule and Supply Curve

1. **Supply** is the relationship between the quantity supplied and the price of the good when all other influences on selling plans remain the same. The supply gives the quantity supplied at all prices.

2. The **supply schedule** is a list of the quantities supplied at each different price when all other influences on selling plans remains the same.

3. The **supply curve** is a graph of the relationship between the quantity supplied and the price when all other influences on selling plans remain the same. Supply curves are upward sloping.

D. Individual Supply and Market Supply

1. The **market supply** is the sum of the supplies of all sellers in a market.

     a. The market supply curve is the horizontal summation of all the individual supply curves.

E. Changes in Supply

1. When the price of the good changes, there is a **change in the quantity supplied,** which is illustrated by a movement along the supply curve.

2. When any other influence on selling plans changes, there is a **change in supply,** which is illustrated by a shift in the supply curve. Factors that change supply are:

     a. Prices of related goods. An increase in the price of a substitute in production (a product that can be produced in place of another good) decreases the supply of the good. An increase in the price of a complement in production (a product that is produced along with another good) increases the supply of the good.

     b. Prices of resources and other inputs.

     c. Expectations

     d. Number of sellers

     e. Productivity

3. When supply increases, the supply curve shifts rightward; when supply decreases, the supply curve shifts leftward.

4.3 Market Equilibrium

A. Market Equilibrium

Market equilibrium is when the quantity demanded equals the quantity supplied so that buyers' plans and sellers' plans are consistent.

1. The **equilibrium price** is the price at which the quantity demanded equals the quantity supplied.
2. The **equilibrium quantity** is the amount bought and sold at the equilibrium price.

B. Price: A Market's Automatic Regulator

1. The **law of market forces** is the tendency for the price to fall when there is a surplus and to rise when there is a shortage.
   a. If the price is above the equilibrium price, there is a surplus, in which the quantity supplied exceeds the quantity demanded.
   b. If the price is below the equilibrium price, there is a shortage, in which the quantity supplied is less than the quantity demanded.
   c. At the equilibrium price, there is no tendency for the price to change.

C. Effects of Changes in Demand

1. If the demand for a product increases, the demand curve shifts rightward. The equilibrium price rises and the equilibrium quantity increases.
2. If the demand for a product decreases, the demand curve shifts leftward. The equilibrium price falls and the equilibrium quantity decreases.
3. When demand alone changes, the supply curve does *not* shift.

D. Effects of Changes in Supply

1. If the supply of a product increases, the supply curve shifts rightward. The equilibrium price falls and the equilibrium quantity increases.
2. If the supply of a product decreases, the supply curve shifts leftward. The equilibrium price rises and the equilibrium quantity decreases.
3. When supply alone changes, the demand curve does *not* shift.

E. Changes in Both Demand and Supply

1. When both the demand and supply of a product increase, both the demand and supply curves shift rightward. The equilibrium quantity increases but the effect on the equilibrium price is ambiguous.
2. When both the demand and supply of a product decrease, both the demand and supply curves shift leftward. The equilibrium quantity decreases but the effect on the equilibrium price is ambiguous.
3. When the demand increases and the supply decreases, the demand curve shifts rightward and the supply curve shifts leftward. The equilibrium price rises but the effect on the equilibrium quantity is ambiguous.
4. When the demand decreases and the supply increases, the demand curve shifts leftward and the supply curve shifts rightward. The equilibrium price falls but the effect on the equilibrium quantity is ambiguous.
5. When both the demand and supply changes, the effect on either the price or the quantity can be determined, but the effect on the other variable is ambiguous unless we know the magnitude of each change.

■ Lecture Launchers

1. You can launch your lectures about supply and demand by using a story made famous by Milton Friedman. Ask the class if someone has a regular pencil. Have a student hold up the pencil and ask the class to think about how that pencil got into this student's hand. Note that someone grew a tree and made the wood, someone made the graphite center, someone grew the rubber that made the eraser, someone made the brass eraser holder, someone made the yellow paint, and someone assembled all these bits. Shippers, wholesalers, and a retailer all played a part in getting that pencil to your student's hand. Emphasize that no one told anyone that this student wanted a pencil. Markets did all this work. Use this example of the power of the market to segue into the study of demand and supply.

2. To start your discussion about demand, pick a good (say a slice of pizza) and propose the number of slices a person would be willing to buy for $4 a slice. Choose one slice. Now pick a student and ask the student if you reduced the price to $3 a slice, how much pizza would he or she be willing to buy. Next ask the same student how much he or she would buy at $2 per slice and then ask about $1 a slice. It can be helpful for *you* to pick the initial price and quantity so the student has a starting point for the subsequent choices. You are then guaranteed of an easy-to-graph relationship between price and quantity. For example, without your starting point, the student might say that he or she wouldn't buy a slice for more than $1. Do this same experiment for one or two more students. Use the data provided by your volunteer students by collecting the demand schedule on the board. Then take the time to graph the demand curve, explicitly labeling the axes. You can then refer to the schedule and make the point that as the price of a good falls the students are willing to buy more slices, and that as the price of the slice rises the students are willing to buy fewer slices. Then inform the students that they have just "discovered" the law of demand! Finally, use the demand curve you plotted. Move between several points on the curve, emphasizing that these "movements along the demand curve" are also known as a change in the quantity demanded and are the result of changes in the price of a slice of pizza.

3. The difference between a "change in the quantity demanded" and a "change in demand" (as well as the analogous "change in the quantity supplied" and "change in supply") can create confusion for students. If you're willing, you can lessen the confusion by always referring to changes in demand as "shifts in the demand curve." If you prefer to have students distinguish between changes in demand and changes in the quantity demanded, you might plan to spend more time emphasizing these distinctions. It helps to create a table for students to use when organizing their thoughts on how these factors affect the demand curve. For example, list the factors in one column, use another column to note whether the factor increases or decreases, and then in another column note which direction the curve shifts. You cannot do enough examples of how these factors shift the demand curve.

4. The law of market forces is important, so you want your students to grasp why prices are driven to the equilibrium. You can choose a good, like concert tickets to the hottest band (whichever one it happens to be that month). Draw a supply and demand diagram with a reasonable equilibrium price and quantity. Ask the students what would happen if the concert promoter decided to charge only $10 per ticket. Would crazy students be lining up before dawn to buy them? Yes! Explain that this is a case of excess demand. Ask them what could the promoter do to get the crowds to go away? Hopefully they will answer, "Raise ticket prices!" Show them how the market pressures the price to rise to equilibrium. Use the graph to show how the promoter and crazy students move up their respective supply and demand curves.

    You can do the same thing for excess supply. Let the promoter try to sell tickets for $1,000 each. Again, move down along the supply and demand curves as the market pressures the price to fall.

5. The ability to use the supply and demand model to determine the impact on the price and quantity from a change is crucial. Students grasp of this material is greatly improved if you draw examples. It's easier not to use specific numbers for these examples, especially when both supply and demand curves shift, because the graphs can get littered with numbers. But, the more examples you use and the more real world the examples, the more your students will comprehend how to use the supply and demand model.

■ Land Mines

1. When developing the law of demand and demand curves, emphasize that the quantities chosen (given the prices) represent what a person is *willing* to do, and that this combination of price and quantity is not what necessarily occurs in the market. Remind them that you don't know the market equilibrium price and quantity until you add in the supply curve. It also reinforces the idea that their *willingness* to pay X dollars for a good doesn't mean that's what they have to pay.

2. Use the same approach when developing the law of supply and supply curves. The supply schedule and curve represent a firm's *willingness* to supply goods at various prices. Just because a firm is *willing* to produce a certain output at a certain price doesn't mean this is what actually occurs. Remind students that they have to consider the demand curve to find out what actually happens. Students seem to understand the behavior behind the demand curve, but tend to find the logic behind the supply curve more difficult. This could be because most of them have never acted like a firm. That's why I always say, "Suppose you own a pizza parlor (or whatever good you're using). What would YOU do as the owner if the price of pizza rose?"

3. When graphing the supply and demand curves, you cannot stress enough that price goes on the vertical axis and quantity belongs on the horizontal axis. I joke with my students that they can do it the other way but it will

probably hurt their chances of getting an A on the exam. In fact, *every* time I draw a graph, I always describe what I'm drawing: "Here's the vertical axis with price and the horizontal axis with the quantity."

4. Using the text's "rightward" and "leftward" shifts of demand and supply curves is much better than saying they shift up or down, especially for shifts of the supply curve. Then, when you draw a curve shifting, be careful to draw the arrows in the horizontal direction. Because a rightward shift in the supply curve makes it "look" like it is getting lower, students want to say this is a decrease in supply. By sticking with "rightward" shifts, an increase in supply or demand is always shown by a rightward shift and a decrease is always shown by a leftward shift. I always tell students that at least one of them will make the mistake of shifting the supply curve the wrong way, and challenge them not to be that student.

5. I always tell students that they stand a much better chance of doing well on the exam if they DRAW the question. Tell them it's much easier to see the effects of a change in demand or a change in supply (or both) on the equilibrium price and quantity if they draw the change.

ANSWERS TO CHECKPOINT EXERCISES

■ CHECKPOINT 4.1: Demand

1a. Assume there are four services provided by the Internet: e-mail, information on Web pages, information on fast breaking news, and entertainment. The only substitute for Internet e-mail service, if a person is interested in the speed of service, is the telephone. For bulky or unique items (like large documents, magazines, bills, photographs) or if you don't mind waiting for news, postal services are substitutes. In terms of Web pages, some provide a great deal of information and others provide minimal, basic information on their firms. If you need the basic information and you want it fast, there are no real substitutes for the Internet. If you want detailed information, substitutes for the Internet are phone calls or literature sent from the firm. For information on fast breaking news, possibly radio or television is a substitute. For entertainment, substitutes abound. For instance, listening to music can be done by accessing an Internet radio station or, as substitutes, a local radio station or a CD. The Internet has cartoons, for which comic books and cartoons on television are substitutes. More generally, anything that provides entertainment substitutes for the Internet's entertainment services, though some (watching a movie on a DVD) may not be a particularly close substitute.

1b. The complements to the Internet are computers, phone lines, modems, cable modems and DSL lines provided by the phone service.

1c. The main developments are quicker and cheaper computers and modems and more Internet providers supplying better service. Additionally, more people now own computers.

1d. This question asks which factors have shifted the demand curve for Internet services. The new, cheaper computers and modems (complements that also represent increases in preferences) have shifted the demand curve rightward. More people now own computers, and this change in the number of buyers also shifts the demand curve rightward.

1e. The increase in quantity demanded occurs when the supply curve shifts. An increase in the number of providers and an increase in technology shift the supply curve rightward. When the supply curve shifts, you move down along the demand curve.

■ CHECKPOINT 4.2: Supply

1a. A truck is a substitute in production for an SUV. If the price of a truck rises, an auto maker will produce more trucks and fewer SUVs. The supply curve for SUVs shifts leftward as shown in Figure 4.1.

FIGURE 4.1
Practice Problem 1a

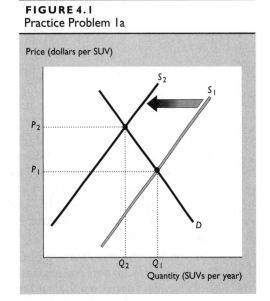

1b. When the price of an SUV falls, there is a movement down along the supply curve for SUVs. This outcome is shown in Figure 4.2 in which the price falls from P_1 to P_2, and the quantity supplied de-creases from Q_1 to Q_2.

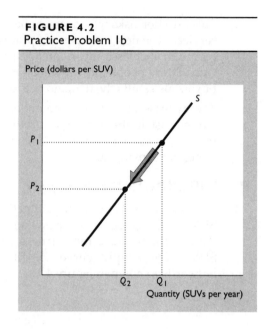

FIGURE 4.2
Practice Problem 1b

1c. If we expect the price of SUVs to fall next year, suppliers will increase the current supply in order to take advantage of current higher prices. The supply curve shifts rightward, as shown in Figure 4.3 with the shift from S_1 to S_2.

1d. To replace the defective engines, the auto maker incurs higher production costs. This cost increase decreases the supply and shifts the supply curve leftward, as was illustrated in Figure 4.1.

1e. The new robot technology decreases production costs for SUVs. This change increases the supply of SUVs and the supply curve for SUVs shifts rightward, as illustrated in Figure 4.3.

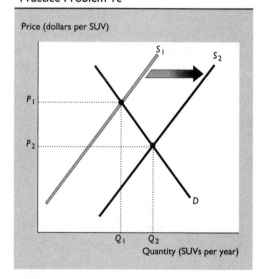

FIGURE 4.3
Practice Problem 1c

■ CHECKPOINT 4.3: Market Equilibrium

1a. The market equilibrium is a price of $7.00 and 200 CDs.

1b. If the price of a CD is $6.00, there will be an excess demand, or shortage, of CDs. Inventories of CDs will be depleted and stores will be crowded with people trying to buy these "cheap" CDs. As a result, the price of CDs will rise.

1c. If the demand for CDs increases by 100 at each price, the new equilibrium price will be $8.00 and 250 CDs a day will be bought. At the old equilibrium price of $7.00 a CD, there is a shortage of CDs, so the price rises.

1d. The new equilibrium price will be $6.00 for a CD and the new equilibrium quantity will be 225 CDs a day. These events shift the demand curve leftward and the supply curve rightward. The supply curve will shift further than the demand curve. As a result, there is a surplus at the initial price. The equilibrium price therefore falls and the equilibrium quantity increases.

ANSWERS TO CHAPTER CHECKPOINT EXERCISES

1a. The Foundations Web site shows there are 54 bottlers along with 900 brands. The market looks competitive.

1b. Suppose the average price of a liter of bottled water was $1.10 in 1998 and 100 million bottles were sold. By 2000, the average price of a bottle of water has decreased to $0.96 while 230 million bottles are sold. The demand has increased as people's preferences for bottled water increased. At the same time, more bottlers have entered the market and increases in productivity have made bottling cheaper. These events increased the supply. Hence the demand curve and supply curve have both shifted rightward. Because the supply curve shifted more than the demand curve, the equilibrium price has fallen and equilibrium quantity has risen.

1c. The increase in preferences for bottled water has decreased the demand for soft drinks.

1d. An increase in fitness centers has increased the demand for bottled water and decreased the demand for soft drinks.

2a. True. Allowing African bananas to be sold in the United States increases the number of sellers of bananas. As Figure 4.4 illustrates, the change in supply shifts the supply curve for bananas in the United States rightward from S_1 to S_2. This shift leads to a movement down along the demand curve for bananas, as illustrated, which results in an increase in the equilibrium quantity (from Q_1 to Q_2) and a decrease in the equilibrium price (from P_1 to P_2).

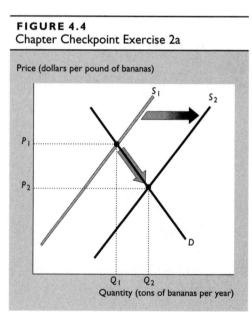

FIGURE 4.4
Chapter Checkpoint Exercise 2a

Price (dollars per pound of bananas)

Quantity (tons of bananas per year)

2b. False. As basketball becomes less popular, the demand for basketball shoes will decrease as people will switch from buying basketball shoes to soccer shoes. The demand curve for basketball shoes will shift leftward and the price will fall. As the price falls, there is a movement along the supply curve and a decrease in the quantity supplied.

Some students may suggest that the supply also decreases, as basketball shoe producers switch to soccer shoes. You might count this answer as correct, but it is a more long-run answer because the decrease in supply will not occur immediately. If the student notes that both the supply of basketball shoes and the demand for basketball shoes decrease, then the price will rise only if the supply decreases by more than the demand.

2c. True. People prefer to ski in the winter when skiing conditions are best. As the weather becomes warmer in the spring, skiing conditions deteriorate, and people prefer to ski less. As a result, in the spring, the demand curve for skiing in Aspen shifts leftward from D_1 to D_2 as shown in Figure 4.5. The price falls from P_1 to P_2 and there is a movement along the supply curve. Demand decreases and the quantity supplied decreases.

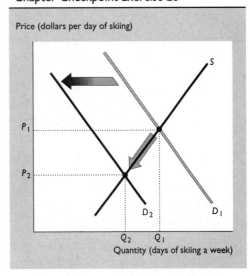

FIGURE 4.5
Chapter Checkpoint Exercise 2c

2d. False. Frozen yogurt and ice cream are substitutes. As frozen yogurt becomes cheaper, some people will switch from buying ice cream to buying frozen yogurt. The demand for ice cream will decrease and the demand curve for ice cream will shift leftward. The price will fall and as a result, there will be a movement along the supply curve. Less ice cream will be consumed. However, the price of ice cream will fall rather than rise, as the question suggested.

3a. Apple juice and orange juice are substitutes. If apple juice becomes cheaper, people will substitute apple juice for orange juice. The demand for orange juice will decrease. The demand curve for orange juice shifts leftward and the equilibrium price and quantity of orange juice decrease.

3b. Apple juice and orange juice are substitutes, and as the price of apple juice falls, the demand for orange juice decreases. This causes the demand curve for orange juice to shift leftward. As the wage rate paid to orange grove workers increases, the costs to produce orange juice rise. As a result, the supply of orange juice decreases and the supply curve of orange juice shifts leftward. The net effect of these events causes the equilibrium quantity to decrease but has an undetermined effect on equilibrium price. If the supply decreases more than the demand, and the shift in the supply curve is greater than the shift in the demand curve, the price rises. However, if the demand decreases more than the supply, and the shift in the demand curve is greater than the shift in the supply curve, the price falls.

3c. As orange juice becomes more popular, the demand increases and the demand curve for orange juice shifts rightward. The cheaper machine lowers the production costs of orange juice, thereby increasing the supply of orange juice and shifting the supply curve of orange juice rightward. As a result, the equilibrium quantity definitely increases. If the shift in the supply curve is greater than the shift in the demand curve, the equilibrium price falls. If the shift in the demand curve is greater than the shift in the supply curve, the equilibrium price rises.

3d. If joggers switch from bottled water to orange juice, the demand for orange juice increases and the demand curve for orange juice shifts rightward. As a result, the equilibrium price and quantity rise.

4a. As more people buy new cars, which use the new fuel, the demand for gasoline will decrease. Thus the demand curve for gasoline shifts leftward, from D_1 to D_2 in Figure 4.6. As a result, the equilibrium price falls from P_1 to P_2 and the equilibrium quantity decreases from Q_1 to Q_2.

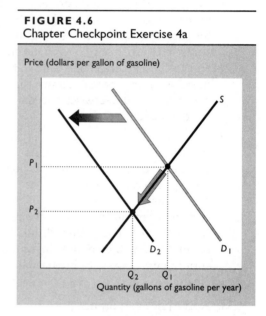

FIGURE 4.6
Chapter Checkpoint Exercise 4a

4b. Because used cars can't use the new fuel, fewer people will demand used cars. The demand curve for used cars shifts leftward. As a result, the equilibrium price falls and the equilibrium quantity decreases.

5a. The market equilibrium occurs at a price of $5 and 140 mouse pads. At the price of $5, the quantity supplied equals the quantity demanded.

5b. At a price of $7, quantity demanded equals 120 mouse pads and quantity supplied equals 160 mouse pads. There is a surplus of 40 mouse pads per week. Store owners want to sell this surplus because it is sitting on their shelves. To accomplish this goal, store owners reduce the price of a mouse pad. As the price falls to $6 per pad, even though the quantity supplied decreases and the quantity demanded increases, there is still a surplus. Finally, store owners reduce the price to $5, at which time the market reaches equilibrium and the quantity of mouse pads demanded equals the quantity supplied.

5c. As a result of the decrease in the price of a computer, the quantity of mouse pads demanded at each price increases by 20. The table shows the new demand schedule. From the table, the new equilibrium price is $6 a mouse pad and the new equilibrium quantity is 150 mouse pads a week.

Price (dollars per pad)	Quantity demanded	Quantity supplied
	(mouse pads per week)	
3	180	120
4	170	130
5	160	140
6	**150**	**150**
7	140	160
8	130	170

5d. The new voice recognition software decreases the quantity of mouse pads demanded by 10 at each price. The demand for mouse pads decreases. At the same time, the quantity of mouse pads supplied increase by 30 at each price. That is, the supply of mouse pads increases. At the initial price of $5 a mouse pad, the quantity demanded is 140 mouse pads and the quantity supplied is 170 mouse pads. At $5 a mouse pad, there is a surplus of mouse pads. The price will fall until the surplus disappears. The new equilibrium price is $3 a mouse pad, and the new equilibrium quantity is 150 mouse pads a week.

6.   The first statement is false. As more people own computers, the demand for Internet service will increase and so the price of Internet service will rise. The second statement is also false. As the demand for Internet service increases, the demand curve shifts rightward and there is a movement along the supply curve and a change in the quantity supplied but not a change in supply.

ADDITIONAL EXERCISES FOR ASSIGNMENT

■ Questions

1.   For each of the questions below, decide whether the event leads to a shift in the demand curve, a shift in the supply curve, a movement along the demand curve, or a movement along the supply curve. Explain your answer.

  a.   What happens to the demand curve for pumpkins in October?
  b.   What happens to the supply curve of new homes if the price of land increases?
  c.   Companies can produce both cardigan sweaters and pull-over sweaters. What happens to the supply curve of cardigan sweaters if the price of pull-over sweaters increases?
  d.   What happens to the demand curve for bottled water in summer?
  e.   What happens to the demand curve for gasoline if 20 percent of all new cars are required to be electric powered?
  f.   What happens to the supply curve of pigs feet if the price of fried pork rinds decreases?

2.   What happens to equilibrium price and quantity of each good described in the situations described below. Explain and illustrate your answer.

  a.   Sunnyvale is named the most livable city in the United States. At the same time, the wages of homebuilders, electricians, and plumbers in Sunnyvale increase. Describe what happens to the new home market in Sunnyvale.
  b.   The price of airline fuel falls by 10 percent. At the same time, people's incomes increase and they prefer to fly to their vacation destinations. Describe what happens to the market for airline travel.
  c.   Installation costs for small satellite TV dishes fall by 10 percent. At the same time, network owners increase the cost of programming packages shown via satellite TV dish systems. Describe what happens in the market for small satellite TV dishes.

■ Answers

1.   a.   As people prepare for fall holidays, people increase their preferences for pumpkins. As a result, there is a shift rightward in the demand curve for pumpkins.

b. Land is a resource used in the production of new homes. As the price of land increases, housing costs increase and the supply curve of new houses shifts leftward.

c. Cardigan sweaters and pull-over sweaters are substitutes in production. If the price of a pull-over sweater increases, there will be a decrease in the supply of cardigan sweaters. The supply curve of cardigan sweaters shifts leftward.

d. People exercise more in the summer and spend more time outside getting thirsty. As a result, there is a increase in the demand for bottled water during the summer and the demand curve for bottled water shifts rightward.

e. As more cars are required to be electric powered, the demand for gasoline decreases. The demand curve for gasoline shifts leftward.

f. Pigs feet and fried pork rinds are complements in production. If the price of fried pork rinds decreases, the supply of pigs feet decreases and the supply curve of pigs feet shifts leftward.

FIGURE 4.7a
Additional Exercises 2a

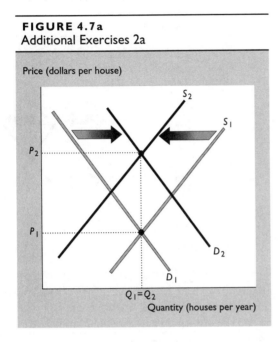

FIGURE 4.7b
Additional Exercises 2a

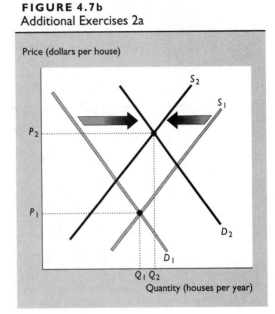

2a. As people hear how nice it is to live in Sunnyvale, the demand for new homes in Sunnyvale increases and the demand curve shifts rightward, from D_1 to D_2. At the same time, an increase in building costs decreases the supply of new homes, so the supply curve shifts leftward from S_1 to S_2. As all three graphs show, the equilibrium price of new homes increases, from P_1 to P_2 in the figures. What happens to equilibrium quantity depends on which curve shifts the most. If the curves shift the same amount, as in Figure 4.7a, the equilibrium quantity does not change. If the demand curve shifts more, as in Figure 4.7b, the equilibrium quantity increases. If the supply curve shifts more, as in Figure 4.7c, the equilibrium quantity decreases.

FIGURE 4.7c
Additional Exercises 2a

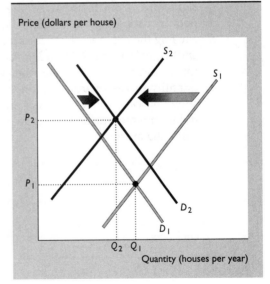

FIGURE 4.8a
Additional Exercises 2b

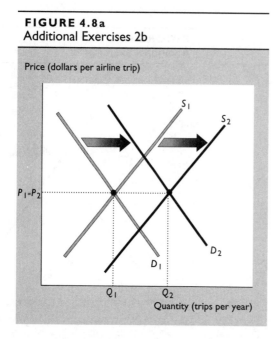

FIGURE 4.8b
Additional Exercises 2b

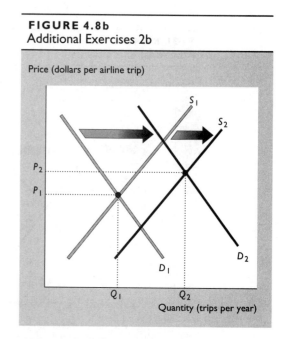

2b. As the price of airline fuel falls, airlines' costs fall. The supply of airline travel increases and the supply curve of airline travel shifts rightward, from S_1 to S_2. At the same time, people decide to take more airline trips, causing the demand curve for airline travel to shift rightward from D_1 to D_2. As a result, all three figures show that the equilibrium quantity increases from Q_1 to Q_2. The figures show, however, that the effect on the price is indeterminate unless you know which curve shifts the most.

FIGURE 4.8c
Additional Exercises 2b

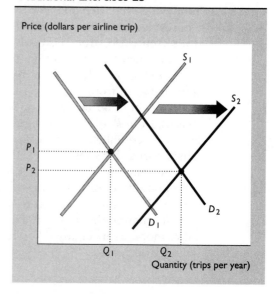

FIGURE 4.9a
Additional Exercises 2c

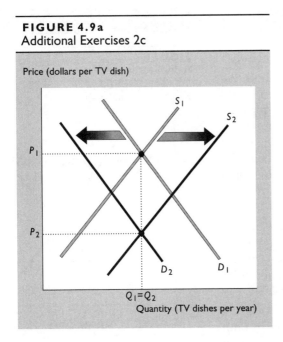

FIGURE 4.9b
Additional Exercises 2c

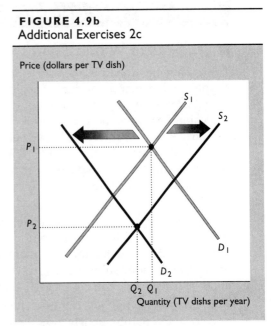

2c. A decrease in installation costs reflects a decrease in production costs. Thus the supply curve of satellite TV dishes shifts rightward, from S_1 to S_2 in the figures. At the same time, the price of a complement (programming) increases. This price hike leads to the demand curve for satellite dishes shifting leftward, in the figures, from D_1 to D_2. As a result, each figure demonstrates that the equilibrium price of satellite dishes decreases from P_1 to P_2. However, as the figures also demonstrate, the effect on the quantity is ambiguous.

FIGURE 4.9c
Additional Exercises 2c

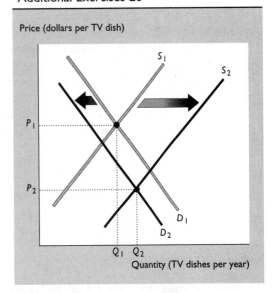

ANSWERS TO ECONOMICS IN THE NEWS

■ Expensive Winter Looms

The events mentioned in the article affect both the supply and demand for fuel. The low crude oil inventories reflect low supply; the pipeline explosion decreases the supply; and, if a hurricane had struck, the supply would have been decreased still more. Thus, all the events that affect the supply of fuel operate to decrease it, so the supply curve shifts leftward, from S_1 to S_2 in Figures 4.10 and 4.11.

At the same time, however, the demand for fuel changes. With consumers using more electricity, the demand for fuel increases. Hence the demand curve shifts rightward, as shown by the shift from D_1 to D_2 in Figures 4.10 and 4.11.

Comparing the two figures shows that the price of fuel unambiguously rises because in both figures the price rises. (The price rises to P_2 in both figures.) But the effect on the quantity of fuel is ambiguous. If the supply shift is larger, as in Figure 4.10, the quantity decreases. If, however, the demand shift is larger, as in Figure 4.11, the quantity increases. Hence, without further information about the relative magnitudes of the effects mentioned in the article, it is impossible to determine if the equilibrium quantity of fuel increases, decreases, or even stays the same. (The quantity stays the same when the two shifts are the same size.)

FIGURE 4.10
Economics in the News

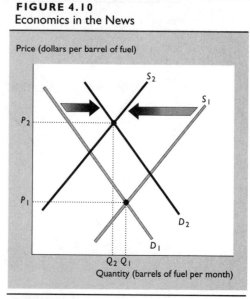

FIGURE 4.11
Economics in the News

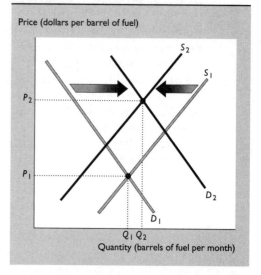

USING EYE ON THE GLOBAL ECONOMY

■ A Change in the Demand for Roses

Use the data to show how a supply and demand diagram is drawn. Remind students that price belongs on the vertical axis, that quantity belongs on the horizontal axis, that the demand curve is downward sloping, and the supply curve is upward sloping. Show that the curves intersect at $40 and 6 million bunches of roses. You also can use the story and data to show how a change in preferences affects the demand for roses. In February, the demand curve for roses shifts rightward. Using this adjusted diagram, you can show that if the price remained at $40, there would be excess demand for roses. You can explain how this shortage pressures the price to rise to the new equilibrium of $80 and 24 million bunches.

USING EYE ON THE PAST

■ Changes in the Supply of Oil

You can use the data and story to review the factors that shift the supply curve. Remind students to analyze separately each event (technological advances, etc.). With a number of events occurring at one time, students are likely to make mistakes in figuring out how equilibrium prices and quantities will be affected. By dissecting the events (instead of lumping them together) they are more likely to get the correct answer.

72

Elasticities of Demand and Supply

Chapter **5**

CHAPTER OUTLINE

1. Define, explain the factors that influence, and calculate the price elasticity of demand.

    A. Percentage Change in Price
        1. The Midpoint Method
    B. Percentage Change in Quantity Demanded
        1. Minus Sign
    C. Elastic and Inelastic Demand
    D. Influences on the Price Elasticity of Demand
        1. Substitution Effects
            a. Luxury Versus Necessity
            b. Narrowness of Definition
            c. Time Elapsed Since Price Change
        2. Income Effect
    E. Computing the Price Elasticity of Demand
        1. Slope and Elasticity
        2. A Units-Free Measure
    F. Elasticity Along a Linear Demand Curve
    G. Total Revenue and the Price Elasticity of Demand
    H. *Your* Expenditure and *Your* Elasticity of Demand
    I. Applications of the Price Elasticity of Demand
        1. Farm Prices and Total Revenue
        2. Addiction and Elasticity

2. Define, explain the factors that influence, and calculate the price elasticity of supply.

    A. Elastic and Inelastic Supply
    B. Influences on the Price Elasticity of Supply
        1. Production Possibilities
            a. Time Elapsed Since a Price Change
        2. Storage Possibilities
    C. Computing the Price Elasticity of Supply

3. Define and explain the factors that influence the cross elasticity of demand and the income elasticity of demand.

    A. Cross Elasticity of Demand

    B. Income Elasticity of Demand

CHAPTER ROADMAP

■ Where We Are

In this chapter we begin to examine what demand and supply curves can tell us besides the equilibrium price and quantity. The price elasticity of demand tells us how the quantity demanded changes in response to a change in price and also tells us how total revenue changes when the price changes. We use the price elasticity of supply to tell us how quantity supplied changes in response to a change in price. Finally, we use the cross elasticity of demand and the income elasticity of demand to tell us how quantity demanded changes in response to a change in price of another good or income, respectively.

■ Where We've Been

We have now examined why we study economics and have built basic models, such as the production possibilities frontier and the supply and demand framework, that we will use throughout the rest of the course to help us understand the motivations behind firms' and consumers' actions.

■ Where We're Going

The next chapter continues to use the supply and demand framework to study the efficiency and fairness of markets. Consumer surplus and producer surplus will be introduced. We return to the concept of efficiency and also study occasions when the market is inefficient.

IN THE CLASSROOM

■ Class Time Needed

You can complete this chapter in no more than two sessions. Take the necessary time to explain the idea of percentage changes and explicitly go over each of the calculations in computing the different elasticities. Provide as many real world examples as you can while focusing on how your students encounter these cases.

By providing these examples and the intuition that goes with them, your students will find this information more applicable and easier to understand.

An estimate of the time per checkpoint is:

- 5.1 The Price Elasticity of Demand—30 to 60 minutes
- 5.2 The Price Elasticity of Supply—15 minutes
- 5.3 Cross Elasticity and Income Elasticity—15 minutes

■ Extended Lecture Outline

5.1 The Price Elasticity of Demand

The **price elasticity of demand** is a measure of the extent to which the quantity demanded of a good changes when the price of the good changes and other influences on buyers' plans remain the same.

A. Percentage Change in Price
   1. The midpoint method uses the average of the initial price and new price in the denominator when calculating a percentage change. Because the average price is the same between two prices regardless of whether the price falls or rises, the midpoint method is a better way to calculate the percentage change in price.
      a. Using the midpoint formula, the percentage change in price equals:
      $$\left(\frac{\text{New price} - \text{Initial price}}{(\text{New price} + \text{Initial price}) \div 2} \right) \times 100.$$

B. Percentage Change in Quantity Demanded
   Use the midpoint method when calculating the percentage change in quantity:
   $$\left(\frac{\text{New quantity} - \text{Initial quantity}}{(\text{New quantity} + \text{Initial quantity}) \div 2} \right) \times 100.$$

   1. Minus Sign
      Because a change in price causes an opposite change in quantity demanded, in calculating the price elasticity of demand we focus on the magnitude of the change by using the absolute value. That is, we ignore the minus sign.

C. Elastic and Inelastic Demand
   The price elasticity of demand falls into three categories:
   1. **Elastic demand**—the percentage change in the quantity demanded exceeds the percentage change in price (which means the elasticity is greater than 1).
   2. **Unit elastic demand**—the percentage change in the quantity demanded equals the percentage change in price (which means the elasticity equals 1).
   3. **Inelastic demand**—the percentage change in the quantity demanded is less than the percentage change in price (which means the elasticity is less than 1).
   4. There are two other special cases:
      a. **Perfectly elastic demand**
      b. **Perfectly inelastic demand**

D. Influences on the Price Elasticity of Demand
   1. Substitution Effect
      If good substitutes are readily available, demand is elastic. If good substitutes are hard to find, demand is inelastic.

2. Three factors determine how easy substitutes are to find:
    a. Luxury versus necessity—there are few substitutes for necessities (so demand is price inelastic) and there are many substitutes for luxuries (so demand is price elastic).
    b. Narrowness of definition—the more narrowly defined the good is, the more elastic its demand. The more broadly defined the good, the less elastic its demand.
    c. Time elapsed since price change—the longer the time that has passed since the price change, the more elastic is demand.
3. Income Effect
   The larger the portion of your income spent on the good, the more elastic is demand because a price change has a large, noticeable impact on your budget. The smaller the portion of your income spent on the good, the less elastic is demand.
E. Computing the Price Elasticity of Demand
   1. The formula used to compute the price elasticity of demand is:

$$\text{Price elasticity of demand} = \frac{\text{Percentage change in quantity demanded}}{\text{Percentage change in price}}.$$

   a. If the price elasticity of demand is greater than 1 (the numerator is larger than the denominator), demand is elastic.
   b. If the price elasticity of demand is equal to 1 (the numerator equals the denominator), demand is unit elastic.
   c. If the price elasticity of demand is less than 1 (the numerator is less than the denominator), demand is inelastic.
   2. Slope and elasticity
      The slope of a demand curve measures the responsiveness of quantity demanded to a change in price, but it is not a units-free measure of this responsiveness.
   3. A units-free measure
      The percentage change in price and the percentage change in quantity demanded (the denominator and numerator of the elasticity formula) are independent of the units of measurement. Hence the elasticity formula produces a units-free measure of responsiveness.
F. Elasticity Along a Linear Demand Curve
   Along a straight-line demand curve, the slope is constant, but the elasticity changes.
   1. At the midpoint of a linear demand curve, the elasticity equals 1 and demand is unit elastic.
   2. Above the midpoint of a linear demand curve, elasticity is greater than 1 and demand is elastic.
   3. Below the midpoint of a linear demand curve, elasticity is less than 1 and demand is inelastic.
G. Total Revenue and Price Elasticity of Demand
   1. **Total revenue** equals (the price of the good) × (the quantity of the good sold).
   2. The **total revenue test** tells us what happens to total revenue when the price of a good changes. The price change's impact on total revenue depends on the elasticity of demand.
      a. If elasticity is greater than 1, an increase in price decreases total revenue. Price and total revenue move in opposite directions.
      b. If elasticity equals 1, an increase in price does not change total revenue.
      c. If elasticity is less than 1, an increase in price increases total revenue. Price and total revenue move in the same direction.
H. *Your* Expenditure and *Your* Elasticity of Demand
   When the price of a good increases, your expenditure on that good depends on the elasticity of your demand for that good.

    a. If your demand is elastic, your expenditure on the good decreases when the price rises.
    b. If your demand is unit elastic, your expenditure on the good does not change when the price rises.
    c. If your demand is inelastic, your expenditure on the good increases when the price rises.
I. Applications of the Price Elasticity of Demand
  1. Farm Prices and Total Revenue
    a. Because the demand for agricultural products is inelastic, a crop failure that boosts the price of an agricultural product leads to an increase in total revenue for all farmers taken together.
  2. Addiction and Elasticity
    a. Nonusers' demand for addictive goods is elastic, so a tax that increases the price of these goods decreases spending by nonusers.
    b. Addicts' demand is inelastic, so a tax or legislation that increases the price of addictive substances increases the expenditure on the goods and does little to deter use.

5.2 The Price Elasticity of Supply

The **price elasticity of supply** is a measure of the extent to which the quantity supplied of a good changes when the price of the good changes and other influences on sellers' plans remain the same.

A. Elastic and Inelastic Supply
  1. The price elasticity of supply falls into three categories:
    a. **Elastic supply**—the percentage change in the quantity supplied is greater than the percentage change in price.
    b. **Unit elastic supply**—the percentage change in the quantity supplied equals the percentage change in price.
    c. **Inelastic supply**—the percentage change in the quantity supplied is less than the percentage change in price.
  2. There are two special cases of price elasticity:
    a. **Perfectly elastic supply**
    b. **Perfectly inelastic supply**
B. Influences on the Price Elasticity of Supply
  1. Production possibilities
    a. How rapidly the cost of increasing production rises and the time elapsed since the price change influence the elasticity of supply.
  2. Storage possibilities
    a. Storable goods have a more elastic supply that goods that cannot be stored.
C. Computing the Elasticity of Supply
  1. The formula used to compute the price elasticity of supply is:

$$\text{Price elasticity of supply} = \frac{\text{Percentage change in quantity supplied}}{\text{Percentage change in price}}.$$

    a. If the price elasticity of supply is greater than 1 (the numerator is larger than the denominator), supply is elastic.
    b. If the price elasticity of supply is equal to 1 (the numerator equals the denominator), supply is unit elastic.

c. If the price elasticity of supply is less than I (the numerator is less than the denominator), supply is inelastic.

5.3 Cross Elasticity and Income Elasticity

A. **Cross Elasticity of Demand**

The cross elasticity of demand is a measure of the extent to which the demand for a good changes when the price of a substitute or complement changes, other things remaining the same.

1. The formula used to calculate the cross elasticity of demand is:

$$\text{Cross elasticity of demand} = \frac{\text{Percentage change in quantity demanded of a good}}{\text{Percentage change in price of one of its substitutes or complements}}.$$

2. The cross elasticity of demand for a substitute is positive.
3. The cross elasticity of demand for a complement is negative.

B. **Income Elasticity of Demand**

The income elasticity of demand is a measure of the extent to which the demand for a good changes when income changes, other things remaining the same.

1. The formula used to calculate the income elasticity of demand is:

$$\text{Income elasticity of demand} = \frac{\text{Percentage change in quantity demanded}}{\text{Percentage change in income}}.$$

2. For a normal good, the income elasticity of demand is positive.
3. When the income elasticity of demand is greater than I, demand is income elastic. This outcome occurs when the quantity demanded increases more quickly than income increases.
4. When the income elasticity of demand is between 0 and I, demand is income inelastic. This outcome occurs when the quantity demanded increases, but more slowly than income increases.
5. For an *inferior* good, the income elasticity of demand is less than 0. This outcome occurs when the quantity demanded for a good decreases as income increases.

■ Lecture Launchers

1. If students only focus on categorizing the types of elasticity and whether the elasticities are negative or positive, or whether they are greater or less than 1, they can be overwhelmed and miss the interesting decision-making information the numbers provide. A great way to preview the importance of elasticities is to choose two volunteers to play "manager." Let one be the manager of a firm that produces food and let the other be the manager of a firm that produces furniture. Tell each of them that the survival of their firms depend on them raising total revenues. Ask the furniture manager what he or she thinks should be done to raise revenues. The most likely answer is to raise prices. Then ask the food manager what he or she thinks should be done. The answer is also likely to be to raise prices. Then ask your students whom they would rather work for, the manager that will lose his or her job or the one that will get to keep his or her job. Try to get your students to commit to one of the "companies" because they will be more likely to pay attention to the lecture to see if they are right or wrong. Explain that today's lecture will provide the answer to your question. As you start explaining the elasticity of demand, but before you get to total reve-

nue, ask your students if any are willing to switch managers. The smarter ones should leave the furniture manager because the demand for furniture is elastic and so raising the price will decrease total revenue!

2. Another interesting aspect of elasticity is how a government raises tax revenues. You can ask students if it will be easier to raise tax revenues if the government raises taxes on cigarettes or on Pepsi. You can try to promote discussion by claiming that a lot more Pepsi is sold than cigarettes and that the government would be better off taxing by Pepsi. Alternatively, you might get some smokers to assert that they would be willing to pay most any price for a cigarette. Tell the students that if they pay attention to to-day's lecture, they'll find out the answer! Then, at the appropriate point in your lecture, be certain to explicitly point out to the students that imposing a tax on cigarettes will surely raise significantly more revenue than a tax on Pepsi.

■ Land Mines

1. To show the importance of a units-free measure of elasticity, you can cal-culate the slope of a demand curve when the vertical axis is measured in dollars and again when it is measured in cents. For instance, assume a de-mand curve for tacos, such that when the price rises from $1.00 to $1.05, the quantity demanded decreases from 50 to 45 tacos. The slope of the demand curve with the price measured in dollars is 0.01. Then, draw the identical demand curve, only this time measure the price in cents. Thus when the price rises from 100 cents to 105 cents, the quantity demanded decreases from 50 to 45 units and so the slope in this case is 1.00. Point out that having the slope of the identical(!) demand curve change simply because the units of the price change is surely not a good feature. (In addition, the slope changes when the quantity units change.) For this reason, economists do not use the slope as their measure of sensitivity. They use elasticity because elasticity is calculated using (unit-free) percentage changes and so elasticity does not change if the units of the price (or the quantity) are changed.

2. Elasticity is a subject that can overwhelm students by the many details. Be sure to stress the common features of all the different elasticities. For in-stance, all elasticities measure how strongly people respond to a change in some factor (though the factor varies with each elasticity); all elasticities use percentage changes; and all elasticities divide the percentage change in the quantity by the percentage change in the relevant factor. Of these features, the most important is the fact that elasticities measure responsiveness. Stress this fact and your students will find it significantly easier to compre-hend all the myriad details.

ANSWERS TO CHECKPOINT EXERCISES

■ CHECKPOINT 5.1 Price Elasticity of Demand

1a. The percentage change in price is 10 percent. The midpoint method gives the percentage as $\left(\dfrac{\$2.10 - \$1.90}{(\$2.10 + \$1.90)/2} \right) \times 100.$

1b. The percentage change in quantity is 20 percent. The midpoint method gives the percentage as $\left(\dfrac{11\,\text{million} - 9\,\text{million}}{(11\,\text{million} + 9\,\text{million})/2} \right) \times 100.$

1c. The demand for spring water is elastic because the percentage change in quantity demanded is greater than the percentage change in price.

1d. The demand for Pepsi might well be less elastic because fewer excellent substitutes exist for Pepsi. Coke and perhaps R.C. Cola are very close substitutes, but other sodas, such as Mountain Dew, are less close substitutes. In the meanwhile, *any* brand of water, Aquafina, Polar, etc., or even plain drinking water are excellent substitutes for the spring water.

1e. The price elasticity of demand = (20 percent/10 percent) = 2.0.

1f. The price elasticity of demand has been calculated for the range between two prices, $1.90 a bottle and $2.10 a bottle. The price at which the elasticity of 2.0 applies is the average price of $2.00 a bottle.

1g. The change in total revenue = −$2,000,000. This amount is the difference between the initial total revenue of $20,900,00 (= $1.90 × 11 million bottles) and the new total revenue of $18,900,000 (= $2.10 × 9 million bottles). Hence the seller's total revenue decreases by $2 million.

1h. The demand for spring water is unit elastic at a price lower than $2.00 a bottle. Why? At $2.00 a bottle, the elasticity equals 2.00. Moving downward along a linear demand curve, the elasticity falls in value. Hence moving downward along the demand curve to lower prices, the elasticity is falling in value until ultimately (at a price of $1.50 a bottle) the elasticity will equal 1.00.

■ CHECKPOINT 5.2 Price Elasticity of Supply

1a. The supply of long grain rice is inelastic. The percentage change in the quantity supplied is less than the percentage change in the price.

1b. Once the seed has been planted, the supply of rice becomes fixed for that period making supply inelastic. Once harvested, rice is a storable good which makes supply more elastic.

1c. The price elasticity of supply = (17 percent/40 percent) = 0.425.

1d. If price remains low, fewer farmers will raise rice. As the price stays low, the weakest farmers will drop out of the market, perhaps by switching to growing other crops. Thus as more time passes, the quantity supplied decreases by more and hence supply becomes more elastic.

■ CHECKPOINT 5.3 Cross Elasticity and Income Elasticity

1a. The cross elasticity of demand of soda with respect to burgers is equal to (67 percent/−13 percent) = −5.15, where the percentages are from using the midpoint method.

1b. Soda and burgers are complements because they are goods that are used together. The negative cross elasticity of demand reflects this fact.

1c. The cross elasticity of demand of pizza with respect to burgers is equal to (−67 percent/−13 percent) = 5.15, where the percentages are (again) from using the midpoint method.

1d. Pizza and burgers are substitutes because they are foods that can be used in place of each other. The positive cross elasticity of demand reflects this fact.

1e. The demand for soda has increased and the demand curve has shifted rightward. The demand for pizza has decreased and the demand curve has shifted leftward.

2a. The income elasticity of demand for macaroni and cheese is equal to (−20 percent/10 percent) = −2.00.

2b. Macaroni and cheese is an inferior good because as Jody's income increases, she consumes less of it. The result that the income elasticity is negative reflects this fact.

2c. The income elasticity of demand for chicken is equal to (5 percent/10 percent) = 0.50.

2d. Chicken is a normal good because as Jody's income increases, she consumes more of it. The result that the income elasticity of demand is positive reflects this fact.

2e. The demand for chicken is income inelastic because the quantity demanded of chicken increases at a slower rate than Jody's income increases.

ANSWERS TO CHAPTER CHECKPOINT EXERCISES

1a. The demand for home heating oil is inelastic because the percentage change in quantity demanded is less than the percentage change in price.

1b. The price elasticity of demand = (2 percent)/(20 percent) = 0.10, where the fact that the change in the quantity of heating oil demanded has a negative sign is ignored, as is conventional.

1c. Because the demand for home heating oil is very inelastic, it is likely to be a necessity.

1d. Total revenue increases as the price of home heating oil increases. The increase in total revenue occurs because home heating oil is a necessity (its demand is inelastic) and as its price rises, the percentage decrease in the quantity demanded is a smaller amount than the percentage increase in the price.

1e. The cross elasticity of demand for home heating oil with respect to wool sweaters equals 0.50. To calculate this answer, use the formula for the cross elasticity of demand, specifically

$$\left(\frac{\text{Percent change in quantity of sweaters demanded}}{\text{Percent change in price of heating oil}}\right) = \left(\frac{10\,\text{percent}}{20\,\text{percent}}\right) = 0.50.$$

1f. Home heating oil and sweaters are substitutes because as the price of home heating oil rises, you can stay warm by using less home heating oil and putting on a sweater. The fact that they are substitutes is reflected by the result that the cross elasticity of demand is positive.

2. Because the price elasticity of demand for cookies is 1.5, Pete should lower the price of cookies in order to raise his total revenue. The fact that demand is elastic means that a decrease in the price of cookies will bring about a larger percentage increase in the quantity demanded than the percentage drop in price.

3a. Because the total revenue did not change, the percentage change in bananas demanded must match the percentage increase in price. Using the midpoint method, the percentage increase in the price equals ($1.00/$1.50) = 66.67 percent. Hence the quantity of bananas demanded must have decreased by 66.67 percent.

3b. The demand for bananas is unit elastic because the percentage increase in the price equaled the percentage decrease in the quantity of bananas purchased.

4. The 5 percent increase in the price (the tuition) has resulted in a 2 percent increase in the quantity of enrollments. Hence the price elasticity of supply is (2 percent)/(5 percent) = 0.40.

5a. The demand for club memberships increases with income, so it is a normal good. Because the quantity demanded increased more (15 percent) than did income (10 percent) the demand for club memberships is income elastic.

5b. The demand for spring water increases with income, so it is a normal good. Because the quantity demanded increased less (5 percent) than did income (10 percent) the demand for spring water is income inelastic.

5c. The demand for soft drinks decreases with income, so it is an inferior good.

5d. The demand for club memberships is income elastic, (15 percent/10 percent) = 1.5. The demand for spring water is income inelastic, (5 percent/10 percent) = 0.5.

5e. Club memberships and spring water are normal goods. Soft drinks are an inferior good.

6a. The price elasticity of demand for bus rides is inelastic. The fact that it is inelastic can be seen by the point that the price elasticity of demand, 0.5, is less than 1.0. When the elasticity is less than 1.0, an increase in the price of a bus fare brings about a percentage decrease in the number of bus rides demanded that is smaller than the percentage increase in price.

6b. An increase in the price of bus fares would increase the bus company's total revenue. Because the demand is inelastic, an increase in the price of the fare will lead to a smaller percentage decrease in the quantity of bus rides demanded than the percentage increase in the fare. For example, if fares increased by 10 percent per ride, then bus ticket sales would only decrease by 5 percent and so the company's total revenue would increase.

6c. Bus rides and gasoline are substitutes. As the price of gasoline increases, it becomes more expensive to drive your car and you might decide to take a bus to work. This observation is borne out by the fact that the cross elasticity of demand between bus rides and gasoline is positive, indicating that the two are substitutes.

6d. If the price of gasoline increases by 10 percent and the price of bus fares does not change, the number of bus rides increases. Using the cross elasticity of demand of 0.2, bus rides will increase by (10 percent) × (0.2) = 2 percent. It is important to note that the increase in the number of bus rides occurs because the demand curve for bus rides shifts rightward (as a result of an increase in the price of gasoline). An increase in the number of bus rides does not occur as a result of a movement along the demand curve for bus rides.

6e. If incomes increase, fewer people will ride the bus because bus rides are an inferior good (the income elasticity of demand is negative). To determine the decrease in rides, use the income elasticity of demand. The decrease in rides equals (−0.1) × (5 percent) = −0.5 percent.

6f. In Pioneer Ville, a bus ride is an inferior good because as income increases, fewer bus rides are demanded. This point is reflected in the fact that the income elasticity of demand is negative.

6g. In Pioneer Ville, bus rides and gasoline are substitutes because as the price of gas increases, the quantity of bus rides demanded increases. This point is reflected in the fact that the cross elasticity of demand is positive.

ADDITIONAL EXERCISES FOR ASSIGNMENT

■ Questions

1a. Suppose that Podunk University wins the 2002 college basketball championship. As a result, Podunk U's fans increase their demand for tickets for the 2003 season. Podunk U. plays in an arena that seats 7,000 people. Describe the supply of basketball tickets at Podunk U. and draw a supply curve for tickets.

1b. Podunk U.'s economist has calculated the price elasticity of demand for tickets to be 0.50. Podunk U.'s president is committed to increasing the total revenue collected by the university. To do so, should Podunk raise or lower its ticket prices?

2. Draw a straight-line demand curve and note three points on the curve. Point A should have an elasticity greater than 1, point B should have an elasticity equal to 1, and point C should have an elasticity less than 1.

■ Answers

1a. The supply is perfectly inelastic because the number of seats can only be supplied in a fixed quantity. Figure 5.1 illustrates the supply curve.

1b. If the university wants to increase its total revenue, it should increase ticket prices. Demand for tickets is inelastic (0.5), so even if ticket prices are increased, the percentage decrease in the quantity of tickets demanded will be less than the percentage increase in the price. Hence, assuming Podunk U.'s economist is correct, raising ticket prices will increase total revenue.

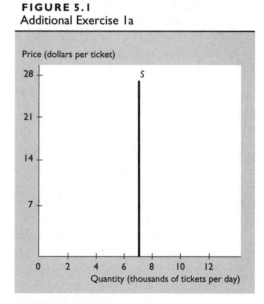

FIGURE 5.1
Additional Exercise 1a

2. Although your students' demand curves will be different from the demand curve in Figure 5.2, there are certain features that must be the same. First, point B, the point with the unit elasticity, must be at the midpoint of the demand curve. Second, point A, the point at which the elasticity exceeds 1.0, must lie above point B on the demand curve. And third, point C, the point at which the elasticity is less than 1, must lie below point B on the demand curve.

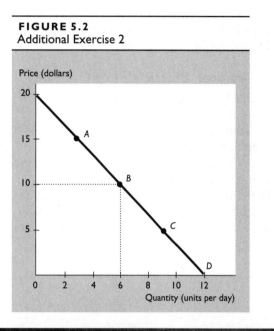

FIGURE 5.2
Additional Exercise 2

ANSWERS TO ECONOMICS IN THE NEWS

■ The Energy Market

1. The demand for oil is inelastic. Hence any decrease or impending decrease in the production of oil will send the price much higher.
2. The effect of the "jawboning" would depend on factors that are outside the strict province of economics. Jawboning depends on a political process, that is, can the United States convince the producing nations' that it is in their best interests to increase the quantity of oil they pump and drop the price?
3. The demand for oil is inelastic, so a rise in the price of oil increases producers' total revenue. Indeed, in the short run the demand is quite inelastic, so a rise in the price of oil significantly increases producers' total revenue.

USING EYE ON THE GLOBAL ECONOMY

■ Price Elasticities of Demand

Often the relatively theoretical nature of economics takes students by surprise. They expect a typical business course in which only "practical, real-world" issues are studied. Elasticity is precisely the sort of "practical, real-world" concept that can appeal to this set of students. The price elasticities of demand in this "Eye on the Global Economy" can be used in test questions, to make the questions more realistic. However, you also can use them in a class discussion by asking your students about a few of the goods. For instance, you could ask them what they guess is more elastic, the demand for motor vehicles (cars) or housing? The demand for furniture or food? The demand for metals or fish? Ask the students to explain their answers and then present them with the actual rankings from this Eye on the Global Economy.

■ Income Elasticities of Demand

In much the same way as with the Eye on the Global Economy that covered the price elasticity of demand, you can use this Eye on the Global Economy to interest your students by having them guess between goods as to which good is the most income elastic. For instance you could ask them to rank movies, haircuts, cars, clothing, and food with respect to their income elasticity. This sort of exercise has at least two effects, both beneficial. First, it introduces the students to thinking about the real world and its relationship to the more abstract concepts used by economists. Second, it gives them a vested interest in determining if their ranking was correct and hence increases their interest in the class.

Efficiency and Fairness of Markets

Chapter 6

CHAPTER OUTLINE

1. Distinguish between value and price and define consumer surplus.
- A. Efficiency: A Refresher
  1. Marginal Benefit
  2. Marginal Cost
  3. Allocative Efficiency
- B. Demand and Marginal Benefit
- C. Consumer Surplus

2. Distinguish between cost and price and define producer surplus.
- A. Supply and Marginal Cost
- B. Producer Surplus

3. Explain the conditions in which markets are efficient and inefficient.
- A. Efficiency of Competitive Equilibrium
- B. The Invisible Hand
- C. Obstacles to Efficiency
  1. Externalities
  2. Public Goods
  3. Monopoly
  4. Price Ceilings and Price Floors
  5. Taxes, Subsidies, and Quotas
  6. Underproduction
  7. Overproduction

4. Explain the main ideas about fairness and evaluate claims that competitive markets result in unfair outcomes.
- A. It's Not Fair If the Result Isn't Fair
  1. Utilitarianism
  2. The Big Tradeoff
  3. Make the Poorest as Well Off as Possible
- B. It's Not Fair If the Rules Aren't Fair
  1. A Price Hike in a Natural Disaster

CHAPTER ROADMAP

■ Where We Are

We explore the conditions of market efficiency and whether market outcomes are fair. We make the distinctions between value and price (facing consumers) versus cost and price (facing producers). By equating marginal benefit and marginal cost, we see that the market produces an efficient outcome. In some cases though, there are factors that prevent this efficient outcome.

■ Where We've Been

We've explored the motivation behind studying economics. We've also developed the supply and demand models that help us visualize how markets operate and demonstrate the efficient allocation of resources.

■ Where We're Going

The next chapter continues to use the supply and demand framework to commence study of government intervention into the market. The next chapter studies taxes, price ceilings, and price floors. It demonstrates how these polices can lead to inefficiency.

IN THE CLASSROOM

■ Class Time Needed

You can complete this chapter in one session, or perhaps a little more. But because this material is so important, you might consider giving it extra time, say up to two sessions.

An estimate of the time per checkpoint is:

- Efficiency: A Refresher—5 to 10 minutes
- 6.1 Value, Price, and Consumer Surplus—10 to 25 minutes
- 6.2 Cost, Price, and Producer Surplus—10 to 25 minutes
- 6.3 Are Markets Efficient?—15 to 25minutes
- 6.4 Are Markets Fair?—10 to 15 minutes

■ Extended Lecture Outline

6.1 Value, Price, and Consumer Surplus

A. Efficiency: A Refresher

1. **Marginal benefit** is the benefit that a person receives from consuming one more unit of a good.

   a. As more of a good is consumed, the marginal benefit of each additional unit decreases.

   b. The marginal benefit curve slopes downward to reflect decreasing marginal benefit.

2. **Marginal cost** is the opportunity cost of producing one more unit of a good.

   a. As more of a good is produced, the marginal cost of each additional unit increases.

   b. The marginal cost curve slopes upward to reflect increasing marginal cost.

3. Allocative efficiency

   a. To determine whether resources are being used efficiently, marginal benefit must be compared to marginal cost.

   b. The efficient use of resources occurs at the intersection of the marginal benefit and marginal cost curves, where production is such that marginal benefit equals marginal cost.

B. Demand and Marginal Benefit

1. The value of another unit of a good or service is its marginal benefit. The value is equal to the maximum price people are willing to pay for a given quantity of the good.

2. A demand curve is a marginal benefit curve.

3. The demand curve for Good A shows the dollar's worth of other goods and services that we are willing to give up to get one more unit of Good A.

C. Consumer Surplus

1. **Consumer surplus** equals the marginal benefit of a good minus the price the person must pay for the good.

6.2 Cost, Price, and Producer Surplus

A. Supply and Marginal Cost

1. The cost of producing one more unit of a good is that good's marginal cost.

2. The marginal cost of a good determines the quantity supplied of the good.

3. The supply curve shows the minimum price that producers must receive to produce a certain amount of the good.

4. A supply curve is a marginal cost curve.

5. The supply curve for Good A shows the dollar value of other goods and services that must be forgone to get an additional unit of Good A.

B. Producer surplus

Producer surplus equals the price a firm sells a good for minus the marginal cost of producing the good.

6. 3 Are Markets Efficient?

A. Efficiency of Competitive Equilibrium

Efficiency occurs at the competitive market equilibrium because that is where marginal benefit equals marginal cost.

B. The Invisible Hand

The invisible hand concept was first suggested by Adam Smith.

1. The invisible hand asserts that competitive markets ensure efficient use of resources.

2. Everyday we encounter markets that allocate resources to the uses in which they are most highly valued.

C. Obstacles to Efficiency

There are a number of factors that can prevent competitive markets from producing the efficient amount of a good.

1. Externalities
   a. An *externality* is a cost or benefit from a production activity that falls on someone other than the producer or consumer.
2. Public Goods
   a. A public good is a good or service consumed freely by everyone at the same time. The production of public goods in an unregulated market would be less than the efficient level.
3. Monopoly
   a. A monopoly is a firm that is the only producer in the market. A monopoly produces too little of the good compared to the efficient level.
4. Price Ceilings and Price Floors
   a. A price ceiling is the maximum price that legally can be charged for a good; a price floor is the minimum price that legally can be charged for a good.
5. Taxes, Subsidies, and Quotas
   a. Taxes, subsidies, and quotas result in inefficiency.
6. Underproduction occurs when too little of a good is produced compared to the efficient level. At this level of production, marginal benefit exceeds marginal cost.
7. Overproduction occurs when too much of a good is produced compared to the efficient level. At this level of production, marginal cost exceeds marginal benefit.
   a. When an inefficient amount of a good is produced, there is a loss of consumer and producer surplus. The loss is called a **deadweight loss.**

6.4 Are Markets Fair?

A. It's Not Fair If the Result Isn't Fair

This approach to fairness concludes that unequal incomes are unfair.

1. **Utilitarianism** (a nineteenth century idea) claimed that income must be transferred from the rich to the poor until incomes are equal across all people.
2. Promoting income equality creates the **big tradeoff** because redistribution decreases efficiency.
3. John Rawls also suggested transferring income from the rich to the poor, but not necessarily until incomes are equal. His version requires making the poorest as well off as possible.

B. It's Not Fair If the Rules Aren't Fair

This idea is based on the symmetry principle and private property rights.

1. The **symmetry principle** is the idea that people in similar situations should be similarly treated.
2. Robert Nozick suggests that fairness follow two rules:
   a. The state should legislate and enforce private property rights.
   b. Private property should be transferred voluntarily, for example, by market transactions.
3. Enforcing private property rights and voluntary exchange ensures allocative efficiency in the absence of external costs, external benefits, public goods, monopolies, price ceilings, price floors, taxes, subsidies, or quotas.

■ Lecture Launchers

1. Launch your lecture by drawing a demand curve and telling your students that this curve has two interpretations. The common interpretation, that the students have seen many times before, starts at a price, goes horizontally to the demand curve, and then down vertically to the quantity. The interpretation of this approach is the "standard" one: At the given price, the demand curve shows the quantity demanded. But then point out to the students that it is possible to pick a quantity, go vertically up to the demand curve, and then horizontally to the price. The interpretation of this method differs from the first. The interpretation here is that for the given quantity, the demand curve shows the maximum price for which someone is willing to buy the selected quantity. Point out that the maximum price equals the value to the consumer and that the value also equals the marginal benefit. Thus you have demonstrated to the students that the demand curve is the same as the marginal benefit curve. (When I make this demonstration, I use actual numbers for the price and quantity because I think using numbers makes the otherwise abstract discussion more concrete and approachable, but you can opt to forgo numbers and use symbols. The choice is yours.)

2. To launch into a discussion of consumer surplus, draw a downward sloping demand curve and a horizontal line representing the market price. (Again, the choice is yours whether to use numbers or abstract symbols.) Remind the students that the market demand curve represents demand from all individuals. Start at a high price on the demand curve and ask if the person represented by this point would be willing to buy the good for the market price. Students will say "yes." Move to another point at a lower price and again ask your students if the person represented by this point would be willing to buy the good at the market price. Again, the answer will be "yes." Finally, move to the market price and ask if the person would be willing to buy the good for this price. You might get some "no's," but most students will answer "yes." Now you can go back to the distances between the points you've chosen and the market price and get students to discuss which person receives the largest benefit from his or her purchase. Tell students that the difference between the demand curve and the price represents the consumer surplus.

■ Land Mines

1. The consumer surplus, producer surplus, and deadweight loss are all generally triangular in shape. Indeed, if you draw only linear demand and supply curves and do not make either curve vertical or horizontal, these surpluses and any deadweight loss are triangles. Thus it is a good idea to remind your students of the formula for calculating the area of a triangle. Make sure to do several examples of the calculation for both consumer and producer surplus. Remind them that this area represents a dollar value. This reminder is especially useful when you quantify the deadweight losses created by monopolies, quotas, subsidies, etc. Many students just see the

loss to society as a loss of jobs or less output, but you can create more intuition by putting the loss in dollar terms.

2. It always helps to use colored chalk, overheads, or PowerPoint slides when dividing up the supply and demand graph into producer surplus, consumer surplus, deadweight loss, and the cost of production. By using colored chalk or the other techniques, you can refer to area by color ("The red area shows consumer surplus and the green area shows the deadweight loss.") The size of the areas are much more apparent. Additionally, you don't need to go back to the screen or board to try to outline the area.

ANSWERS TO CHECKPOINT EXERCISES

■ CHECKPOINT 6.1 Value, Price, and Consumer Surplus

1a. The value of the 30th can of soft drink is $0.50.

1b. A consumer is willing to pay $1.50 for the 10th can of soft drink.

1c. The consumer surplus is the difference between what a consumer is willing to pay for the 10th can and what he or she actually pays. The consumer's value for the 10th can is $1.50 and he or she pays $0.50, so the consumer surplus equals $1.00

1d. Thirty cans of soft drink are bought. The consumer surplus is the area below the demand curve and above the market price. Calculating the area of this triangle as 1/2 the base times the height shows that consumer surplus equals $22.50.

1e. The total amount paid = 30 cans × $0.50 = $15.00.

1f. The total benefit = $15.00 + $22.50 = $37.50.

1g. If the price of soft drinks rises to $1.00 per can, consumer surplus falls to $10.

■ CHECKPOINT 6.2 Cost, Price, and Producer Surplus

1a. The marginal cost of the 30th can is $2.00 per can.

1b. The minimum supply price of the 10th can is $1.00.

1c. The producer surplus of the 10th can is $0.50 because the price is $1.50 and the minimum supply price is $1.00. Producer surplus equals $1.50 – $1.00.

1d. Twenty cans of soft drinks are sold and the producer surplus equals the area of the producer surplus triangle, or $10.

1e. The total revenue = 20 cans × $1.50 = $30.00.

1f. The total cost can be calculated as the odd shape under the supply curve. Alternatively, the cost equals the total revenue minus the producer surplus = $30.00 – $10.00 = $20.00.

1g. If the price falls to $1.00, total revenue = $10.00. Producer surplus decreases to $2.50.

■ CHECKPOINT 6.3 Are Markets Efficient?

1a. The equilibrium price and equilibrium quantity are $1.25 and 15 cans.

1b. At market equilibrium, consumer surplus = $5.63.

1c. Producer surplus = $5.63.

1d. The market is efficient because 15 cases are produced and this is the production for which the marginal cost equals marginal benefit. Resources are efficiently used.

1e. If output is limited to 10 cans per day, the market is not efficient because when 10 cans are produced, the marginal cost ($1.00) does not equal marginal benefit ($1.50). The market is underproducing.

1f. The deadweight loss equals $1.25.

1g. If the government requires 20 cans to be produced each day, the market is not efficient because at 20 cans, the marginal cost ($1.50) does not equal marginal benefit ($1.00). The market is overproducing.

1h. The deadweight loss equals $1.25.

■ CHECKPOINT 6.4 Are Markets Fair?

1a. The people who value the water the most will consume the water because they will be the people willing to pay a high price for the water.

1b. The consumers who drink the water are the consumers who receive the consumer surplus.

1c. Presuming there are no resales of water from one buyer to another at a higher price than the store charges, the store selling the water receives the producer surplus. If there are resales, then the reselling purchasers also receive producer surplus.

1d. The outcome is efficient.

1e. The outcome is unfair based on the fair-results principle because poor people can't afford to buy the water. Hence the water will be shared unequally. The outcome is fair based on the fair-rules principle because the store's property rights are enforced and there is voluntary exchange between the store and buyers.

1f. The outcome is fair based on the fair-rules idea and unfair on the fair results idea.

ANSWERS TO CHAPTER CHECKPOINT EXERCISES

1a. The efficient quantity is 200 sandwiches.

1b. If 200 sandwiches are produced, the price will be $4 per sandwich. Figure 6.1 can be used to calculate the consumer surplus. The consumer surplus equals the area of the triangle above the price and below the demand curve. This amount is $400.

1c. Once again, Figure 6.1 can be used, this time to calculate the producer surplus. The producer surplus equals the area of the triangle below the price and above the supply curve. This amount is $400.

1d. If only 100 sandwiches are produced, the deadweight loss equals $200.

1e. In one view, rationing sandwiches might be fair based on the "fair results" principle because everyone has an equal number of sandwiches. On the other hand, because Sandwiches To Go, Inc. is restricting the number of sandwiches it produces, some customers are likely to go without. If the "fair results" view incorporates these consumers into the picture, then the rationing is unfair because not every consumer has a sandwich. The "fair rules" approach is likely to consider the rationing fair, because all exchanges are voluntary. But, it is worth noting that Sandwiches To Go, Inc. is acting like a monopoly by restricting its production and thereby creating a deadweight loss.

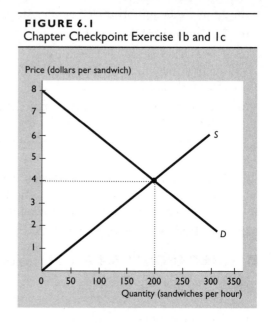

FIGURE 6.1
Chapter Checkpoint Exercise 1b and 1c

2a. Consumer surplus decreases after the flood and producer surplus increases after the flood.

2b. The allocation of resources is efficient before and after the flood because the market operates at equilibrium, where marginal cost equals marginal benefit.

2c. If the government rationed sandbags, the effect on the producer surplus of the companies selling sandbags depends on the price the government paid. If the government paid the higher, post-flood price, the firms' producer surplus is unchanged. If, however, the government required the companies to sell the sandbags to the government at the lower, pre-flood price, the firms' producer surplus decreased. Presumably the government hands out the sandbags for "free" so that everyone gets an equal share. In this case, people who have low marginal benefit from a sandbag (people who live on high ground!) will sell their sandbags to people whose marginal benefit is higher, presumably because their homes are lower. The families selling the sandbags gain producer surplus. The consumer surplus with the government rationing will increase. Why? After all, the price of a sandbag with the rationing and resales will be the same as the price without the government intervention. The point is, however, that some families with high marginal benefit will get some sandbags from the government for "free." These people's consumer surplus will increase.

2d. The rationing outcome is efficient as long as the government allows people to resell the sandbags. These resales allocate the sandbags to the families that place the highest value on them and hence is necessary for the allocation to be efficient. If the government allows no resales, then the allocation will be inefficient.

2e. Assuming the government allows resales, the resulting distribution is unfair according to the fair results view because sandbags are unequally shared. Because the government must raise taxes to finance its purchase of sandbags and taxes are not voluntary, the outcome is unfair according to the fair rules view.

3. The students will find the question of efficiency difficult because they have not yet studied price discrimination. Price discrimination, such as that in the question, helps move the economy toward efficiency from a strict single-price monopoly outcome. But the students will not yet realize this point. Hence the students' answers should be in terms of whether this arrangement sets the marginal benefit of attendance equal to the marginal cost. The arrangement is not fair under the fair results view because not everyone can attend. Indeed, this scheme violates the symmetry principle because some students will pay less (and be able to attend) than similarly situated non-students (who will not be able to attend). Because the scheme violates the symmetry principle, fairness using a fair rules approach is also problematic, though at least all exchanges are voluntary.

4. The compensation arrangement is efficient as long as the marginal benefit of winning (as well as coming in second) equals the marginal cost. The fair results approach to fairness would assert that the compensation scheme is unfair because income is not equally distributed. The fair rules approach would assert that the scheme is fair because the players voluntarily enter the tournament and the symmetry principle is not violated.

5. The compensation for male and female golfers might well differ because of different levels of revenue that the tours are able to collect. The men's golf tour is more popular and therefore gets higher paying sponsors and sells its shows to television networks for higher prices, resulting in a bigger economic pie to split among its players. Women's golf is less popular and so cannot attract as many high-paying sponsors. In tennis, however, the popularity of women's tennis is comparable to that of men's tennis. Thus, the compensation arrangements might well be efficient and would definitely be efficient if they are such that the marginal benefit of winning equals the marginal cost. The compensation arrangements are definitely unfair under the "fair results" approach because incomes are quite different among winners and losers and among men and women golfers. The compensation arrangements are fair under the "fair rules" approach.

6. Under a fair rules approach, it is fair that Tiger Woods wins as many tournaments as he does because he puts in many hours of practice. If a rule limiting wins was enacted, the "fair-rules" principle would be violated be-

cause Tiger would not be able to sell his private property (his golf skills). Under a fair results approach, Tiger is definitely unfair because his income soars well beyond that of any other golfer. A fair results proponent would argue in favor of a rule limiting the number of times a golfer can win because a limit would help equalize incomes.

ADDITIONAL EXERCISES FOR ASSIGNMENT

■ Questions

1. The figure shows the market for electrical generators before and after a hurricane, with the demand curves labeled "before" and "after."

1a. What is the producer surplus and consumer surplus before the hurricane?

1b. What is the producer surplus and consumer surplus after the hurricane?

1c. What is the equilibrium price and quantity after the hurricane? Is this outcome efficient?

1d. Under which rule is the outcome after the hurricane fair?

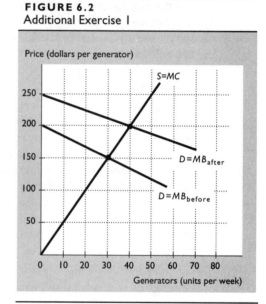

FIGURE 6.2
Additional Exercise 1

2. Figure 6.3 shows the market for carnations. In recent years, the U.S. government has removed quotas on imported carnations. Suppose that in 1990, the United States only allowed florists to import 30 tons of carnations each week. The price at that time was $400 per ton of carnations. Today, the quotas have been removed and florists now import 60 tons of carnations and the price is $300 per ton of carnations.

2a. What were the producer and consumer surplus while the quota was in effect? What was the deadweight loss?

2b. What is the producer and consumer surplus now that the quota has been removed?

2c. Which outcome is efficient, with the quota or without?

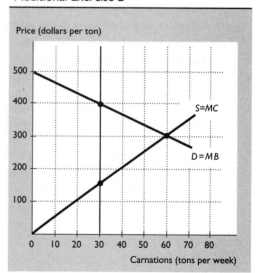

FIGURE 6.3
Additional Exercise 2

■ Answers

1a. Before the hurricane, the producer surplus = $2,250 and the consumer surplus = $750.

1b. After the hurricane, the producer surplus = $4,000 and the consumer surplus = $1,000.

1c. The equilibrium price is $200 and the equilibrium quantity is 40 generators per week. The outcome is efficient because the marginal benefit equals the marginal cost.

1d. According to the "fair-rules" principle, the outcome is fair because there is voluntary exchange of private property.

2a. While the quota was in effect, producer surplus was $9,750 and consumer surplus was $1,500. The deadweight loss was $3,750.

2b. With the quota removed, producer surplus is $9,000 and consumer surplus is $6,000.

2c. The situation without the quota is efficient because without the quota, the marginal benefit of carnations equals the marginal cost.

USING EYE ON THE U.S ECONOMY

■ The Invisible Hand and e-Commerce

You can use this example to graphically show consumer and producer surplus and how they differ for different individuals. Remind students that market demand curves are the addition of individual demand curves and therefore consumer surplus differs across people. (The same is true for supply curves.) As a result, as the cold drink vendor sells cold drinks, most people receive a consumer surplus from their purchase (the market price is less than the value they place on the drink). And the vendor is receiving producer surplus from selling cold drinks (the market price is greater than his marginal cost). That's typically the end of the story.

For the man on the bench though, it's not the cold drink that provides the consumer surplus, but the umbrella, so he offers to buy the umbrella. Once the man on the bench makes the offer for the umbrella, the vendor realizes that he can realize a producer surplus from selling the umbrella, too. What price did the man offer for the umbrella? A price low enough to provide him some consumer surplus. What price was the vendor willing to accept? A price high enough to provide him some producer surplus.

USING EYE ON THE GLOBAL ECONOMY

■ Are Mega-Mergers Efficient or Inefficient?

Use this story to highlight differences between efficiency and fairness as seen by producers and consumers. While firms claim to merge to create more efficiency, the decrease in the number of firms leads to movement away from an efficient market outcome. Monopolies result in underproduction but higher profits for the firms.

In terms of fairness, firms' abilities to merge without the government's inhibiting this transfer of private property is "fair" under the fair rules principle. But for consumers, the monopoly ends us transferring wealth from consumer to producers and creating a bigger income inequality which is "not fair" under the fair-results principle.

ANSWERS TO ECONOMICS IN THE NEWS

■ Internet Auctions for College Placement

1. The price of a college, that is, the tuition, changes the quantity demanded, not the demand. Other factors affect the demand. For example, if the economy experiences a recession, there are fewer job opportunities and more students choose to attend college, which increases the demand. In addition, as salaries of college graduates continue to increase relative to high school graduates, the demand for college places increases. And, the demand for different colleges is affected by their reputations.

2. Along a supply curve for college places, as the price of a degree rises, colleges provide more spaces. This effect, however, refers to a change in the quantity supplied and not the supply. Some factors that affect the supply would be technology and the political climate toward education. For example, with technological advances, colleges can provide more spaces using distance learning. And, if politicians come to more closely realize the value to a young person of obtaining a college degree, they might build more colleges.

3. The equilibrium price and quantity are determined by the intersection of the supply and demand curves.

4. The service provided will:
   a) increase the number of students attending college.
   b) depending on the relative shifts of the supply and demand curves, tuition may increase or decrease.
   c) consumer surplus increases.
   d) producer surplus increases.
   e) assuming there were inefficiencies in the market prior to the service, the deadweight loss decreases.

5. Gainers are students who receive better college offers and more financial aid benefit from the service. The schools who attract better students also benefit.

    The losers are the students who would have received better college offers with an inefficient market and colleges that lose the best students to colleges making more lucrative offers.

Government Influences on Markets

Chapter 7

1. **Explain the effects of taxes on goods and labor and determine who pays the taxes.**
    - A. Tax Incidence
    - B. Tax Incidence and Elasticities of Demand and Supply
    - C. Tax Incidence and Elasticity of Demand
        1. Perfectly Inelastic Demand: Buyer Pays Entire Tax
        2. Perfectly Elastic Demand: Seller Pays Entire Tax
    - D. Tax Incidence and Elasticity of Supply
        1. Perfectly Inelastic Supply: Seller Pays Entire Tax
        2. Perfectly Elastic Supply: Buyer Pays Entire Tax
    - E. Taxes on Income and Employment
    - F. Taxes and Efficiency

2. **Explain how a rent ceiling creates a housing shortage, inefficiency, and unfairness.**
    - A. A Rent Ceiling
        1. A Black Market
        2. Increased Search Activity
    - B. Are Rent Ceilings Efficient?
    - C. Are Rent Ceilings Fair?
    - D. If Rent Ceilings Are So Bad, Why Do We Have Them?

3. **Explain how the minimum wage creates unemployment, inefficiency, and unfairness.**
    - A. The Minimum Wage
        1. Increased Job Search Activity
        2. Illegal Hiring
    - B. Is the Minimum Wage Efficient?
    - C. Is the Minimum Wage Fair?
    - D. If the Minimum Wage Is So Bad, Why Do We Have It?

CHAPTER ROADMAP

■ Where We Are

We use the supply-demand diagram to study how the government can influence markets. Interventions, such as taxes, price floors, and price ceilings, can prevent markets from efficiently allocating resources. Examples show how these actions impact consumers and firms, how equilibrium prices and quantities change, and how they create deadweight losses.

■ Where We've Been

We've developed the supply and demand model, a tool to use in examining how markets determine their equilibrium prices and quantities. The elasticities of supply and demand reflect how responsive quantities are to a change in price. These ideas play an important role in showing how market interventions create inefficiency and unfairness.

■ Where We're Going

Now that we've become more familiar with how markets work, we closely examine the motivation behind the demand curve and the concepts of consumer choice and utility. After that, we examine supply by focusing on costs, revenues, and industry structure.

IN THE CLASSROOM

■ Class Time Needed

If you have only a little participation and questions from the class, you should try to cover these topics in two sessions. It might be a tight fit. If, however, you have class participation and/or examples you want to present, this material can stretch to three lectures. Start with the discussion of taxes for the first session, even though it might take longer than just one class session. If, as might be likely, you cannot fit both the price ceiling and price floor sections in one session because the tax material "ran long," at least try to mention price floors after you cover price ceilings because you want the students to see that the topics are so closely related.

An estimate of the time per checkpoint is:

- 7.1 Taxes—50 minutes to 65 minutes
- 7.2 Price Ceilings—25 minutes to 45 minutes
- 7.3 Price Floors—25 minutes to 45 minutes

■ Extended Lecture Outline

7.1 Taxes

A. **Tax Incidence**

The division of a tax between the buyer and the seller.

1. Imposing a sales tax on a product decreases the supply.
2. The tax shifts the supply curve leftward and the vertical distance between the supply curve with the tax and the supply curve without the tax equals the amount of the tax.
3. Generally, the quantity decreases and the price rises, but by less than the amount of the tax.

B. Tax Incidence and Elasticities of Demand and Supply

1. For a given elasticity of supply, the buyer pays a larger share of the tax the more inelastic the demand for the good.
2. For a given elasticity of demand, the seller pays a larger share of the tax the more inelastic the supply of the good.

C. Tax Incidence and Elasticity of Demand

1. Perfectly Inelastic Demand: Buyer Pays Entire Tax
2. Perfectly Elastic Demand: Seller Pays Entire Tax

D. Tax Incidence and Elasticity of Supply

1. Perfectly Inelastic Supply: Seller Pays Entire Tax
2. Perfectly Elastic Supply: Buyer Pays Entire Tax

E. Taxes on Income and Employment

1. An *income tax* decreases the supply of labor and the supply of labor curve shifts leftward. The wage received by workers falls and the wage paid by firms rises. The quantity of employment decreases.
2. A **payroll tax** decreases the demand for labor and the demand for labor curve shifts leftward. The wage received by workers falls and the wage paid by firms rises. The quantity of employment decreases.
3. The effect of an income tax is identical to that of a similarly sized payroll tax.

F. Taxes and Efficiency

1. Taxes create a deadweight loss, called the **excess burden.**
2. Consumer and producer surplus decrease and the government collects tax revenue.

7.2 Price Ceilings

A. A **Rent Ceiling**

A rent ceiling is a government regulation that makes it illegal to charge more than a specified rent for housing. A rent ceiling is an example of a **price ceiling,** the highest price at which it is legal to trade a particular good, service, or factor of production.

1. A rent ceiling below the equilibrium rent increases the quantity demanded and decreases the quantity supplied, thereby leading to a shortage.
2. Rent ceilings create a **black market,** an illegal market that operates alongside a government-regulated market.
3. Rent ceilings also create increased **search activity,** time spent looking for someone with whom to do business.
   a. The opportunity cost of a good is equal to its price plus the value of the search time spent finding the good.

B. Are Rent Ceilings Efficient?

Rent ceilings create a deadweight loss. Consumer surplus and producer surplus both decrease and resources are spent on search and evading the rent ceiling.

C. Are Rent Ceilings Fair?

1. Rent ceilings block voluntary exchange and are unfair under the "fair rules" view.

2. Rent ceilings typically do not insure that the poorest are housed, and so rent ceilings are unfair under the "fair results" view.

D. If Rent Ceilings Are So Bad, Why Do We Have Them?

People who gain from rent ceilings (renters who find a low-rent apartment) lobby politicians in favor of rent ceilings.

7.3 Price Floors

A. The Minimum Wage

A minimum wage is a government regulation that makes hiring labor for less than a specified wage illegal. A minimum wage is an example of a **price floor,** the lowest price at which it is legal to trade a particular good, service, or factor of production.

1. A minimum wage above the equilibrium wage rate decreases the quantity of labor demanded and increases the quantity supplied thereby leading to a surplus of labor, that is, unemployment.

2. Minimum wages create increased job search activity as workers look for jobs.

3. Minimum wages also lead to illegal hiring of workers for less than the minimum wage.

B. Is the Minimum Wage Efficient?

The minimum wage creates a deadweight loss. Firms' surplus and workers' surplus both decrease and resources are spent on job search.

C. Is the Minimum Wage Fair?

1. The minimum wage blocks voluntary exchange and is unfair under the "fair rules" view.

2. The minimum wage benefits only those who find jobs and so is unfair under the "fair results" view.

D. If the Minimum Wage Is So Bad, Why Do We Have It?

People who gain from the minimum wage support the minimum wage.

■ Lecture Launchers

1. You can involve students in your lecture on tax incidence by drawing the supply and demand diagram and asking them if a tax was imposed in this market, which curve would be affected? You can ask for a show of hands or a voice vote, but you'll probably get more votes for the demand curve because students see themselves (the consumer) as always paying the entire tax. Of course, the fun part of the lecture is showing how consumers rarely pay the entire tax.

2. Ask the students if they saw the article in the day's local paper that the local government plans to place a $200 limit on rents that landlords could charge for apartments near campus. (Of course this story wasn't in the paper, but students are more likely to pay attention if they think you're serious! Don't tell them this yet though.) Ask them to participate in an informal vote by raising a hand in response to "Who thinks this is a good idea?", "Who

thinks this is a bad idea?", and "Who doesn't care?" (This last one always catches a few honest students who like to chuckle as they raise their hands!)

Then explain to the students that this limit is called a "rent ceiling" and cities across the country have them...so they must be good, right? However, further explain that in this lecture, they'll find out several ways that the government intervenes in markets and that while the ideas might *sound* good, economically they create problems. At the end of the lecture, remark how astute the students were that voted against the price ceilings and definitely be sure to tell the students that the local government isn't really going to impose the rent ceiling.

3. To launch your lecture on the minimum wage, ask the students about jobs around town. Sound them out to see if there are a lot of jobs that pay the minimum wage. (Do not ask a particular student his or her wage, because he or she may be embarrassed if the wage is the minimum wage!) Then, ask the students if they think jobs would be easier or harder to find without the minimum wage. You can easily segue from the students' answers to your lecture on the minimum wage and you also can easily interweave their answers into your lecture.

■ Land Mines

1. Give students the intuition for the leftward shift in the supply curve when a tax is imposed. You also will need to show them that the vertical distance between the two curves equals the amount of the tax. However, remember that in previous chapters there was emphasis on the horizontal nature of the shift, that is, the fact that a decrease in supply is represented by a leftward shift of the supply curve. Tell the students that the curve has shifted leftward, only you do not know by how much. This ignorance is not disastrous, though, because what we are really interested in is the vertical distance and that distance you, as a trained economist, do know! And, after that explain to the students that the vertical shift equals the amount of the tax so that they, too, know!

2. Students have difficulty envisioning why the supply curve shifts with imposition of a tax, especially because they've always believed it's the buyer that pays the tax. They don't seem to realize that it's the firms that are responsible for sending the tax into the government. Remind them that this fact is why it makes sense to shift the supply curve leftward (reflecting this added "cost" to the firm).

3. For the payroll tax, remind students that this tax is paid by the *demanders* of the good. In this case, the demanders are the firms and the good is labor. Be careful here because students can get confused because this tax is reflected as a "minus," that is, the new demand curve is labeled as D − tax. You should convey the intuition that the tax "subtracts" from the demand for labor.

4. When you use a supply and demand diagram to show the effects of a price ceiling and/or price floor, be sure to label all the prices, quantities, *and* the

ceiling or floor. In the case of the price ceiling, clearly label and emphasize the shortage created. In the case of the price floor, clearly label and emphasize the surplus created. As you add more lines to the supply and demand diagram, there is always the chance for confusion. Many times the students leave the labels off, and when they go back to study, they can't remember what that extra line is. So, be sure that you label the lines and stress to your class that they should be doing the same.

Use price ceilings and floors to remind students that any surplus or shortage is a horizontal distance. Some students want to look at vertical distances or areas of triangles as the measure of the surplus or shortage.

ANSWERS TO CHECKPOINT EXERCISES

■ CHECKPOINT 7.1: Taxes

1a. When the government imposes a 20 cent on phone calls and the supply is perfectly elastic, the buyer pays all of the tax.

1b. The tax decreases the number of calls made because the rise in the price of a phone call decreases the quantity demanded.

1c. Because the tax creates a deadweight loss, the market with the tax is inefficient.

1d. The excess burden is the deadweight loss.

2. When the demand is perfectly inelastic or the supply is perfectly elastic, the buyer pays all of a sales tax.

3. The employer (the demander) pays all of a payroll tax when the demand for labor is perfectly inelastic or when the supply of labor is perfectly elastic. In this case, the market is inefficient because the quantity of labor employed decreases.

■ CHECKPOINT 7.2: Price Ceilings

1a. The equilibrium occurs at $125 per week and 1,400 rooms.

1b. At a rent ceiling of $100 per month, the quantity of rooms demanded would be 1,600 and so there would be a shortage of 200 rooms on campus. The allocation would not be efficient because marginal benefit is greater than marginal cost. Both consumer surplus and producer surplus shrink. Students respond by renting off-campus housing. The college can respond to the loss of revenue by increasing other fees or reducing maintenance of on-campus housing. The allocation is not fair because it prevents voluntary exchange and does not necessarily reallocate housing to the poorest students.

1c. The people who gain from the ceiling are those students who get the cheaper apartments on campus. Assuming the enrollment doesn't change, the status of off-campus housing owners remains unchanged because they still rent the same number of apartments at the market equilibrium. The losers are those students are those unable to rent at the $100 ceiling.

1d. Because this is on-campus housing, we would expect the school administration not to "cheat" and create a black market. Black market operations might be the school forcing students to buy a valueless meal package for $25 per week if they live in on-campus housing. However, if a black market develops, the maximum rent that can be charged is $125 dollars. Because the supply of apartments is fixed, so that the supply curve is vertical at 1,400 units, the equilibrium with a black market would be efficient and, setting aside any student's hesitancy to transact in a black market, the equilibrium would be fair.

■ CHECKPOINT 7.3: Price Floors

1a. Equilibrium occurs at a wage rate of $10 per hour and a quantity of 200 tutors.

1b. An $8 per hour minimum wage is ineffective because it is below the equilibrium wage. The equilibrium wage rate remains $10 per hour and the equilibrium quantity remains 200.

1c. At a minimum wage of $15 per hour, only 100 tutors are hired and each receives $15 per hour.

1d. The outcome with the minimum wage rate of $15 is an inefficient outcome because marginal benefit exceeds the marginal cost and there is a deadweight loss. The outcome is not fair either. It benefits only the tutors who get the jobs and the unemployed tutors earn nothing. Students are unable to hire the tutors they want.

1e. If a black market develops and tutors can charge below the minimum wage, the supply curve shows that some are willing to tutor for as little as $5 per hour.

ANSWERS TO CHAPTER CHECKPOINT EXERCISES

1. The government will collect less than $200,000 for each boat sold because the pre-tax price of a boat will fall to less than $1 million. Because boats are luxury goods, the elasticity of demand is greater than 1. Indeed, empirically the elasticity of demand is probably quite elastic because people willing and able to spend $1 million on a boat have many other luxury options available. Hence the tax will fall mainly on the sellers. The tax creates inefficiency because it creates a deadweight loss with a wedge between marginal benefit and marginal cost. The tax is unfair. By the fair-rules concept, the tax is not fair because there is involuntary exchange. By the fair-results concept, the tax might be considered fair because the purpose is to transfer income from the rich to the poor. However, when a boat luxury tax actually was imposed, many fewer boats were produced and many lower-income boat builders lost their jobs.

2. Because sunscreen and sunglasses are necessities, so that the elasticity of demand is less than 1, most of a tax imposed on them will be paid by the buyers. Even though the tax doubles in amount, the quantity purchased will not be halved because the demand is inelastic. The tax is unfair by both principles of fairness. Because the tax represents an involuntary transfer of private property, the tax is unfair by the "fair rules" theory. Because the tax is imposed on a necessity that poor people must buy, the tax is unfair by the "fair results" theory.

3. It is likely that the supply of labor by professional basketball players is quite inelastic because it is not obvious what other professions they would see as good substitutes for basketball. (Football would be a possibility, but the skills—to say nothing of the height—required to excel at basketball seem a different bundle than the skills required to excel at football.) The more inelastic the supply of labor by basketball players, the smaller the decrease in the quantity. Hence, the income tax will raise a lot of revenue because the quantity traded will not decrease by much. The players will pay most of the tax.

4. A payroll tax of 10 percent will raise the same amount of revenue as would a super income tax of 10 percent. The players will continue to pay most of the tax.

5. With the arrival of the Olympics, the demand for housing increased and the demand curve for housing shifted rightward. Homeowners left town and rented out their homes causing the supply of housing to increase and the supply curve to shift rightward. However, the increase in demand was much greater than the increase in supply and, without government intervention in the housing market, rents increased. Everyone willing and able to pay the market price was able to rent a home.

    Now assume that in anticipation of soaring rents, the government imposed a rent ceiling below the equilibrium rent. At the rent determined by the ceiling, the quantity of homes demanded exceeds the quantity supplied. The (apparent) lower rent increases the number of people who want to rent a home and decreases the number willing to inconvenience themselves by offering their home for rent. A shortage of homes would exist. It is likely that a black market would have arisen. In the black market, there would have been occurrences such as prospective landlords offering a house for rent at the ceiling rent only if a car was simultaneously rented for an above-market fee for car rentals. Alternatively, landlords might have rented their house only if a "Special Olympic Party Pack" consisting of a bag of chips and a six-pack of soda were purchased for several hundred dollars.

6a. If oil producing countries increased production so that the equilibrium price ($0.90) fell below the $1.00 ceiling, the ceiling has no effect.

6b. If the equilibrium price of gasoline rose to $2.00, the $1.00 ceiling would create a deadweight loss. This outcome is illustrated in Figure 7.1. The shortage of oil shifts the supply curve from S_1 to S_2. Hence, even though the ceiling price was above the initial equilibrium price and so ineffective, after the decrease in supply the price ceiling is below the new equilibrium price (of $2 per gallon) and so the ceiling has an effect. At the ceiling price, the quantity demanded is Q_d and the quantity supplied is Q_s. A shortage, equal to the amount $Q_d - Q_s$, exists. The market is inefficient because the marginal benefit exceeds the marginal cost. The deadweight loss equals the area of the darkened triangle in the figure.

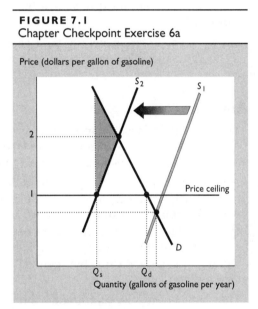

FIGURE 7.1
Chapter Checkpoint Exercise 6a

7. Bakers and copy shop workers will be unaffected by the $5 minimum wage because these workers are already making at least the minimum wage. The gas pump attendants (at least, those that get to keep their jobs) will see their wage rise from $4 to $5 per hour. Some attendants will get laid off.

8. Because the $10 price floor is effectively imposed, the quantity demanded of beef is less than the quantity purchased when the price was $5 per pound. If you were a farmer lucky enough to sell all of your beef at the $10 per pound price, you would support the floor. Because the government does not guarantee to buy the surplus beef, ranchers who cannot sell their cattle at the $10 per pound price are stuck with their cattle. These ranchers want the price floor removed.

ADDITIONAL EXERCISES FOR ASSIGNMENT

■ Questions

1. Your local government notes that 10,000 pizzas are delivered weekly. It imposes a $1 per pizza tax on the delivery of pizza and believes that it will collect $10,000 per week. Is this belief correct? Why or why not?

2. Suppose the government was considering imposing a sales tax on new cartridges used in ink jet printers. Would workers making and distributing ink jet cartridges be in favor of, or in opposition to, such a tax?

3. In order to be effective, a price floor must be below the equilibrium price and a price ceiling must be above the equilibrium price. Is this statement true or false?

4. Union members are generally paid significantly more than the minimum wage. Why, then, do unions support increases in the minimum wage?

■ Answers

1. The belief is incorrect. Imposing a tax on pizza decreases the equilibrium quantity of pizza so that fewer than 10,000 pizzas per week will be delivered. Hence the tax revenue, which is $1 per pizza, will be less than $10,000.

2. A tax on new ink jet cartridges would decrease the equilibrium quantity of new ink jet cartridges, as some people would refill old cartridges, others would print less, and still others would switch to laser printers. Because the quantity of new ink cartridges decreases, firms will lay off or otherwise decrease the quantity of workers employed making these cartridges. Hence, workers making the cartridges generally would oppose the tax out of concern for their jobs.

3. The statement is false and is unfortunately common among students who think of a floor as being beneath their feet (so that a price floor is beneath the equilibrium price) and a ceiling as being above their heads (so that a price ceiling is above the equilibrium price). A price floor sets the lowest price that can legally be charged. Prices cannot (legally) penetrate below the floor. To be effective, the price floor must be set above the equilibrium price because in this case the equilibrium price becomes illegal. Similarly, to be effective a price ceiling (which sets the highest legal price) must be set below the equilibrium price in order to make the equilibrium price illegal.

4. Workers who are paid the minimum wage are generally low-skilled workers while union workers, who are paid more than the minimum age, are generally high-skilled workers. However, low-skilled and high-skilled workers are substitutes. Thus an increase in the minimum wage will cause firms to decrease the quantity of low-skilled workers they demand and increase their demand for high-skilled, union workers. Therefore an increase in the minimum wage helps increase the employment and wages of union members.

ANSWERS TO ECONOMICS IN THE NEWS

■ Deal possible in Congress on minimum wage increase

1. The effect of a $1 increase in the minimum wage depends on whether the new minimum wage is effective (above the equilibrium wage rate) or ineffective (below the equilibrium wage rate). If the new minimum wage is above the equilibrium wage rate, a surplus of labor and hence unemployment would result. If the new minimum wage is below the equilibrium wage rate, it is ineffective and has no effect in the labor market.

    In today's robust economy, the current minimum wage of $5.15 is not effective in many markets. Workers that would typically earn the minimum wage (store clerks, fast food workers, etc.) are earning more that $5.15 in many cases. A $1 increase over two years would probably move the minimum wage above the equilibrium wage rate in more markets and hence would likely increase the unemployment rate somewhat.

2. If the increased minimum wage is above the equilibrium wage rate, the unemployment rate will rise.

3. Tax breaks that reduce the taxes payable by firms if they employ workers earning the minimum wage would increase the demand for labor and shift the demand for labor curve rightward. The effect would be to limit the surplus of labor created by the minimum wage, that is, decrease the unemployment.

USING EYE ON THE PAST

■ An Earthquake and a Rent Ceiling: A Tale of Two Eras in One City

For the first part of the story concerning the 1906 San Francisco earthquake, you can use a supply and demand diagram to show the result of the earthquake reducing the amount of available housing. Be certain that you explain to the students that the earthquake decreases the supply but does not change the demand. Many students reason that the demand for housing increases because there are more (potentially) homeless people after the earthquake. Be sure to eliminate this type of reasoning!

Because there is a free housing market, rents rise to a new equilibrium, in which there is no deadweight loss. Over time, builders (unfettered by rent ceilings) find it profitable to build more apartments, and the market moves toward a new equilibrium of more apartments rented at lower prices. Diagramming this part of the story by showing the supply curve shifting rightward is another opportunity to demonstrate to the students how to use the supply and demand model.

The story also relates the outcome of San Francisco when rent ceilings were re imposed in the 1940s. As a result of a 30 percent increase in population and only a 20 percent increase in supply, there was a housing shortage. The shortage was the result of rent ceilings that had been imposed in the 1940s. Builders, whose profits were constrained by the rent ceilings, chose not to build apartments to meet demand. Again, demonstrate to the students what occurred by showing them how the increase in demand outstripping the increase in supply means that the demand curve shifted rightward farther than the supply curve and, with the rent ceiling in place, a shortage was the result.

USING EYE ON THE U.S. ECONOMY

■ The Federal Minimum Wage

You can use this story to start a discussion about your students' personal experience with the minimum wage. Ask them if any have behaved as Card and Krueger suggest. For example, if they got a wage increase as a result of a minimum wage hike, did they work harder? If any have been managers, ask if they worked to make the firm more efficient. Ask if any know of friends who quit high school to find a minimum wage job.

You can also focus on the economic growth ideas proposed by Welch and Murphy. Ask students for the intuition behind their suggestion that a healthy economy caused a positive relationship between wages and employment.

Externalities

Chapter

8

CHAPTER ROADMAP

■ Where We Are

We'll use the supply and demand curves to show how externalities affect the efficient use of resources. We'll see that external costs result in overproduction and that external benefits result in underproduction. By developing a marginal social cost curve and marginal social benefit curve, we incorporate these external costs and external benefits into the basic supply and demand curve diagram. Finally, we investigate how the government intervenes in the market to promote efficient use of resources.

■ Where We've Been

We've explored the interactions of supply and demand that bring about the efficient use of resources by equating marginal benefit to marginal cost. We use the concept of efficiency in this chapter to discuss the deadweight loss from externalities and how government action can overcome the inefficiency.

■ Where We're Going

After this chapter, we turn to exploring consumer demand in greater detail. We know that the demand curve slopes downward, but in the next chapter we examine the rationale behind people's choices..

IN THE CLASSROOM

■ Class Time Needed

You can complete this chapter in one and a half sessions. This chapter is particularly suitable to the use of current event examples. You can take one class period to cover the mechanics of the marginal social cost curve, marginal social benefit curve, and government intervention. Then you can spend part of the next class period discussing real world examples.

An estimate of the time per checkpoint is:

- 8.1 Negative Externalities: Pollution—25 minutes
- 8.2 Positive Externalities: Education and Research—25 minutes

■ Extended Lecture Outline

8.1 Negative Externalities: Pollution

A. Externalities in Our Daily Lives

An externality is a cost or benefit that arises from a production activity that falls on someone other than the producer; or a cost or benefit that arises from a consumption activity that falls on someone other than the consumer.

1. Negative Production Externalities—an example of which is pollution.
2. Positive Production Externalities—an example of which is producing honey using bees next to an apple orchid.
3. Negative Consumption Externalities—an example of which is smoking in a closed space.
4. Positive Consumption Externalities—an example of which is education.

B. Private Costs and Social Costs

1. There are several types of important costs in analyzing externalities:
   a. A *private cost* is a cost of production borne by the producer of a good.
   b. **Marginal private cost** (MC) is the private cost of producing an extra unit of a good.
   c. **Marginal external cost** is the cost of producing an extra unit of a good borne by people other than the producer.
   d. **Marginal social cost** (MSC) is the marginal cost borne by the producer plus everyone else impacted by a cost from the good.
   e. MSC = MC + marginal external cost.
2. Economists use market prices to determine the opportunity costs of pollution or other activities that produce external costs.
3. The MSC curve lies above the MC curve and both costs increase as output increases.

C. Production and Pollution: How Much?

1. Without regulation, the market equilibrium (as determined by the supply and demand curves) determines the amount of output produced. This equilibrium is inefficient because not *all* costs are being counted.
2. To determine the efficient allocation of resources, you must count all the costs (private and external) when comparing marginal benefit and marginal social cost.
3. An unregulated market creates a deadweight loss.

D. Property rights are legally established rights entitling an owner to determine how his or her property will be used. By assigning property rights, it is possible to reduce the inefficiency created by an externality.

E. The Coase Theorem

The **Coase theorem** is the proposition that if property rights exist, transactions costs are low, and only a small number of parties are involved, then private transactions are efficient.

1. The Coase theorem implies that if property rights exist and are enforced (and transactions costs are low), it doesn't matter who (the polluter or the victim) owns the property rights.
2. **Transactions costs** are the opportunity costs of making a transaction.

F. Government Actions in the Face of External Costs

The government uses three main tools to deal with external costs:

1. Emissions charges are per unit pollution fees charged by the EPA to polluters.
2. Marketable permits are pollution limits assigned to firms by the government. Firms can buy and sell these permits depending on their needs.

   3. Taxes are an incentive for polluters to cut back on the amount of the external costs they produce.

8.2 Positive Externalities: Education and Research
   A. Private Benefits and Social Benefits
      1. There are several types of benefits important in analyzing externalities:
         a. A *private benefit* is a benefit gained only by the consumer of a good or service.
         b. **Marginal private benefit** is the private benefit from an additional unit of a good or service.
         c. **Marginal external benefit** is the benefit from an additional unit of a good or service received by people other than the consumer.
         d. **Marginal social benefit** (*MSB*) is the marginal benefit enjoyed by society (by both consumers of the good and others).
         e. *MSB = MB +* marginal external benefit.
      2. Without government intervention, society will underproduce a good that generates an external benefit.
   B. Government Actions in the Face of External Benefits
      1. **Public provision** is the production of a good or service by a public authority that receives funding from the government.
      2. A **private subsidy** is a payment that the government makes to the producer of a good. The subsidy reduces the provider's costs and increases the production of the good.
      3. A **voucher** is a token or coupon that the government provides to consumers, which they can use to buy specific goods or services. A voucher increases the demand for a good, leading to an increase in production.
      4. A **patent** or **copyright** is a government-granted right to the inventor of a good to exclusively produce, use or sell the invention. A patent or copyright is the legal device used to guarantee **intellectual property rights**.

■ Lecture Launchers

1. Launch your Chapter 8 lecture by asking your students if they have seen the movie *Erin Brokovich*. It's a great (not necessarily in a review sense, but in an economic sense!) movie that shows how pollution creates external costs and how residents required Pacific Gas & Electricity (PG&E) to account for both private costs and external costs in the use of hexavalent chromium (chromium 6). PG&E used the chemical to clean its equipment. According to the movie, PG&E improperly discharged the chemical and polluted the ground and water, causing death and disease. The movie starts with PG&E recognizing there is a problem because it offers a homeowner $55,000 for his home and medical bills. The movie ends with this family receiving $5 million from PG&E. PG&E now claims that chromium 6 is not deadly if you drink it, only if you inhale it and that it presents no external costs. Still, PG&E settled the case for $330 million.

2. I ask students why do we have plenty of cows while rhinos are almost extinct. They want to answer that rhinos are exotic or that the rhino's environment is deteriorating. You can remind students that the buffalo wasn't exotic and they had plenty of space to roam and still they were almost ex-

tinguished. The difference between cows and rhinos (and buffaloes in the 19th century) is that someone *owns* the cows (someone has the property rights to the cows), but no one owns the rhinos. Because no one had property rights to the rhino, there was no benefit to anyone for the rhino to stay alive; they would be hunted to extinction. In South Africa, though, black and white rhinos are growing in number because of "game privatization." According to *Smithsonian* magazine (March 2001), private landowners in South Africa are converting their farms to private reserves to breed, raise, and sell rhinos (and other endangered species). You can even hunt white rhinos today (but not black ones). Mark Englezakis (a lodge owner quoted in the magazine) understands the benefits of property rights: "The cow is mine, it's worth money, so I've got to protect it," he says. He adds that by giving him the right to sell a rhino and earn the benefits (profits), he's also willing to raise and protect rhinos. "For wildlife to survive, it has to become a cow," he adds.

3. In Cobb County, Georgia (just outside of Atlanta) residents 65 and older are not required to pay "school taxes." You might need to explain how school taxes work and that in most areas, all homeowners are required to pay property taxes to provide public education. You might ask students "Does this mean that these people no longer benefit from an educated public?" and promote discussion along these lines.

■ Land Mines

1. This chapter tests students' graphing abilities with the addition of the marginal social cost curve and the marginal social benefit curve. Using colored chalk, colored markers on the overhead, or colored lines on your PowerPoint slides is very helpful in distinguishing these different lines.

2. Draw the supply (marginal cost) curve for a plant that pollutes. Remind students that this curve represents the quantity of other goods that the producer must forgo to produce one more unit of the good. Pick a point on the curve and say "To increase the production of electricity one more unit, the graph shows that the producer must forgo $100 (or whatever price and quantity you have chosen). If I tell you that the utility is polluting the environment, should we (as a society) make them give up more?" Most students will answer "yes" and you can plot a point higher on the graph (at the same quantity). Do the same analysis for other production points and you now have a new supply curve, the marginal social cost (*MSC*) curve. Remind students that the area between the curves is the "penalty" for the production of pollutants or marginal external cost. Make sure to show that the *MSC* curve (by intersecting with the demand curve at a different point) reduces the amount of pollution. You also can do a similar analysis for the *MSB* curve.

3. To clarify the effects of the government's options of using public provision, private subsidies, and vouchers to deal with external benefits, draw all three options as headings across the board at one time. Under each heading, start with identical supply and demand curves that result in underpro-

duction. Add the *MSB* curve in each case. Start with the voucher case first because it is the simplest and show how the voucher increases demand so that it becomes the same as the *MSB* curve. You can then show how a subsidy shifts the supply curve creating the same outcome. Compare the value of the subsidy with voucher's value…it's the same. Then draw the public provision case showing how the taxpayer foots the bill (the same amount in the two other cases) and produces the efficient amount. Review how each option produces the same outcome for the same "price" and that it's just the process to the efficient outcome that differs.

ANSWERS TO CHECKPOINT EXERCISES

■ CHECKPOINT 8.1 Negative Externalities: Pollution

1a. The efficient quantity is 20 tons per week.
1b. The price of the permit is $50, the marginal external cost when 20 tons per week are produced.
1c. The factory buys the permits and the town sells the permits.
1d. If the factory received all the permits, the townspeople would buy the permits for $50 per ton.
1e. If the townspeople received all the permits, the factory would buy the permits for $50 per ton.

■ CHECKPOINT 8.2 Positive Externalities: Education and Research

1a. The equilibrium tuition is $12,000 and the equilibrium number of students is 5,000.
1b. The efficient number of students is 15,000.
1c. The government will charge a tuition of $4,000 because that is the tuition necessary to have 15,000 enrolled.
1d. The subsidy must be $8,000.
1e. The voucher must be for $8,000.

ANSWERS TO CHAPTER CHECKPOINT EXERCISES

1a. Larry will be willing to pay Tom up to $25 to not smoke. Tom's net benefit from smoking is $18 (the marginal benefit minus the price of the cigar). The Coase theorem says that in this case, with Tom and Larry meeting at Tom's home, Larry will pay Tom some amount between $18 to $25 not to smoke and Tom will not smoke.

1b. If Tom and Larry meet at Larry's house, Tom is willing to pay up to $18 to be allowed to smoke. But Larry will accept nothing less than $25 to allow Tom to smoke. Hence Tom cannot offer enough to Larry, so Tom will not smoke. Note that in both parts (a) and (b), the efficient outcome, Tom not smoking, is attained regardless of who is given the property right, that is, regardless of who owns the house in which the meeting occurs.

2a. Larry will be willing to pay Tom up to $20 to not smoke. Tom's net benefit from smoking is $23 (the marginal benefit minus the price of the cigar). When Tom and Larry meet at Tom's house, Larry cannot offer enough to Tom to make Tom quit smoking, so Tom will smoke.

2b. If Tom and Larry meet at Larry's house, Tom is willing to pay up to $23 to be allowed to smoke. And Larry will accept anything more than $20 to allow Tom to smoke. Hence Tom will offer Larry some amount between $20 and $23 and Tom will smoke. Note that as in Exercise 1, in both parts of this exercise, the efficient outcome (in this case, Tom smoking) is attained regardless of who is given the property right, that is, regardless of whose house the meeting occurs.

3a. With no pollution control, the marginal cost to the firm of polluting is $0. Thus the firm will pollute until the marginal benefit from so doing equals $0, which implies that the there will be 100 percent pollution.

3b. The amount of pollution is efficient when the marginal cost of further pollution reduction equals its marginal cost. The marginal benefit can be measured by the change in the amount of property tax citizens are willing to pay. For instance, the marginal benefit of reducing pollution from 10 percent to 20 percent is $135, the increase in the property tax citizens are will-ing to pay. The marginal cost of

Pollution cut (Percentage)	Marginal benefit (dollars)	Marginal cost (dollars)
10	150	10
20	135	15
30	120	20
40	105	25
50	90	30
60	75	35
70	60	40
80	45	45
90	30	50

pollution reduction is measured by the change in the total cost of pollution reduction. For instance, the marginal cost of reducing pollution from 10 percent to 20 percent is $15, the increase in the firm's total cost. The com-plete marginal benefit and marginal cost schedules are in the table. The ta-ble shows that the efficient amount of pollution reduction is 80 percent.

3c. If the city owns the steel mill, then pollution will be cut by 80 percent.

3d. If the city is a company town, pollution will be cut by 80 percent. The Coase theorem points out that regardless of whether the city owns the mill or the mill owns the city, the amount of pollution is the efficient amount.

4a. With no public college and no government involvement, 1 million students will enroll in college and the tuition will be $5,000 per year.

4b. The efficient number of students is 2 million. The proper government subsidy is $2,000, which will lead to 2 million students enrolling.

4c. If the government offers a $2,000 voucher, the efficient number of students, 2 million, enroll.

5. With the reduction in cost to $3,500 a year, 1.75 million students will enroll in college when there is no government involvement. (This answer assumes that the demand curve between 1 and 2 million students is linear.) The efficient number of students is 8 million, because this is the number of students for which the marginal social benefit ($3,500, the sum of the private benefit, $500, plus the marginal external benefit, $3,000) equals the marginal cost. The proper government subsidy is $3,000 and the proper government voucher is a $3,000 voucher.

6. Research provides external benefits that go unaccounted for without government protection. Patent and/or copyright protection shift the demand curve for research rightward by the amount of the discovery's external benefit. The rightward shift in the demand curve generates a higher equilibrium quantity of research than would otherwise occur.

7. Your students answers will vary, depending on your state and the region they select.

ADDITIONAL EXERCISES FOR ASSIGNMENT

■ Questions

1. Figure 8.1 shows the cost and benefit curves facing a scenic seaside village that has a factory producing both paper and water pollution next to it.

   a. If property rights are not assigned and there is no government intervention, how much paper is produced and what is the price?

   b. If property rights to the water are assigned, how much paper is produced? Does it matter whether the town or the factory is assigned the property rights?

   c. If the city wants to tax the factory to achieve the efficient amount of pollution, what must the tax be and what will be the city's tax revenue?

FIGURE 8.1
Additional Exercise I

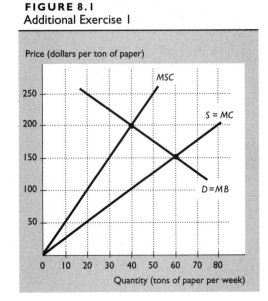

2. The figure shows the market for college education.
    a. What is the efficient number of students?
    b. If the government decides to provide public colleges, in order to attain efficiency, what must the tuition equal? How much of the cost of a student will be funded by taxes and how much will be paid for by the student?

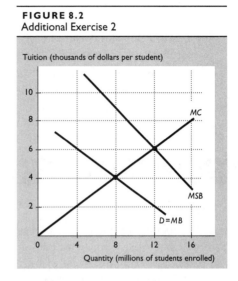

FIGURE 8.2
Additional Exercise 2

■ Answers

1a. With no property rights and no government intervention, the quantity of paper is determined by the demand and supply curves and is 60 tons of paper at a price of $150 per ton.

1b. If property rights to the water are assigned, the efficient amount of paper is produced, 40 tons. The Coase theorem points out that it does not matter to whom the property rights are assigned.

1c. To attain efficiency, the tax must equal the marginal external cost at the efficient quantity, which is $100 per ton. With this tax, 40 tons of paper are produced, so the city collects ($100 per ton) × (40 tons) = $4,000 per week in tax revenue.

2a. The efficient number of students is 12 million because that is the quantity for which the marginal social benefit, *MSB*, equals the marginal cost, *MC*.

2b. To have 12 million students enroll, the demand curve demonstrates that the tuition must be $2,000. The marginal cost is $6,000, so with the student paying $2,000, taxpayers must pay $4,000 per student.

ANSWERS TO ECONOMICS IN THE NEWS

■ Golf Club Squeals over Pig Farm Neighbor

1. The news article describes the problem of external costs. The farm produces odors that are an external cost to the golfers.

2. The Coase solution would be to assign property rights to the air. The property rights would be assigned to either the farm or the golf course. As long as the transactions costs are low, this solution would work regardless of which party was assigned the rights.

3. The Coase solution runs into the problem of the number of parties that must negotiate. Unless the club negotiates for all golfers, the number of golfers that must negotiate with the farm would be large and hence reaching a Coase solution would be difficult. If the club is a private club and able to negotiate for all its members, then the Coase solution is feasible.

4. The government can impose a tax equal to the marginal external cost. The tax shifts the marginal cost curve leftward reducing the amount of pollution. A correct assessment of the marginal external cost produces a tax that reduces the amount of pollution to the efficient level.

USING EYE ON THE U.S ECONOMY

■ Pollution Trends

This article focuses on the three main types of pollution: air, water and land. The story notes that most types of air pollution have decreased over the past 25 years. These results show that the cost of reducing some contaminants (lead and sulfur dioxide) is lower than other contaminants (nitrogen dioxide and ozone). If the costs were equally low, we would see all types of pollution decrease by similar percentages. You can ask students when or how they think the most common types of pollutants will effectively be reduced. Their answers should contain intuition about comparing the opportunity cost of reduction versus pollution and the ability to assign property rights.

USING EYE ON THE GLOBAL ECONOMY

■ A Carbon Fuel Tax?

This story highlights three aspects of carbon emissions: the debate over the danger of carbon emissions, the comparison of today's costs to reduce pollution versus the benefits that accrue in the future, and the role of developing countries in increasing pollution.

The debate over the danger of carbon emissions means that it will be difficult to get the U.S. government to agree on any tax imposition. If scientists would agree on the emissions' negative (or negligible) effects, a meaningful policy might well adopted in the United States. As long as developing countries' governments subsidize the pollution, actions in the United States will account for a decreasing portion of the world's total. Attempts to reduce pollution will have to focus more on these countries than on the United States.

You can ask students how much are they willing to pay for cleaner air, land, and water. For example, electricity deregulation is supposed to allow you to choose among various utility providers. Some providers will claim "clean" production of electricity, while others will offer electricity at the lowest price. Ask your students which provider they would pick. How many of those choosing the "green" provider are willing to pay higher prices? How much higher?

Ask your students how many of them buy the "green" paper towels and napkins in the grocery store. They are usually higher priced and lower quality. How many of them are willing to give up their cars for public transportation? These choices represent the opportunity cost of reducing pollution. Obviously, in some cases, the costs are too high.

Public Goods and the Tax System

Chapter 9

CHAPTER OUTLINE

1. **Distinguish between public goods and private goods, explain the free-rider problem, and explain how the quantity of public goods is determined.**
   A. Public Goods
   B. The Free-Rider Problem
   C. The Marginal Benefit of a Public Good
   D. The Marginal Cost of a Public Good
   E. The Efficient Quantity of a Public Good
   F. Private Provision
   G. Public Provision
      1. The Principle of Minimum Differentiation
   H. The Role of Bureaucrats
   I. Rational Ignorance
   J. Why Government is Large and Grows
      1. Voter Preferences
      2. Inefficient Overprovision
   K. Voter Backlash

2. **Explain the effects of income taxes and review the main ideas about the fairness of the tax system.**
   A. Income Taxes
      1. Personal Income Tax
      2. Corporate Income Tax
   B. The Effects of Income Taxes
      1. Taxes on Labor Income
      2. Taxes on Capital Income
      3. Taxes on Land and Other Unique Resources
      4. Why We Have a Progressive Income Tax
   C. Is the Tax System Fair?
      1. The Benefits Principle
      2. The Ability-to-Pay Principle
         a. Horizontal Equity
         b. Vertical Equity
         c. The Marriage Tax Problem

CHAPTER ROADMAP

■ Where We Are

We'll discuss the characteristics of public goods and the free-rider problem. We'll see that without government intervention, the efficient amount of public goods will not be produced. In order to provide these public goods, the government must levy taxes. The second part of the chapter reviews the U.S. tax system, the effects of taxes on resources, and the fairness of taxes.

■ Where We've Been

We've explored the interactions of supply and demand that bring about the efficient use of resources by equating marginal benefit to marginal cost. We've extended the supply and demand model to show how externalities affect the efficient use of resources. We saw that external costs result in overproduction, that external benefits result in underproduction and how the government intervenes in the market to promote efficient use of resources.

■ Where We're Going

After this chapter we turn to exploring consumer demand in greater detail. We know that the demand curve slopes downward, but in the next chapter we examine the rationale of maximizing utility. We see that by maximizing utility, people's choices lead to a downward-sloping demand curve. We also explore the paradox of value.

IN THE CLASSROOM

■ Class Time Needed

You can complete this chapter in one to one and one half class sessions.

An estimate of the time per checkpoint is:

- 9.1 Public Goods and the Free-Rider Problem—25 to 50 minutes
- 9.2 The Tax System—25 to 30 minutes

■ Extended Lecture Outline

9.1 Public Goods and the Free-Rider Problem

A. Public Goods

Public goods are goods or services that everyone can consume at the same time and from which no one can be excluded. Pure public goods are nonrival and nonexcludable (national defense).

1. **Private goods** are goods or services that can only be consumed by one person at a time and only by those people who have purchased it. Pure private goods are rival and excludable (food).
2. A **nonrival good** is good that when consumed by one person does not decrease the quantity available for someone else.
3. A **rival good** is a good that when consumed by one person, decreases the quantity of the good available for someone else.
4. A **nonexcludable** good is one from which it is technologically impossible or very costly to prevent people from consuming.
5. A good is **excludable** if it is possible to prevent a person from enjoying the benefits of the good.
6. A mixed good is a good that exhibits qualities of each dimension. For example, a good might be nonrival, but excludable (cable television) or rival, but nonexcludable (clean air).

B. The Free-Rider Problem

1. A **free rider** is a person who consumes a good without paying for it.
2. Because no one can be excluded from consuming a public good, public goods create a free-rider problem. As a result, the market underproduces public goods.
3. The government intervenes in the market to ensure the efficient quantity of a public good is provided.

C. The marginal benefit curve of a public good is determined by *vertically* adding the marginal benefit curves of all the consumers in the economy.

D. The marginal cost of a public good, as for any other good, increases as production of the good increases.

E. The efficient quantity of a public good is determined by the intersection of the marginal benefit and marginal cost curves.

F. Public goods will not be provided by a private firm because of the free-rider problem. If a private firm decided to provide a public good, free riders would consume the good without paying for it and the firm would earn no revenue. The firm could not stay in business providing the public good.

G. Competition in the political marketplace can help ensure the production of the efficient quantity of a public good.

1. This efficient outcome occurs if voters and political parties are well-informed.
2. Political parties and firms adopt the **principle of minimum differentiation.** The idea is that, in order to appeal to the maximum number of voters or customers, political parties and firms act alike (either by locating in similar areas or by making similar products for firms or adopting similar platforms for political parties).

H. Bureaucrats play a role in providing an efficient level of public goods. Depending on the power of the bureaucrats, interest groups and voters, either the efficient level or overproduction might occur.

I. Rational Ignorance

Rational ignorance is the decision by voters not to acquire more information because the marginal cost of obtaining the information is greater than the marginal benefit.

1. Voters (who are consumers of public goods) sometimes adopt the strategy of rational ignorance, which allows bureaucrats to make decisions about the provision of public goods.
2. Producers of public goods (who are also voters) exert influence on political parties and bureaucrats to increase the amount of public goods to be provided.

J. The government is large and still growing because the demand for public goods increases at a faster rate than the demand for private goods. There are two possible reasons for this outcome:

1. Voter preferences

There is a positive relationship between voters' incomes and their demand for public goods. Because incomes have risen, the demand for public goods has also risen.

2. Inefficient overproduction

Rational ignorance combined with bureaucrats' desires for larger budgets result in the rise in public goods.

K. Voters can decrease the size of government by choosing to have private firms produce public goods or by not voting for politicians that support large government.

9.2 The Tax System

A. Income taxes are imposed on the incomes of individuals and corporations.

1. Personal income tax
   a. **Taxable income** = total income − personal exemptions − standard deduction.
   b. A **marginal tax rate** is the percentage of an additional dollar of income that is paid in tax. The marginal tax rate a person pays depends on his or her taxable income.
   c. The **average tax rate** is the percentage of income that is paid in taxes. For the U.S. personal income tax, the average tax rate is less than the marginal tax rate.
   d. A **progressive tax** is one for which the average tax rate increases as income increases. A **proportional tax** is one for which the average tax rate is the same at all income levels. A **regressive tax** is one for which the average tax rate decreases as income increases.

2. Corporate income tax
   a. The government taxes the profits earned by corporations.
   b. The corporate income tax taxes corporate income twice, once as profits and again as individuals earn income via the firm's dividends.

B. The Effects of Income Taxes

Tax incidence describes which party (the supplier or the demander) bears the tax. Excess burden is the deadweight loss generated by a tax. Government taxes fall on three sources of income (labor, capital, and land or other unique resources) and each kind of tax creates an incidence, a tax burden, and a deadweight loss depending on the particulars of the market.

1. Taxes on Labor Income
   a.. Different labor groups, each with their own unique elasticity of demand, have different incidences of taxation.
   b. Taxes on labor income result in deadweight losses. The deadweight loss for high-wage workers exceeds that for low-wage workers.

2. Taxes on Capital Income
   a. Capital income is income accruing from people's earnings on assets such as bank deposits, bonds, and stock dividends.

    b. The supply of capital is highly elastic because capital can readily move from one country to another, seeking the highest return.

    c. Because capital income taxes decrease the quantity of capital, the capital stock is smaller than it would be otherwise. Additionally, the marginal product of labor and labor income are negatively affected.

  3. Taxes on Land and Other Unique Resources

    a. Landowners bear the entire tax burden on their property because the supply of land is perfectly inelastic. There is no deadweight loss from a tax on land.

    b. Other unique resources include a media star's unique talent.

  4. Why We Have a Progressive Income Tax

  We have a progressive tax system because it is supported by the political equilibrium. The median voter is a low-income voter. The median voter model predicts that these voters put politicians in office that support the progressive tax system.

C. Is the Tax System Fair?

Fairness of a tax system is based on two principles:

  1. The Benefits Principle

  The **benefits principle** states that people should pay taxes equal to the benefits they receive from public services.

  2. The Ability-to-Pay Principle

  The **ability-to-pay principle** states that people should pay taxes based on how easily they can bear the burden. This principle compares taxpayers on two dimensions.

    a. **Horizontal equity,** which implies that people with the same ability-to-pay, should pay the same amount.

    b. **Vertical equity,** which implies that people with the greater ability-to-pay, should pay a greater portion of the taxes.

    c. The **marriage tax** problem occurs because the U.S. tax system taxes a married couple as one taxpayer (not two individuals) resulting in a larger tax burden.

■ Lecture Launchers

1. Tell students that you are going to classify goods (and services) today and you'll be using this classification to see which goods should be provided by the government versus private firms. Use a grid similar to the one in the text, with "rivalry" along one axis and "excludability" along the other. Explain the definitions of rival goods and excludable goods. Then start naming goods: cable TV, broadcast TV, radio broadcasts, oceans, lakes stocked with fish, cars, air, etc. Make sure to get a meaningful range of goods to fill the areas on your grid. Then ask students which ones need government provision. Use their answers to define public goods.

2. Most texts list a lighthouse as a pure public good. In fact, you might have used it in your lecture. Depending on the circumstances though, a lighthouse (or other goods) does not always fit into one category. There is evidence from the United Kingdom that in the 18th century, that the Crown granted owners the right to build lighthouses via patents. The owners then sent agents to ports and were empowered to collect fees from sailors who had benefited from sailing past the lighthouse. And, when the lighthouse

saw a ship whose owner refused to pay, the lighthouse would sometimes be turned off(!). You can use this historical story in the discussion of private firms providing public goods.

3. The debate in Congress over campaign financing (such as the debate over the McCain-Feingold bill in 2001) addresses (at least to one degree) the rational ignorance/informed voter topic. There also are third party, union, and free-speech issues involved, but you can concentrate on the rational ignorance/informed voter division. In general, political lobbyists spend hundreds of millions of dollars (via soft money contributions) delivering their preferences to politicians. As a result, economists might claim that typical voters exhibit rational ignorance because these voters see a low marginal benefit in becoming an informed voter (the large contributors "capture" the politicians). By limiting contributions, proponents of campaign finance change hope one result is to decrease the power of large political contributors and thereby increase voters' interest in elections.

■ Land Mines

1. Students sometimes find it difficult to distinguish between nonrival and rival goods, especially when there is a large supply of a good. Remind students that even McDonald's hamburgers are rival goods. You eating a burger prevents me from eating the same burger, even though "billions and billions" have been sold!

2. Spend time on determining the marginal benefit of public goods. The vertical summation of individual marginal benefit curves is not always an easy concept to grasp (especially if your students are used to the horizontal summation for private goods). Remind students that because private goods are rival (each demander needs to have his or her *own* unit of the good), we add quantities at each price. On the other hand, public goods are nonrival (the unit of a good that satisfies the demand for one person is the same unit that also satisfies the demand by another person). As a result, we add prices at each quantity (a vertical sum). Take the time to work through an example using prices and quantities, comparing the different approaches.

ANSWERS TO CHECKPOINT EXERCISES

■ CHECKPOINT 9.1 Public Goods and the Free-Rider Problem

1a. The Grand Canyon is a public good (it is essentially nonexcludable and usually nonrival, except for high-peak vacation time). Because the government charges an admission fee, there is not a free-rider problem.

1b. Street lighting is a public good (nonrival and nonexcludable). Residents are taxed to prevent the free-rider problem.

1c. Flood control is a public good (nonrival and nonexcludable). Through taxation, the free-rider problem is avoided.

1d. The beach at Santa Monica is a public good (nonrival, except on crowded days and nonexcludable). Area residents are taxed to maintain the beach, but visitors to the area (who don't pay local taxes) are free riders.

2a. A private company would provide four fire stations, if they could force people to pay for them. If the private company could not overcome the free-rider problem, it would provide no stations.

2b. The efficient quantity is four stations.

2c. In a single-issue election, four stations would be produced.

■ CHECKPOINT 9.2 The Tax System

1a. California's personal income tax is progressive; its corporate income tax is proportional; its sales tax and excise tax are regressive.

2a. Figure 9.1 illustrates the marginal tax rates in Australia.

2b. It is likely that Australia has the most progressive income tax because the marginal tax rate in Australia is distinctly higher than in the United States. As a result, the average tax rate in Australia rises enough so that it exceeds the average tax rate in the United States.

2c. Over the range of income from $1 to $5,400, the average tax rate is 0 percent. Over the range of income from $5,401 to $20,700 the average tax rate rises from 0 percent to 14.8 percent. Over the range of income from $20,700 to $38,000, the average tax rate rises from 14.8 percent to 23.5 percent. Over the range of income from $38,000 to $50,000, the average tax rate rises from 23.5 percent to 28.2 percent. And for incomes higher than $50,000, the average tax rate rises from 28.2 percent to (its limiting value of) 47 percent.

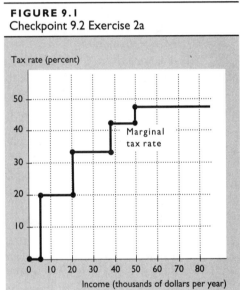

FIGURE 9.1
Checkpoint 9.2 Exercise 2a

ANSWERS TO CHAPTER CHECKPOINT EXERCISES

1a. The millennium celebrations were a public good (nonexcludable and non-rival). There was a free-rider problem because New York City did not put up gates and charge an entrance fee to enter Times Square.

1b. The Santa Monica freeway is generally a public good but not during Friday afternoon rush hour. At that time, the freeway is nonexcludable but it is ri-val. One person's consumption of the freeway's services deprives another person because the first person adds to congestion and slows the traffic. There is a free-rider problem because the government does not charge a toll for traveling on the road.

1c. Sewerage service is not a pure public good because, even though it is nonrival, it is excludable. Indeed, there is not a free-rider problem because if you do not pay your bill, you are excluded by not receiving the service.

1d. The railway system is a private good (excludable and rival). People, or firms, must pay for the use of riding on the rails and for the rails' upkeep. Amtrak, for instance, is a "private corporation" whose stock is owned by the federal government. If Amtrak's revenue's fall short of its costs, the federal government provides funds to pay expenses.

1e. For some uses, the Great Lakes are a public good. For instance, for scenery, they are nonrival and nonexcludable. For other purposes, such as boating, they can be excludable by charging for use of boat ramps or marina slots.

2a. The efficient capacity is 2.5 million gallons per day.

2b. If the city installs the system, everyone pays $50.

2c. If voters are well-informed, a system with a capacity of 2.5 million gallons will be installed.

2d. If voters are rationally ignorant, bureaucrats will install a system with a capacity of greater than 2.5 million gallons because bureaucrats want to maximize their budgets.

3. Your students' answers will depend on your state.

4a. Ohio has the more progressive tax rate. It takes a larger percentage of income (7.228 percent versus 4.5 percent) as income increases.

4b. A voter referendum would not change either tax because the median voter supports the redistribution of income from the rich to the poor through a progressive tax.

4c. Because the elasticities are (assumed) the same in both states, the factor that creates a difference in the deadweight tax is the size of the tax. The tax on low-income residents is lower in Ohio, so the deadweight loss from low-income workers is lower in Ohio. However, the tax on high income workers is lower in Connecticut, so the deadweight loss on high-income workers is lower in Connecticut.

5. Both the benefits principle and the ability-to-pay principle conclude that if the existing taxes are fair, it is fair for a state to not have an income tax. However, it is most likely that the benefits principle will conclude that in states with no income taxes, the existing taxes—sales taxes, property taxes, excise taxes, etc—are fair. The ability-to-principle likely will suggest that higher-income people should pay a greater share of those states' taxes than is currently the case.

6. California has an income tax whereas Florida does not, so definitely (!) California's income tax is higher than Florida's. California's excise taxes are generally higher than Florida's, with the only exception being wine. On wine, California imposes an excise tax of 20 cents a gallon while Florida imposes an excise tax of $2.25 a gallon. This difference is perhaps not surprising because California has a large wine industry while Florida has almost none.

ADDITIONAL EXERCISES FOR ASSIGNMENT

■ Questions

1. Classify each of the following as a public or private good based on the degree of rivalry and exclusion it exhibits.
   a. Fish in the ocean
   b. A parade

2. The table shows the marginal cost and marginal benefit data for a water treatment plant.
   a. What is the efficient capacity for the plant?
   b. In a single-issue election for the size of the water treatment plant, what size plant will be approved?
   c. If a private firm were to provide the water treatment service, what plant size will be built?

Quantity (millions of gallons per day)	Marginal cost (cents per gallon cleaned)	Marginal benefit (cents per gallon cleaned)
0	2	10
1	4	8
2	5	7
3	6	6
4	8	4

■ Answers

1a. Fish are not a pure public good. They are nonexcludable, because you can't stop a fisherman from trying to catch a fish. But they are rival: If one fisherman catches a fish, no other fisherman can catch the same fish.

1b. Most parades are public goods. No one tries to exclude anyone and, as long as the route is long enough, one person watching doesn't prevent others from watching. For popular parades, like Macy's Thanksgiving Day Parade, people are excluded from watching (tickets are sold) and are rival (one person getting a spot prevents others from doing the same).

2a. The efficient plant size will have a capacity to clean 3 million gallons of water.

2b. In a single-issue election where voters are informed, a plant with the capacity to clean 3 million gallons of water will be approved. If voters exhibit rational ignorance, bureaucrats will be able to build a larger plant.

2c. Unless the private firm had the right to collect payments to water users, it will not build the plant. Some neighborhoods do have private water treatment plants. Each homeowner is charged a monthly fee for using the plant.

ANSWERS TO ECONOMICS IN THE NEWS

■ The U.S. Election is About Missiles

1. The two broad views are whether or not to deploy a national missile defense shield. President Bush is broadly in favor of deployment, while Democrats are generally opposed.

2. The social costs of a national missile defense are the opportunity cost of what could be done with the resources used to construct the shield if the shield is not deployed. The social benefits of the shield are the increased safety felt by Americans who believe the shield will work and, if the shield is ever put to the test and passes, immense benefits will be the lives and property saved.

3. The missile defense shield, like virtually all national defense, is a public good.

USING EYE ON THE U.S PAST

■ Defense Spending in the United States

The article provides data on the level of defense spending in the United States and reasons for its decline. Most students have very little perspective on the last 20 years of defense spending, so you can take some time to review the defense history in the United States. You can let students predict under what events the level of defense spending would change.

USING EYE ON THE GLOBAL ECONOMY

■ The End of the Cold War

The story discusses the decrease in U.S. defense spending since the collapse of the Soviet Union. It compares the change in defense spending across several groups of countries, including NATO, OECD states, and the "threat states." The article points out that the decrease occurred as countries compared the marginal benefits to the marginal costs of providing the defense.

You can draw a marginal benefit/marginal cost diagram and ask students how the (political) market responded to the collapse of the Soviet Union. As the article states, the marginal benefit of providing a high-level of defense decreased. As the marginal benefit curve shifted leftward, the efficient amount of defense spending decreased. You can discuss why the United States responded to a greater degree than did other countries.

■ Taxes Around the World

The article provides average tax rates for a number of countries. Remind students what a marginal tax rate means: "If you make $100,000 in Sweden, the government gets *half* of that last dollar earned." Ask students how that would affect their work habits. You can also remind them that marginal income tax rates in the U.S. have been as high as 91 percent. Then ask students the conditions under which they would be willing to pay higher taxes (free day care, larger unemployment benefits, better roads, etc.).

Consumer Choice and Demand

Chapter

10

CHAPTER OUTLINE

CHAPTER ROADMAP

■ Where We Are

In this chapter, we uncover the consumer's behavior that leads to a downward-sloping demand curve. The consumer maximizes utility by allocating his or her entire budget while equating the marginal utility per dollar spent across all goods. As a result, the demand curve reflects choices a consumer is willing to make that maximize his utility. The chapter concludes by investigating the paradox of value, the point that water, which is a necessity to life, is cheap while diamonds, which are useless compared to water, are expensive.

■ Where We've Been

The first two sections of the book focused heavily on supply and demand. The supply and demand model was developed and then extended to show how externalities affect the efficient use of resources. The model shows that external costs result in overproduction and that external benefits result in underproduction. The last chapter further used the supply and demand model to cover the characteristics of public goods, the free-rider problem, and the U.S. tax system.

■ Where We're Going

After this chapter, the focus turns to exploring the supply curve in greater detail. Chapter 11 looks at a firm's production choices and its total product function. After examining the firm's production, we examine its costs and its cost curves in the short run and in the long run.

IN THE CLASSROOM

■ Class Time Needed

You can complete this chapter between two and a half class sessions to three class sessions, depending the mathematical level of your class.

An estimate of the time per checkpoint is:

- 10.1 Consumption Possibilities—30 to 40 minutes
- 10.2 Marginal Utility Theory—50 to 80 minutes
- 10.3 Efficiency, Price, and Value—25 to 40 minutes

■ Extended Lecture Outline

10.1 Consumption Possibilities

Our consumption choices are determined by our income and the prices of goods.

A. The Budget Line

The **budget line** describes the limits to consumption possibilities; it shows which purchases are affordable and which are not.

1. The budget line is calculated by determining the different combinations of goods that can be afforded given prices and a person's income.

2. Shown with the quantity of goods measured on both axes, good x on the x-axis and good y on the y-axis, the budget line is downward sloping. The horizontal intercept reflects the quantity of good x that can be purchased when none of good y is purchased. Likewise, the vertical intercept reflects the quantity of good y that can be purchased when none of good x is purchased.

B. Changes in Prices

1. If the price of good x falls, the budget line rotates outward and consumption possibilities increase.

2. If the price of good x rises, the budget line rotates inward and consumption possibilities decrease.

C. Prices and the Slope of the Budget Line

1. The slope of the budget line is an opportunity cost (the ratio of good x's price divided by good y's price), which means that it is a **relative price.**

2. Moving along the budget line, the consumer faces a tradeoff. The consumer must give up some of good x in order to obtain more of good y, and vice versa.

D. A Change in the Budget

1. When the budget increases, the budget line shifts outward and the slope does not change.

2. When the budget decreases, the budget line shifts inward and the slope does not change.

10.2 Marginal Utility Theory

The budget line shows the choices that are available, but it doesn't tell us which of those choices the person makes. People make these choices based on preferences.

A. **Utility** is the satisfaction received from consuming a good.

1. Temperature: An Analogy

Like temperature, we cannot observe utility, but nonetheless utility theory helps us make predictions about people's consumption choices.

B. **Total utility** is the total benefit a person receives from consuming a good. As more of a good is consumed, a consumer's total utility increases.

C. Marginal Utility

Marginal utility is the extra utility received from consuming one more unit of a good. A person experiences **diminishing marginal utility** because each additional unit of a good provides less and less utility.

D. Maximizing Total Utility

Maximizing total utility is the goal of each consumer. A consumer uses a **utility-maximizing rule** to achieve this outcome. The rule has two requirements:

1. The consumer must allocate his or her entire budget.

2. The consumer must equalize the marginal utility per dollar spent across all goods. The **marginal utility per dollar spent** is the increase in total utility resulting from the last dollar spent on a good.

E. Finding the Demand Curve

The demand curve for a good can be derived by varying the price of the good and using marginal utility theory to determine how the quantity demanded changes.

F. Marginal Utility and the Elasticity of Demand

1. When the marginal utility declines sharply as more of a good is consumed, a fall in the good's price requires only a small change in consumption to equate the marginal utility per dollar spent on it to the marginal utility per dollar spent on other goods. As a result, the quantity demanded increases very little and so the demand is inelastic.

2. When the marginal utility declines slowly as more of a good is consumed, a fall in the good's price requires a large change in consumption to equate the marginal utility per dollar spent on it to the marginal utility per dollar spent on other goods. As a result, the quantity demanded increases significantly and so the demand is elastic.

G. The Power of Marginal Analysis

Marginal analysis can be used to determine a consumer's utility maximizing combination of goods. For example, if the marginal utility per dollar spent is greater for good x than for good y, the person will allocate more of the budget to good x because this change will increase the person's total utility. As more of that good is consumed, the marginal utility of the last unit decreases, which means that the marginal utility per dollar spent on that good also decreases. At the same time, as less of the other good is consumed, its marginal utility increases, as does the marginal utility per dollar spent on it. As a person's budget is reallocated according to this process, eventually the marginal utility per dollar spent is equal for all goods, and the person is maximizing utility.

10.3 Efficiency, Price, and Value

A. Consumer Efficiency

An individual's demand curve reflects his or her utility maximizing choices and is an efficient use of resources.

B. The paradox of value describes why we are willing to pay only a low price for water (which has high total utility and low marginal utility), but willing to pay a much higher price for diamonds (which have low total utility and high marginal utility).

1. The paradox is explained using the concepts of total utility and marginal utility.

2. Marginal utility is reflected in the price of a good and total utility is reflected in the value of a good.

3. *Consumer surplus* also explains the paradox of value because water has a huge consumer surplus and diamonds a much smaller consumer surplus.

■ Lecture Launchers

1. Use the paradox of value to start your lecture. Ask students how much they are willing to pay for a gallon of water. Of course, they'll answer a relatively low amount. Then ask them how much they would be willing to pay for a diamond. Most students will answer hundreds or thousands of dollars. Then ask them "Why?" Remind them that water is essential for life and that it makes no sense to be willing to spend so little for such a valuable item. Spark some more discussion by asking them their willingness to pay

for water (versus willingness to pay for diamonds) if they were lost in the desert. If no one provides the correct answer (and most students won't unless they've read the chapter), tell them they'll "get it" if they'll pay attention to the lecture! Act like a magician willing to reveal the secret of a trick! When you finish the day's lecture, ask students if they can explain the paradox. Reassure them this topic is difficult to understand. In fact, so difficult that until the concepts of utility and marginal utility were discovered in the 1800s, the paradox could not be explained.

2. Once you have introduced the idea of marginal utility, ask your students why a vending machine, which requires payment for each snack purchased, must be used to sell snacks while a newspaper can be sold out of a box that allows anyone to take more than one paper. In other words, papers are sold using the honor system. If students fail to respond using marginal utility analysis, prompt them by asking, "If snacks were sold using the honor system, would some people take more than they paid for?" Then ask, "Why don't people take more than one paper?" See if the students can discover diminishing marginal utility on their own. If not, explain why different sales techniques are used: Because the marginal utility of a paper diminishes so rapidly, there is little concern that people will take more than one. When you have formally taught diminishing marginal utility, tie your lecture back into this example.

■ Land Mines

1. Students are introduced to another curve in this chapter, the budget line. Remind students that this line is not a demand curve nor a production possibility frontier. Point out the differences: A demand curve is graphed in price/quantity space and shows how the quantity demanded of a product depends on its price; a budget line is graphed in good A/good B space and shows what can be afforded; and although a *PPF* is also graphed in good A/good B space, it applies to a nation as whole and shows what can be produced.

2. To help students remember how the budget line shifts when the prices of goods change, suggest they should assume they spend ALL of their income on either good. For example, suppose apples are on the *x*-axis, and oranges are on the *y*-axis. Ask students, "What happens if the price of apples increases?" Tell them to assume that they hate apples and regardless of the price of apples, they spend their entire budget on oranges. Because the price of oranges doesn't change, ask how the change in the price of apples impacts the number of oranges they can buy. Point out the *y*-intercept and stress the fact that this is the consumption point at which all the income is spent on oranges. Make it clear that this point does not change when the price of apples rises. Then turn to the *x*-axis and tell students that they now buy only apples and no oranges. Discuss with them that the *x*-intercept shows the maximum number of apples they can buy when they spend all their income on apples. While pointing out the *x*-intercept, ask students what happens to the number of apples they can buy when the price of ap-

ples rises? When they answer "fewer apples," move your finger leftward along the x-axis and make a mark. Then draw the new budget line: the y-intercept does not change while the x-intercept rotates inward, making the budget line steeper. The point of this exercise is to focus on the intercepts and not the slope. For many students, this is an easier method of determining the change in the budget line. To complete the exercise, let the price of oranges fall and go through the same mechanics.

3. When you use the marginal utility per dollar approach to explain utility maximization, you should be prepared for students' questioning the reality of the idea that they actually equate marginal utility per dollar before making a consumption decision. Some will say, "I've never calculated the marginal utility of any item I've ever purchased. This material doesn't make any sense." Suggest to these students that they should "buy into the story for the time being" because this approach is one of the easiest ways to explain utility maximization. Let them know that by the end of class, they will see that this is a good way to explain consumer behavior and the demand curve. You can use the newspaper/snack example, in Lecture Launcher 2, to convince students that almost everyone (whether consciously or not) behaves as predicted by marginal utility theory. If people behaved otherwise, newspaper publishers wouldn't sell newspapers like they do! By tying this everyday behavior to the marginal utility per dollar spent approach and the derivation of demand curves, students can see that (whether they are aware of it or not), they *do* behave as predicted by the theory.

ANSWERS TO CHECKPOINT EXERCISES

■ CHECKPOINT 10.1 Consumption Possibilities

a.   The affordable combinations of cake and pasta are:
     0 cake and 4 pastas ($24 spent)
     1 cake and 3 pastas ($22 spent)
     2 cakes and 2 pastas ($20 spent)
     3 cakes and 2 pastas ($24 spent)
     4 cakes and 1 pasta ($22 spent)
     5 cakes and 0 pasta ($20 spent)
     6 cakes and 0 pasta ($24 spent)

b.   Figure 10.1 shows Martha's budget line.

c.   At the initial prices, when the price of a cake is $4
     and the price of a dish of pasta is $6, the relative
     price of a cake is ($4/$6) = 2/3 of a cake for a dish
     of pasta. If the price of a dish of pasta falls to $3,
     the relative price of cake increases from 2/3 of a
     dish of pasta to 1 1/3 dishes of pasta. In other
     words, when the price of a dish of pasta falls to
     $3, the consumer must forgo 1 1/3 dishes of pasta
     if the consumer purchases 1 cake.

d.   If the price of a dish of pasta falls, the budget line
     rotates outward and becomes flatter. The vertical
     intercept stays the same, while the horizontal
     intercept increases.

          If the price of a cake falls, the budget line
     rotates outward and becomes steeper. The
     horizontal intercept stays the same, while the
     vertical intercept increases.

          If Martha's budget decreases, the new budget line shifts inward and is
     parallel to the old budget line.

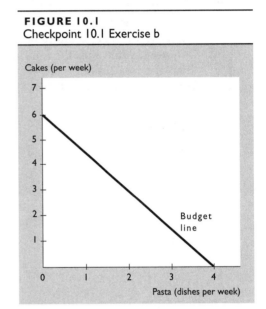

FIGURE 10.1
Checkpoint 10.1 Exercise b

■ CHECKPOINT 10.2 Marginal Utility Theory

a.   The total utility of the 3rd movie is 84 units of utility and the total utility of
     the 2nd movie is 60 units of utility. Therefore the change in total utility,
     which equals the marginal utility, (84 units of utility) − (60 units of utility) =
     24 units of utility.

b.   The marginal utility per dollar spent on movies when Wendy sees 3 movies
     is 24/$8 = 3 units of utility per dollar spent on the 3rd movie.

c.   The total utility of the 4th taco is 30 units of utility and the total utility of
     the 3rd taco is 27 units of utility. Therefore the marginal utility of the 4th
     taco equals (30 units of utility) − (27 units of utility) = 3 units of utility.

d.   The marginal utility per dollar spent on the 4th taco is 3/$2 = 1 1/2 units of
     utility per dollar spent on the 4th taco.

e. Wendy is not maximizing her utility. She is not allocating (spending) all of her income because she is spending only $20. And the marginal utility per dollar spent on a taco is 4 1/2 units of utility per dollar, which does not equal the marginal utility per dollar spent on a movie, which is 3 1/2 units of utility per dollar. To maximize her utility, Wendy should buy 1 more taco. If she buys 1 more taco, she will consume 3 tacos and 2 movies. This combination allocates all of her income and sets the marginal utility per dollar spent on a taco equal to that of a movie, with both equal to 3 1/2 units of utility per dollar.

■ CHECKPOINT 10.3 Efficiency, Price, and Value

On the margin, the economics book is more valuable. That is, the marginal utility from the economics book exceeds the marginal utility from another gallon of water. But, the total utility from the economics book is *much* less than the total utility from water. Even an economist can live without an economics book but not even an economist can live without water!

ANSWERS TO CHAPTER CHECKPOINT EXERCISES

FIGURE 10.2
Chapter Checkpoint Exercise 1a

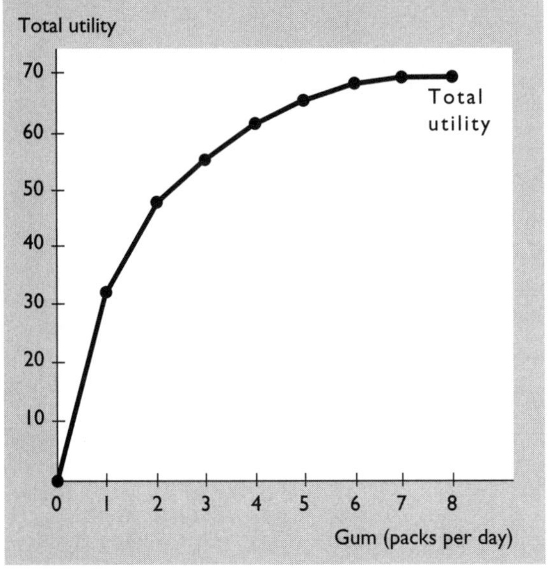

FIGURE 10.3
Chapter Checkpoint Exercise 1a

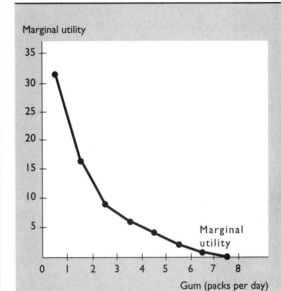

1a. The figures are above. Comparing the figure above to Figure 10.5 on page 241 in the text, the graphs show that the marginal utility from gum decreases more rapidly than does the marginal utility from bottled water.

1b. Based on marginal utility, Tina's demand for gum is less elastic than her demand for water because her marginal utility decreases more steeply for gum.

1c. If Tina's budget increases, she'll consume more water and gum because they are both normal goods. Between the two, she will consume relatively more water because its marginal utility does not decrease as rapidly as gum's marginal utility.

1d. If Tina's budget increases and the price of water increases, Tina will consume more gum. The impact on Tina's consumption of water is ambiguous. The increase in the budget implies more water will be consumed, but this increase can be offset by the increase in the price of water.

2a. The total utility from consuming 4 cakes and 1 pasta is 51 units of utility.

2b. The marginal utility from the third cake is 7 units.

2c. The marginal utility per dollar spent on the third cake is (7/$4) = 1 3/4 units of utility per dollar.

2d. The marginal utility from the second dish of pasta is 16 units of utility.

2e. The marginal utility per dollar spent on the second dish of pasta is (16/$2) = 2 units of utility per dollar.

2f. Martha is maximizing utility because she equates the marginal utility per dollar spent for cake and pasta and she allocates (spends) her entire budget.

3a. When the price of a cake is $4 and the price of a dish of pasta is $8, Martha buys 2 cakes and 2 dishes of pasta. If the price of a dish of pasta falls to $4, Martha buys 2 cakes and 4 dishes of pasta. This combination maximizes Martha's utility because it allocates (spends) her entire income and equates her marginal utilities per dollar.

3b. One point is a price of $8 for a dish of pasta and quantity of 2 dishes; another point is a price of $4 for a dish of pasta and a quantity of 4 dishes.

3c. Martha's demand for pasta is unit elastic over the price range between $8 and $4.

3d. When the price of a cake is $4, the price of a dish of pasta is $8, and Martha has $40 to spend, she will buy 4 cakes and 3 dishes of pasta. This combination maximizes Martha's utility because it allocates (spends) her entire income and equates the marginal utility per dollar spent on cake to the marginal utility per dollar spent on pasta, with both equal to 1 1/2 units of utility per dollar.

4a. The relative price of pizza is ($4 per pizza)/($1 per cola) = 4 colas per pizza.

4bi. Tim's consumption possibilities increase because his budget line rotates outward.

4bii. Tim will change his lunch purchases to equate the marginal utility per dollar spent on each good.

4biii. Most likely, Tim will increase the quantity of pizza he consumes.

5a. Because the price of a sandwich is 1 2/3 times greater than the price of a coffee and Josie is maximizing utility, the marginal utility of the last sandwich must be 1 2/3 times greater than the marginal utility received from the last coffee. When the marginal utility of the sandwich is 1 2/3 times larger than the marginal utility of the coffee, Josie will be equating the marginal utility per dollar spent for coffee and sandwiches.

5b. Josie's allocation is efficient because she maximizes her utility. By maximizing her utility, she is making the best use of her scarce resources, that is, her income.

ADDITIONAL EXERCISES FOR ASSIGNMENT

■ Questions

1. The table has Bobby's total utility from popcorn and soda. Assume the price of popcorn is $2, the price of a cola is $1, and Bobby's budget is $10.

    a. List the affordable combinations of cola and popcorn that are on Bobby's budget line.

    b. What is the utility maximizing combination of cola and popcorn ?

Popcorn		Soda	
Bags (per week)	**Total utility**	**Cans (per week)**	**Total utility**
0	0	0	0
1	40	1	30
2	60	2	50
3	70	3	65
4	75	4	75

2. Using the data above, assume that Bobby's budget increases to $12 but the prices of popcorn and cola do not change. What happens to the relative prices of popcorn and cola?

■ Answers

1a. The affordable combinations are 0 popcorn and 10 colas; 1 popcorn and 8 colas; 2 popcorns and 6 colas; 3 popcorns and 4 colas; 4 popcorns and 2 colas; and 5 popcorns and 0 cola.

1b. To maximize utility, Bobby buys 4 colas and 3 popcorns. This combination allocates the entire budget and equates the marginal utility per dollar spent of 10 units of utility per dollar.

2. Because neither the price of popcorn nor cola changes, the relative prices do not change. A change in a person's budget does not change relative prices.

ANSWERS TO ECONOMICS IN THE NEWS

■ Coca-Cola Sells Bottled Water in the United States

1. Coke entered the bottled water market because they saw consumer's preferences switching to water instead of soda and coffee.

2. The article states that the relative price of water has decreased. If the price of a good decreases, the marginal utility of that good must decrease in order to keep marginal utility per dollar spent equal across goods. Because the marginal utility of a good decreases as more of that good is consumed, the quantity of water consumed must have increased.

USING EYE ON THE U.S ECONOMY

■ Relative Prices on the Move

The article provides data on relative prices. Use the data to show students that, contrary to what they might have predicted, the relative prices of many of the goods they buy have changed, with some falling and others rising. You can present the material by listing a number of the items on the board (or overhead) and then poll students what they think has happened to the relative price. They will probably find it surprising to see the relative price of fruits and vegetables has risen while the relative prices of cars and soft drinks have fallen.

■ Rational Choices in Beverage Markets

The article and data provide a good example of reallocating budgets after the prices of goods have changed. The story provides a good explanation of what happens to demand for a good when its price changes as people attempt to equate marginal utility per dollar spent. Ask your students why they think these changes occurred. In other words, did the changes occur because people's tastes changed or because other factors, such as supply, changed?

USING EYE ON THE PAST

■ Jeremy Bentham, William Stanley Jevons, and the Birth of Utility

The story provides background material to use for the lecture launchers. You can remind students that these ideas are "discoveries" in terms of economics and they allow economists to explain or better understand concepts such as the demand curve and the paradox of value.

Appendix: Indifference Curves

APPENDIX ROADMAP

■ Where We Are

The appendix to Chapter 10 takes a different approach to explaining consumer behavior by using indifference curves. Instead of equating marginal utility per dollar spent across goods, consumers achieve consumer equilibrium by deciding whether different combinations of goods make them better off, worse off, or leave them indifferent. The combinations among which consumers are indifferent lie along an indifference curve and the consumer equilibrium is the combination that is on the budget line and on the highest attainable indifference curve. A (downward-sloping) demand curve is derived using indifference curves and budget lines.

■ Where We've Been

Chapter 10 used marginal utility theory to study the consumer's equilibrium choice of goods and services as well as to derive a consumer's (downward sloping) demand curve.

■ Where We're Going

The next chapter starts our examination of firms by studying their production and how production relates to costs. None of the material in this appendix are used in Chapter 11 or any of the following chapters.

IN THE CLASSROOM

■ Class Time Needed

Depending on your class's mathematical sophistication, you might decide to make this appendix optional. If you cover it in class, you should spend between one to one and a half class sessions on it.

■ Extended Lecture Outline

A.1 Indifference curves

A. An Indifference Curve

An **indifference curve** is a line showing combinations of goods among which a person is indifferent. That is, a person does not prefer one of the combinations represented on the indifference curve to any other combination on the same curve. The curve is graphed showing the quantity of one good on one axis and the quantity of another good on the other axis.

1. A consumer prefers any combination above the indifference curve to a combination on the indifference curve. The combinations above the indifference curve are on higher indifference curves.
2. A consumer prefers any combination on the indifference curve to any combination below the indifference curve. The combinations below the indifference curve are on lower indifference curves.
3. A preference map shows a series of indifference curves reflecting a person's preferences for two goods.

B. Marginal Rate of Substitution

The **marginal rate of substitution** (MRS) is the rate at which a consumer is willing to substitute one good for another good. The MRS is the magnitude of the slope of the indifference curve.

1. If the slope is steep, the MRS is high.
2. If the slope is flat, the MRS is low.
3. The fact that the indifference curves are bowed toward the origin reflects diminishing marginal rate of substitution.

C. Consumer Equilibrium

A person is at *consumer equilibrium* when the person is on the budget line and is on the highest indifference curve. At this point, the MRS equals the relative price of the two goods.

D. Deriving the Demand Curve

To derive the demand curve using indifference curves, change the price of one of the goods. The budget line rotates, and the consumer moves to a new equilibrium point, determined by new budget line and the highest indifference curve. Then plot the prices of the good and the quantities consumed at each price, which yields the demand curve.

■ Lecture Launchers

1. Students need to be told why they are studying indifference curves. Indeed, many students think indifference curves impractical and so are less than eager to study them. Motivation is necessary! One way to motivate students

is by pointing out that the material will be on their test. But that is perhaps not the best way. Launch your lecture on indifference curves by reminding students that economists are social scientists. (Depending on your personality, you can even preen a bit when you mention this fact!) As social scientists, we are interested in humans and their behavior. Tell your students that the indifference curve theory you will present is one way economists have of studying people's behavior. Point out to them that indifference curves might not seem as "practical" as, say, elasticity, but not everything a scientist does has immediate practicality.

■ Land Mines

1. The most dangerous error students can make in this appendix is to think that the indifference curve is the same as the demand curve. This error arises because both slope downward and both have the quantity of a good measured along the *x*-axis. Be sure to stress that they are different. Point out that the indifference curve is truly more basic because we use indifference curves to derive the demand curve. Hence an indifference curve and a demand curve are quite different curves.

ANSWERS TO APPENDIX CHECKPOINT EXERCISES

1a. The relative price of cola is ($3 per can of cola)/($3 per bag of popcorn) = 1 bag of popcorn per can of cola.

1b. The opportunity cost of a can of cola is the same as its relative price, 1 bag of popcorn per can of cola.

1c. The budget line is in Figure A10.1.

1d. Sara buys 2 bags of popcorn and 2 cans of soda because that is the combination of popcorn and soda that is on her budget line and on the highest indifference curve.

1e. The marginal rate of substitution is equal to the slope of the budget line, 1 bag of popcorn per can of cola.

2a. Sara buys 1 bag of popcorn and 6 cans of soda because that is the combination of popcorn and soda that is on her budget line and on the highest indifference curve.

2b. One point on Sara's demand curve is from the answer to exercise 1 part (d): when the price of a can of cola is $3, the quantity Sara demands is 2 cans. The other point on the demand curve comes from part (a) of this question, that when the price of a can of cola is $1.50, the quantity Sara demands is 6 cans.

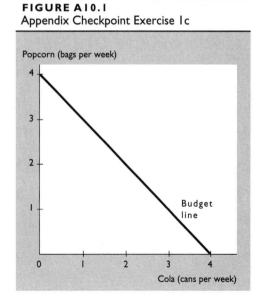

FIGURE A10.1
Appendix Checkpoint Exercise 1c

3a. The relative price of a can of root beer ($5 per can of cola)/($10 per CD) = 1/2 of a CD per can of root beer.

3b. The opportunity cost of a can of root beer is the same as its relative price, 1/2 of a CD per can of root beer.

3c. The budget line is in Figure A10.2.

3d. Marc buys 2 cans of root beer and 1 CD because that is the combination that is on his budget line and on the highest indifference curve.

3e. The marginal rate of substitution is equal to the slope of the budget line, 2 cans of root beer per CD.

4a. Marc now buys 3 CDs and 1 can of root beer.

4b. One point on Marc's demand curve for CDs comes from the answer to exercise 3, part (d), that when the price of a CD is $10, the quantity Marc demands is 1 CD. Another point come from the answer to part (a) of this question, that when the price of a CD is $5, the quantity Marc demands is 3 CDs.

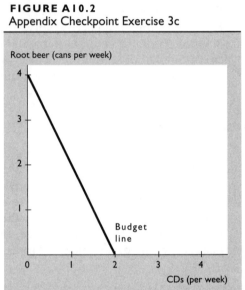

FIGURE A10.2
Appendix Checkpoint Exercise 3c

5a. If the sales tax is replaced with a consumption tax, the relative price of haircuts (a service) increases and the relative price of floppy disks (a good) decreases.

5b. If haircuts are on the horizontal axis, the budget line rotates inward.

5c. If the relative price of floppy disks falls and the relative price of a haircut rises, most consumers buy more disks and fewer haircuts.

5d. The type of tax that is best for the consumer depends on the consumer's preferences. If the consumer prefers goods over services, the consumption tax is better. If the consumer prefers services, the sales tax is better.

6a. An increase in income allows Jim to spend more money on all goods. Assuming all the goods Jim buys are normal goods, Jim will definitely buy more housing, food, and clothing. The fact that vacation travel rises in price makes Jim's purchases of this good ambiguous. His higher income leads Jim to spend more on vacation travel but the higher relative price leads Jim to spend less on it.

6b. Depending on his preferences, Jim might be better off, but we cannot say for sure. For instance, if prior to the changes Jim spent, say, $1 on vacation travel and the rest of his income on the other goods, almost certainly Jim is better off. But, if prior to the changes Jim spent $2,999 on vacation travel and the rest of his income on the other goods, than almost surely Jim is worse off.

6c. If all prices rise by 50 percent while Jim's income increases by 33 percent, Jim's budget line shifts inward and Jim decreases his purchases. Because his budget line shifted inward, signaling a decrease in Jim's consumption possibilities, Jim is worse off.

6d. Your students' answers will not be identical to the answer that follows, but they should be similar. Figure A10.3 divides Jim's purchases into vacation travel and all other goods. (The slope of the budget line is arbitrary; your students might well have different slopes for their budget lines.) The 50 percent increase in prices combined with only a 33 percent increase in income shifts Jim's budget line inward. The slope does not change. Assuming that both goods are normal goods, the figure shows that Jim decreases his purchases of vacation travel and of the other goods as he moves from point *A* to point *B*.

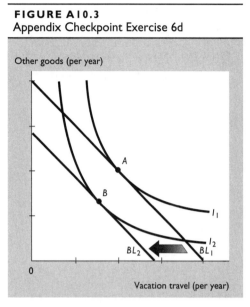

FIGURE A10.3
Appendix Checkpoint Exercise 6d

ADDITIONAL EXERCISES FOR ASSIGNMENT

■ Questions

1. Why are both a budget line and an indifference curve required to determine the consumer's equilibrium?

2. How does an increase in income affect the budget line? The indifference curves?

■ Answers

1. The budget line shows affordable combinations of goods and services. The indifference curves show the consumer's preferences over these affordable combinations. The consumer will select the affordable combination that he or she most prefers.

    Intuitively, a budget line is similar to a menu: it shows what is available. However, what a consumer chooses to consume from a menu depends on the consumer's preferences. For instance, a restaurant might offer liver on the menu, but if a diner hates liver, the diner will not order it. It takes *both* the menu, which shows what is available, and the consumer's preferences, which show what the consumer likes, in order to determine what the consumer will select.

2. An increase in income shifts the budget line outward and does not change its slope. An increase in income has *no* effect on the indifference curves. Although the consumer will move to a new indifference curve, that indif-

ference curve had existed all along, but until the increase in income, had been unaffordable.

Indifference curves capture the consumer's preferences. For instance, a poor person might love lobster as much as a rich person, so their indifference curves are the same. However, the poor person buys less lobster than the rich person because their budget lines differ. Preferences do not depend on income or prices, and so do not change with changes in the consumer's income or the prices of the goods.

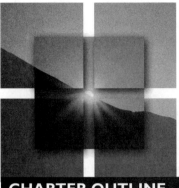

Chapter 11

Production and Cost

CHAPTER OUTLINE

1. Explain how economists measure a firm's cost of production and profit.
- A. The Firm's Goal
- B. Accounting Cost and Profit
- C. Opportunity Cost
  - 1. Explicit Costs and Implicit Costs
- D. Economic Profit

2. Explain the relationship between a firm's output and labor employed in the short run.
- A. The Short Run: Fixed Plant
- B. The Long Run: Variable Plant
- C. Total Product
- D. Marginal Product
  - 1. Increasing Marginal Returns
  - 2. Decreasing Marginal Returns
- E. Average Product
  - 1. Marginal Grade and Grade Point Average

3. Explain the relationship between a firm's output and costs in the short run.
- A. Total Cost
- B. Marginal Cost
- C. Average Cost
- D. Why the Average Total Cost Curve is U-Shaped
- E. Cost Curves and Product Curves
- F. Shifts in the Cost Curves
  - 1. Technology
  - 2. Prices of Factors of Production

4. Derive and explain a firm's long-run average cost curve.
- A. Plant Size and Cost
  - 1. Economies of Scale
    - a. Specialization of Labor
    - b. Specialization of Capital

2. Diseconomies of Scale
3. Constant Returns to Scale
B. The Long-Run Average Cost Curve
1. Economies and Diseconomies of Scale

CHAPTER ROADMAP

■ Where We Are

In this chapter, we define economic costs and profits. We examine the relationship between inputs, costs, and production. This chapter lays the groundwork for the profit-maximizing decisions that are made by firms, which we study in the next several chapters.

■ Where We've Been

We defined what economics means in terms of scarcity, opportunity cost, choice, and efficient use of resources. We've explored the interactions of supply and demand that bring about the efficient use of resources by equating marginal benefit to marginal cost. We've discussed the rationale behind the downward-sloping demand curve using marginal utility analysis.

■ Where We're Going

After this chapter, we look at the demand and marginal revenue curves for firms in different industry structures. By combining the cost, demand, and revenue curves, we will see the profit-maximizing, operating decisions made by these firms.

IN THE CLASSROOM

■ Class Time Needed

You can complete this chapter in between two to three class sessions. However, this is a very important chapter, so do not short change it. If you judge from your class's reaction that you need more time, take it!

An estimate of the time per checkpoint is:

- 11.1 Economic Cost and Profit—15 to 25 minutes
- 11.2 Short-Run Production—45 to 65 minutes
- 11.3 Short-Run Cost—45 to 65 minutes
- 11.4 Long-Run Cost—30 to 40 minutes

■ Extended Lecture Outline

11.1 Economic Cost and Profit

A. The firm's goal is to maximize its profit.
  1. The firm's profit is calculated as total revenue – total cost.
B. Accounting Cost and Profit
  1. Accountants measure cost and profit to ensure firms follow rules imposed by the Internal Revenue Service. Accountants do not consider opportunity costs.
C. Opportunity Cost
  Economists emphasize the fact that resources used to make one good are prevented from being used to make another good.
  1. To ensure the firm obtains these resources, firms must pay resource owners for the use of these factors of production.
  2. A firm's opportunity cost of production is the cost of employing its factors of production.
  3. Opportunity costs are divided into implicit and explicit costs.
    a. An **explicit cost** is the cost paid in money to a factor of production.
    b. An **implicit cost** occurs when a factor of production is used, but it does not receive a direct money payment.
    c. **Economic depreciation,** which is an implicit cost, is the opportunity cost of owning and using capital. Economic depreciation is measured as the change in the market value of capital.
    d. A **normal profit** is the return to entrepreneurship and is part of the firm's costs.
D. Economic Profit
  A firm's **economic profit** equals its total revenue minus its total (opportunity) costs.

11.2 Short-Run Production

A firm's production costs depend on the time frame over which the firm plans to produce output. There are two decision time frames facing firms:
A. The Short Run: Fixed Plant
  The **short run** is a time frame in which the quantities of some resources are fixed.
    a. The resources that cannot be changed are called *fixed inputs*. Fixed inputs are the firm's technology, capital, and management and are called the firm's plant.
    b. The factors that can be changed are called *variable inputs*. Variable inputs include labor.
    c. To change output in the short run, firms must change their variable inputs.
B. The Long Run: Variable Plant
  The **long run** is a time frame in which the quantities of *all* resources can be varied.
    a. Once more plant has been purchased, its costs cannot be changed. The purchase of fixed inputs is a sunk cost. Sunk costs are irrelevant to a firm's decisions.
C. Total product
  The **total product** is the total amount of output produced in a given time period. The total product curve, graphed with the quantity of labor on the *x*-axis and output on the *y*-axis, is upward sloping.
D. Marginal product
  The **marginal product** (*MP*) is the change in total product that results from a one-unit increase in the quantity of labor employed. The marginal product curve is upward sloping, reaches a maximum, and then declines.

1. **Increasing marginal returns** occur when the marginal product of an additional worker exceeds the marginal product of the previous worker.
2. **Decreasing marginal returns** occur when the marginal product of an additional worker is less than the marginal product of the previous worker.
3. The **law of decreasing returns** states that as a firm uses more of a variable input, with a given quantity of fixed inputs, the marginal product of the variable input eventually decreases.

E. Average product

The **average product** (*AP*) is the total product per worker employed and equals total product divided by the quantity of labor. The average product curve is upward sloping, reaches a maximum, and then declines. The marginal product curve intersects the average product curve at the *AP* curve's maximum point.

1. The marginal product and average product are related:
   a. When the marginal product is greater than the average product, the average product is increasing.
   b. When the marginal product is less than the average product, the average product is decreasing.

II.3 Short-Run Cost

A. Total Cost

There are three total cost terms:

1. **Total cost** (*TC*) is the cost of all inputs used in production including both fixed and variable inputs.
2. **Total fixed cost** (*TFC*) is the cost of a firm's fixed inputs.
3. **Total variable cost** (*TVC*) is the cost of a firm's variable inputs.
4. Total cost = total fixed cost + total variable cost.

B. Marginal Cost

Marginal cost (*MC*) is the change in total cost that results from a one-unit increase in output.

C. Average Cost

There are three average cost terms:

1. **Average fixed cost** (*AFC*) equals *TFC/Q*. The *AFC* curve is downward sloping.
2. **Average variable cost** (*AVC*) equals *TVC/Q*. The *AVC* curve is U-shaped.
3. **Average total cost** (*ATC*) equals *TC/Q* or, equivalently, *ATC* = *AFC* + *AVC*. The *ATC* curve is U-shaped and lies above the *AVC* curve. The distance between the *ATC* and *AVC* curves is average fixed costs.
4. The *MC* curve intersects the *ATC* curve and the *AVC* curve at their minimum points.

D. The *ATC* curve is U-shaped because it is the sum of the *AFC* and *AVC* curves. The U-shape reflects the factors that determine the shapes of those two curves:

1. The *AFC* curve is downward sloping because as output increases, the firm spreads its fixed costs over larger and larger amounts of output.
2. The *AVC* curve is U-shaped because of decreasing marginal returns.

E. The cost curves and product curves are linked.

1. In the range of employment and output over which the *AP* curve is upward sloping, the *ATC* curve is downward sloping, and in the range over which the *AP* curve is downward sloping, the *ATC* curve is upward sloping.
2. In the range of employment and output over which the *MP* curve is upward sloping, the *MC* curve is downward sloping, and in the range over which the *MP* curve is downward sloping, the *MC* curve is upward sloping.

F. Cost curves shift in response to changes in two factors:
1. Technology.
   An increase in technology that improves productivity shifts the product curves upward and the cost curves downward.
2. Prices of productive resources.
   An increase in the price of resources increases costs and shifts the cost curves upward. An increase in fixed costs does *not* affect the variable cost or marginal cost curves (*TVC*, *AVC*, and *MC* curves). An increase in variable cost does *not* affect the fixed cost curves (*TFC* and *AFC*). The total cost curves (*TC* and *ATC* curves) are affected by a price change for any resource.

11.4 Long-Run Cost

In the long run, the firm can vary both labor and capital inputs.

A. When a firm changes its plant size, the firm's scale changes.
   When the scale changes, there are three possible effects on costs:
   1. **Economies of scale** occur when increasing capital and labor by the same percentage leads to a greater percentage increase in output and thereby a decrease in average total cost.
      a. Economies of scale result from the specialization of labor and capital.
   2. **Diseconomies of scale** occur when increasing capital and labor by the same percentage leads to a smaller percentage increase in output and thereby an increase in average total cost.
   3. **Constant returns to scale** occur when increasing capital and labor by the same percentage leads to the same percentage increase in output and thereby no change in average total cost.

B. The **long-run average cost curve** (*LRAC*) shows the lowest average cost a firm can produce output when all inputs (both fixed and variable) can be changed. The *LRAC* is divided into segments reflecting the three types of scale:
   1. The downward-sloping portion of the *LRAC* reflects economies of scale.
   2. The flat portion of the *LRAC* reflects constant returns to scale.
   3. The upward-sloping portion of the *LRAC* reflects diseconomies of scale.

■ Lecture Launchers

1. This chapter is incredibly important because it serves as the basis for the next three chapters. You know this fact, I know this fact, but your students don't know this fact. You must tell them this fact because without it you will definitely lose some of the class. How so? They won't realize that this chapter is critical until they are unable to grasp the next three chapters. At that point, several possibilities exist, all unpleasant: These students will flunk the course, these students will drop the course, or these students will camp out in your office. Most likely no one would be happy with any of these outcomes, so launch your lecture by motivating your students with the important information that Chapter 11 is truly a key to Chapters 12, 13, and 14!

■ Land Mines

1. Don't be tempted to draw the curves in this chapter without using any numeric examples. Either make up your own numbers or use the table the text provides, but make sure to provide your students with two things: a preprinted table with the columns labeled (but not filled in) and preprinted

handouts with graphs on which the axes are labeled. If you can, draw the points (not the actual curves) on the graphs that will correspond to the data in the tables.

The table should provide a complete spreadsheet, with labor employment, capital employment, output, *AP, MP, TC, TFC, TVC, ATC, AFC, AVC,* and *MC*. Work through the first part of the table (capital and labor inputs, output, fixed, variable and total costs). Label and draw these graphs. Then turn back to the table, completing the data for the average and marginal cost columns. Finally draw and explain the graphs that relate to these data. This exercise allows students to listen to the intuition and follow the example without being distracted trying to get the layout of the table and graphs correct. You'll also be able to cover more material this way because you won't be waiting for students to catch up.

2. Students are introduced to more graphs in this chapter. When summing up the day's lecture, the clearest way to show the differences (especially with respect to the variables on the axes) is to graph each of the curves on the board at the same time. Suggest that students practice graphing each of the curves many times noting the maximum points, minimum points, and intersections. Tell your students that at times it is important to draw the *ATC* curve and *MC* curve correctly, that is, so that the *MC* curve intersects the *ATC* curve when the *ATC* is at its minimum. You can point out to the students that if they always draw the relationship correctly, they will always draw the relationship correctly (!?)

3. Distinguish between decreasing marginal product in the short run versus diseconomies of scale in the long run. Decreasing returns occur when additional units of labor are combined with a fixed amount of capital. Diseconomies of scale do not occur for the same reason, because in the long run both labor and capital can change. Diseconomies of scale occur because of chaos, organizational overloads, etc.

4. The grade point average versus marginal grade example in the text is outstanding to use in class to describe how the marginal product and marginal cost curves relate to the average product and average cost curves. Once students can tell a story using the same intuition, they find drawing those curves much easier. While you have the curves drawn on the board or overhead, physically "pulllll" the average cost curves down (while marginal cost is below) or pull them up (when the marginal cost curve rises above). Use theatrics: raise your hands over your head and "pull down the curves." If you have a more sports-oriented class, you can try using a batting average percentage and at-bat outcome example (if you had a .300 batting average and you struck out at your next at-bat [the marginal factor], your batting average is pulled down).

ANSWERS TO CHECKPOINT EXERCISES

■ CHECKPOINT 11.1 Economic Cost and Profit

a. Explicit costs are the $150 printer lease and $1,250 for paper, utilities, and postage. Some students might also include the $5,000 paid for the computer. Technically, the computer should probably be depreciated over several years and not all the $5,000 included as a cost the first year. (If the computer is depreciated, the cost will be an implicit cost. See, for instance, the answer to part (b)). If the computer is not included, the explicit costs are $1,400. If the computer is included, the explicit costs are $6,400.

b. The implicit costs are the $40,000 in wages forgone, the $5,000 in rent forgone, the $3,000 in normal profit, the $250 in forgone interest payments on the savings, and the $1,000 in economic depreciation, for a total of $49,250.

c. The economic profit equals $50,000 − ($1,400 + $49,250) = −$650, or in other words, Roma has an economic loss of $650 for the year.

■ CHECKPOINT 11.2 Short-Run Production

a. The total product with 3 workers is 70 lawns mowed and the total product with 4 workers is 94 lawns mowed. Therefore the marginal product of the fourth student is 24 lawns.

b. The average product of the 4th student is (94 lawns)/(4 students) = 23.5 lawns.

c. The marginal product decreases between 3 and 6 students.

d. When the marginal product decreases, eventually it become less than the average product. Before it is less than the average product (that is, when the marginal product, though decreasing, exceeds the average product) the average product increases as more workers are hired. When the marginal product is less than the average product, the average product decreases as more workers are hired.

■ CHECKPOINT 11.3 Short-Run Cost

a. The (total) costs are in the table to the right.

Labor	Output	Total fixed cost	Total variable cost	Total cost
0	0	200	0	200
1	20	200	40	240
2	44	200	80	280
3	70	200	120	320
4	94	200	160	360
5	114	200	200	400
6	120	200	240	440

b. The (average) costs are in the table to the right.

Labor	Output	Average fixed cost	Average variable cost	Average total cost
0	0	xx	xx	xx
1	20	10.00	2.00	12.00
2	44	4.55	1.82	6.37
3	70	2.86	1.71	4.57
4	94	2.13	1.70	3.83
5	114	1.75	1.75	3.50
6	120	1.67	2.00	3.67

c. The marginal cost is in the table to the right.
d. The distance between the total cost and variable cost curves is the same at all levels of output because the distance is equal to total fixed cost. Indeed, note in the answer to part (a), the difference between total variable cost and total cost is always $200, the amount of the fixed cost. The distance is the same because total fixed cost is constant regardless of the level of output.

Labor	Output	Marginal cost
0	0	
		2.00
1	20	
		1.67
2	44	
		1.54
3	70	
		1.67
4	94	
		2.00
5	114	
		6.67
6	120	

■ CHECKPOINT 11.4 Long-Run Cost

a. If Lisa doubles her inputs, and her output less than doubles, Lisa experiences diseconomies of scale. Average total costs rise so that her long-run average cost curve slopes upward.
b. The source of her diseconomies of scale could be management problems when she hires more students and leases more mowers. Trying to organize more mowers and more students across different areas of the town requires more communication and coordination. If she is unable to manage the larger firm as efficiently as she was able to manage the smaller firm, her average total costs will increase.

ANSWERS TO CHAPTER CHECKPOINT EXERCISES

1a. The explicit costs are $10,000 for cards, $5,000 for rent, and $1,000 for utilities. Her cash register is more of an issue. Conventionally, a cash register is depreciated over a number of years and so its cost is always an implicit cost. Some students, however, might implicitly assume that Sonya is running her shop on a cash basis, and so include the cost of the cash register, $2,000, as an explicit cost. If the cash register is not included, the explicit costs equal $16,000 and if it is included the explicit costs equal $18,000.

1b. Sonya's implicit costs are $25,000 in forgone wages, $14,000 normal profit, $60 in forgone interest, and $400 in economic depreciation on the cash register, for a total of $39,460.

1c. Sonya's economic profit equals her total revenue, $58,000, minus her total opportunity costs, the sum of explicit and implicit costs or $55,640. Thus her economic profit is $58,000 − $55,640 = $2,360.

2a. The marginal product and average product schedules are in the table to the right.

Labor	Total product	Average product	Marginal product
0	0	xx	
			20
1	20	20.0	
			24
2	44	22.0	
			16
3	60	20.0	
			12
4	72	18.0	
			8
5	80	16.0	
			4
6	84	14.0	
			2
7	86	12.3	

2b. Marginal returns decrease after the second worker is hired.

2c. The variable costs are the costs of labor; the fixed costs are the costs of the shaping board equipment. The (total) cost schedules are in the table to right.

Labor	Output	Total fixed cost	Total variable cost	Total cost
0	0	300	0	300
1	20	300	1,000	1,300
2	44	300	2,000	2,300
3	60	300	3,000	3,300
4	72	300	4,000	4,300
5	80	300	5,000	5,300
6	84	300	6,000	6,300
7	86	300	7,000	7,300

2d. The total cost minus the total variable cost always equals $300. The difference between the total cost and the total variable cost equals the fixed cost. The total fixed cost is always the same amount ($300 in this case) regardless of the level of output.

2e. The (average) cost schedules are in the table to the right.

Labor	Output	Average fixed cost	Average variable cost	Average total cost
0	0	xx	xx	xx
1	20	15.00	50.00	65.00
2	44	6.82	45.45	52.27
3	60	5.00	50.00	55.00
4	72	4.17	55.56	59.72
5	80	3.75	62.50	66.25
6	84	3.57	71.43	75.00
7	86	3.49	81.40	84.88

2f. The marginal cost schedule is in the table to the right.

Labor	Output	Marginal cost
0	0	
		50.00
1	20	
		41.67
2	44	
		62.50
3	60	
		83.33
4	72	
		125.00
5	80	
		250.00
6	84	
		500.00
7	86	

2g. Len's average total cost is at a minimum between 44 and 60 body boards per day.

2h. Len's average variable cost is at a minimum between 44 and 60 body boards per day.

2i. Though the range of output over which the minimum average total cost and average variable cost occur is the same, we know that the average variable cost equals its minimum at a lower level of output than the average total cost. The average total cost equals the average variable cost plus the average fixed cost. The average fixed cost constantly decreases as output increases. Thus as output increases after the average variable cost reaches a minimum and starts to increase, the average total cost continues to fall for a while because the average fixed cost falls. Eventually, however, the increase in the average variable cost overwhelms the decrease in the average fixed cost and at that level of output, the average total cost begins to increase as output increases.

3a. $A = \$1,050$. A is calculated using $TVC = TC - TFC$. Total cost is given in the row. To calculate total fixed cost, TFC, note that $AFC = TFC \div TP$, or rearranging, $TFC = AFC \times TP$. Multiply the AFC and TP from any row to get

$TFC = \$500$ (approximately, because of rounding). Thus $A = \$1{,}550 - \$500 = \$1{,}050$.

3b. $B = \$1{,}200$. Calculate B by adding $TVC + TFC$, with TFC from part (a) as $\$500$. Then $B = \$700 + \$500 = \$1{,}200$.

3c. $C = \$5$. Calculate C by dividing $TFC \div TP$, or $\$500/100 = \$5$.

3d. $D = \$8.50$. Calculate D by dividing $TC \div TP$ or $\$850/100 = \$8.50$.

3e. $E = \$2.50$. Calculate E as the change in TC divided by the change in TP, or $(\$1{,}550 - \$1{,}200)/(380 - 240) = \$2.50$.

4. The long-run average cost curve, $LRAC$, shows the lowest average total cost of producing any level of output using any combination of fixed and variable inputs. To construct the $LRAC$ curve, calculate the ATC curve for each plant size. Then the ATC that is the lowest for each level of output is part of the $LRAC$ for that level of output.

5. The sources of economies to scale are specialization of labor and capital. The sources of diseconomies of scale are management coordination and communication. In Figure 11.1, economies of scale occur up to point A with long-run average costs declining as output increases. Diseconomies of scale occur at output levels above point A as long-run average costs increase.

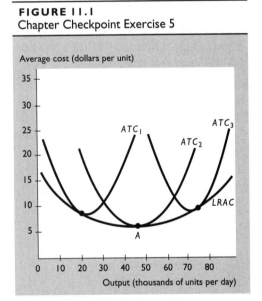

FIGURE 11.1
Chapter Checkpoint Exercise 5

6. Your students' answers will likely differ, but economies of scale occur in industries that are high tech and in agriculture. High tech industries, such as server farms, can service thousands of customers in one location. The ATM example in the book provides a good example of scale.

   In agriculture, large, commercial farms can hire many workers to specialize in the many specific tasks that are required. For instance, on a dairy farm many tasks are required: breeding cows, growing feed, milking, selling, and delivering milk. A large corporate farm can hire specialists for all these tasks, versus a single farmer trying to do all of the jobs on a farm.

7. Your students' answers will likely differ, but diseconomies of scale occur in the electricity industry. We see electrical utilities buying electricity from other suppliers during extreme weather that occurs infrequently. If the utility had built a plant to meet demand on these very cold or very hot

days, it would experience diseconomies of scale. As a result, the utility uses a smaller plant size that minimizes average total cost on normal days (the vast majority of days), but it must buy additional power during extreme weather.

ADDITIONAL EXERCISES FOR ASSIGNMENT

■ Questions

1. Create some hypothetical data for a firm's labor employment and output. Calculate the firm's average product and marginal product schedule. Carefully graph the data. Make sure your graphs are shaped as described in the text.

2. Create hypothetical data for a firm's labor employment, output, and total cost data for a firm. Select wages and the cost of the fixed input and then calculate the marginal cost, average fixed cost, average variable cost, and average total cost schedules and curves. Label the minimum points on the *AVC* and *ATC* curves.

■ Answers

1. Students will all have individual answers. Make sure they understand the meaning of the concave marginal product and average product curves. By having students generate their own data, they get a clearer meaning of how output behaves. Make sure the curves AND the axes are labeled correctly.

2. Students will have individual answers. Make sure graphs and axes are labeled correctly. By generating their own data, students learn the interaction of output and different costs.

ANSWERS TO ECONOMICS IN THE NEWS

■ Chrysler to Cut 26,000 Jobs

1. The effect on Chrysler's cost curves depends on what the student assumes about Chrysler's economies or diseconomies of scale. Closing a plant reduces Chrysler's scale of operations. Chrysler will move to another ATC curve. If Chrysler had been operating where it had economies of scale, closing the plant moves Chrysler to an average total cost curve that lies to the left of the initial curve, as illustrated in Figure 11.2 by the shift from ATC_1 to ATC_2. The average variable cost (not illustrated to avoid complexity) shifts similarly. The marginal cost curve shifts leftward, as illustrated, and the average fixed cost shifts downward, as illustrated.

FIGURE 11.2
Economics in the News Question 1

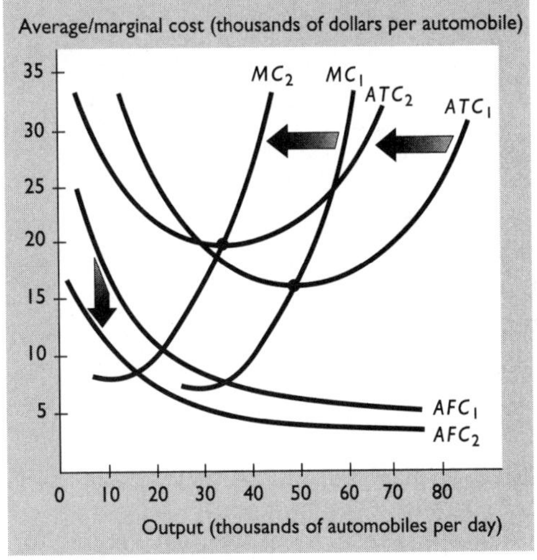

If Chrysler had initially been operating where it had diseconomies of scale, the average total curve again shifts leftward, but the minimum of the new ATC curve lies below the minimum of the old ATC curve. The average variable cost curve shifts similarly to the average total cost curve. The marginal cost curve shifts leftward so that it goes through the minimum points on the new average variable cost and average total cost curves. The average fixed cost curve shifts downward, the same as illustrated in Figure 11.1.

2. Decreasing its labor force has no effect on Chrysler's cost curves, that is, the curves do not shift. Instead, there is a (leftward) movement along the curves.

3. Closing the plant is a long-run change. Decreasing production to two shifts is a short-run change.

USING EYE ON THE U.S ECONOMY

■ The ATM and the Cost of Getting Cash

The article provides interesting data and ATC curves for ATMs. The story and curves clearly show why large banks do a lot of their business via ATMs as a result of a large customer base. Smaller banks, on the other hand, face a small client base and so it is not efficient (cost-effective) for them to provide ATMs to this small number. It is cheaper for the small banks to use tellers.

Ask your students if it would make sense if smaller banks and credit unions would be less likely to charge their own customers for using other banks' ATM machines. You can conduct a quick poll of the class to determine if any of the students have actual experience with this question. The point is that by not charging its customers for using other bank's ATMs, the smaller bank can increase its scale without having to actually change its plant size. The answer to the question depends, in part, on the charges the smaller bank has to pay to allow its customers to be part of the larger network.

Chapter 12

Perfect Competition

CHAPTER ROADMAP

■ Where We Are

In this chapter, we examine the profit-maximizing decisions made by a perfectly competitive firm in the short run and the long run. To do so, we use the groundwork on firms' costs laid in the previous chapter.

■ Where We've Been

Chapter 12 uses the foundation from Chapter 11, which studied firms' production and costs. The cost material covered in Chapter 11 remains important throughout not only Chapter 12 but also Chapters 13, 14, and 15.

■ Where We're Going

After this chapter, we continue studying firms' behavior by looking at the demand and marginal revenue curves for monopolies, oligopolies and monopolistically competitive firms. By combining the cost, demand, and revenue curves, we will see operating decisions faced by these firms and we can compare them with those made by perfectly competitive firms.

IN THE CLASSROOM

■ Class Time Needed

This chapter is very important. Perfect competition is the standard against which other industries are compared, so do not rush through this material. You should plan on spending at least two and a half class sessions and possibly even three.

An estimate of the time per checkpoint is:

- 12.1 A Firm's Profit-Maximizing Choices—60 to 80 minutes
- 12.2 Output, Price, and Profit in the Short Run—30 to 50 minutes
- 12.3 Output, Price, and Profit in the Long Run—30 to 40 minutes

■ Extended Lecture Outline

12.1 A Firm's Profit-Maximizing Choices

A. Perfect Competition

Perfect competition occurs when:
1. A large number of firms are selling identical products to many buyers.
2. There is unrestricted entry into and exit from the market.
3. Established and new firms operate on a level playing field.
4. Sellers and buyers are well informed about prices.

B. Other Market Types
1. A **monopoly** produces a product with no close substitutes and a barrier blocks the entry of new firms. The firm has no competitors.
2. **Monopolistic competition** has many firms competing by making similar but slightly different products.
3. An **oligopoly** has a small number of firms that compete.

C. Price Taker
1. A **price taker** is a firm that cannot influence the price of its product. The market determines the price, and the firm takes it as given.

2. A perfectly competitive firm faces a *perfectly elastic* demand because there are many substitutes for the firm's product.

D. Revenue Concepts
   1. In a perfectly competitive market, the equilibrium price and quantity are determined by the intersection of the market supply and demand curves. This is the price that the firm "takes."
   2. A firm's total revenue = price × quantity. When plotted with total revenue on the vertical axis and quantity on the horizontal axis, a firm's total revenue curve is upward sloping.
   3. **Marginal revenue** is the change in total revenue resulting from a one-unit change in quantity sold.
   4. In perfect competition, marginal revenue equals price because the firm can sell any quantity of its good at the market price.

E. Profit-Maximizing Output
   There is one level of output that maximizes a firm's economic profit. This quantity can be determined in two ways:
   1. Compare total cost to total revenue. Profit reaches a maximum when total revenue exceeds total cost by the greatest amount. Where total cost equals total revenue, the firm has its break-even point and at this quantity, economic profit equals zero.
   2. Compare marginal cost (*MC*) to marginal revenue (*MR*).

F. Marginal Analysis and the Supply Decision
   1. By comparing marginal cost (which increases as output increases) to marginal revenue (which is constant as output increases), a firm determines its profit-maximizing level of output.
   2. If marginal revenue is greater than marginal cost, each extra unit of output sold raises more revenue than it costs to produce the good. When *MR* > *MC*, economic profit increases as output increases.
   3. If marginal cost is greater than marginal revenue, each extra unit of output costs more to produce than it raises in revenue. When *MC* > *MR*, economic profit decreases as output increases (and increases as output decreases).
   4. When *MC* = *MR*, the firm maximizes economic profit.

G. Exit and Temporary Shutdown Decisions.
   1. If the price of a good falls, a firm faces three decisions:
      a. The firm *exits the market* if it incurs an economic loss that it believes is permanent.
      b. The firm *shuts down* if it incurs an economic loss that it believes is temporary and the price is less than average variable cost.
      c. The firm *produces output* if it incurs an economic loss that it believes is temporary and the price is greater than average variable cost.

H. The Firm's Short-Run Supply Curve
   1. The firm's short-run supply curve shows the profit-maximizing quantity as price varies. The firm produces output as long as price is greater than the minimum of average variable cost (*P* > minimum *AVC*).
   2. The firm shuts down if price is less than the minimum of average variable cost (*P* < minimum *AVC*). This price and quantity is called its **shutdown point.**
   3. The firm's supply curve is divided into three sections:
      a. When *P* > minimum *AVC* , the firm's supply curve is the firm's marginal cost curve.
      b. When *P* = minimum *AVC*, the firm is indifferent between producing and shutting down.
      c. When *P* < minimum *AVC*, the firm's supply curve runs along the vertical axis as the firm produces no output.

12.2 Output, Price, and Profit in the Short Run

A. In the short run, the market supply curve shows the quantity supplied at various prices by all the firms in the market put together.

    1. The market supply curve is divided into three sections:

        a. At prices below the minimum *AVC* of any firm, all firms shut down. The market supply is perfectly inelastic and the market supply curve runs along the vertical axis indicating that zero units are supplied.

        b. At a price equal to the minimum *AVC*, firms are indifferent between shutting down and producing. Some produce and some do not. The market supply is perfectly elastic and the market supply curve is horizontal.

        c. At prices greater than the minimum *AVC*, all firms supply output. The market supply curve is the sum of each firm's output at the different prices and is upward sloping.

B. Short-Run Equilibrium in Good Times

    1. The price each perfectly competitive firm takes as given is determined by the intersection of the market supply and demand curves.

    2. If the price is greater than a firm's average total cost, the firm earns an economic profit.

C. Short-Run Equilibrium in Bad Times

    1. If the price (determined by the market) is less than the firm's average total cost, the firm incurs an economic loss.

12.3 Output, Price, and Profit in the Long Run

In the long run, at the profit-maximizing quantity of output, price equals average total cost ($P = ATC$). In the long run, a perfectly competitive firm earns zero economic profit, that is, the firm earns a normal profit.

A. Entry and Exit

Firms enter and exit the market when they expect to earn an economic profit or incur an economic loss, respectively.

    1. The Effects of Entry

If firms in a market are earning an economic profit, new firms are motivated to enter the market. As new firms enter, market supply increases and the price falls. As the price falls, each firm's economic profit decreases. Eventually, the price decreases to where each firm earns zero economic profit (that is, each firm earns a normal profit). New firms stop entering at this point.

    2. The Effects of Exit

If firms are incurring an economic loss, firms are motivated to exit the market. As these firms exit, market supply decreases and the market price increases. As the price increases, each of the remaining firm's economic profit increases. Eventually, the price increases to where each firm earns zero economic profit. Firms stop exiting the market.

B. A Permanent Change in Demand

A permanent change in demand brings about an adjustment from one long-run equilibrium to another.

    1. Suppose the market starts in a long-run equilibrium (where $P = ATC$) and firms earn a zero economic profit. If demand increases permanently, the market price increases.

    2. Because price is greater than average total cost ($P > ATC$), existing firms earn an economic profit and new firms are motivated to enter the market.

3. Entry leads to an increase in the market supply and the price decreases. Eventually, enough firms enter the market and the price falls to where $P = ATC$. Firms earn zero economic profit, so no new firms enter the market and a long-run equilibrium is reached again.

4. The opposite process occurs when there is a permanent change in demand. The decrease in demand produces a lower market price, leading firms to exit the market because $P <$ minimum AVC.

5. As firms exit, supply decreases and the market price increases until all firms earn zero economic profit again. In the long run, there are fewer firms.

6. The price in the new-long run equilibrium might actually be greater than, less than, or equal to the price in the original equilibrium.

C. External Economies and Diseconomies

1. The **long-run market supply curve** shows the relationship between the quantity supplied and price as the number of firms adjust (to permanent changes in demand) to achieve zero economic profit.

2. The behavior of the long-run equilibrium price depends on factors that are out of the firm's control:

   a. **External economies** are factors beyond the firm's control that lower its costs as market output increases. The long-run market supply curve slopes downward in this case and the price decreases in the long run as a result of an increase in demand.

   b. **External diseconomies** are factors beyond the firm's control that increase the firm's costs as market output increases. The long-run market supply curve slopes upward in this case and the price increases in the long run as a result of an increase in demand.

   c. With no external economies or diseconomies, the long-run market supply curve is horizontal.

3. In some cases, the price of a good decreases in the long run even though the market experiences external diseconomies. The price fall occurs because of technological change.

E. Technological changes allow firms to lower their cost of production, which means the firm's cost curves shift downward.

1. Firms adopting the new technology earn an economic profit. These firms have an incentive to stay in the market or enter it using the new technology.

2. Firms that do not adopt the new technology incur an economic loss. These firms exit the industry.

3. As new-technology firms enter the market and old-technology firms exit the market, the price falls and output increases. The market returns to its long-run equilibrium when all firms make zero economic profit while consumers enjoy lower prices and better products.

■ Lecture Launchers

1. Launch your lecture by drawing a spectrum of market types noting the four market structures to be studied in this and the next two chapters (Chapter 12 Perfect Competition, Chapter 13 Monopoly, Chapter 14 Monopolistic Competition and Oligopoly). Let your students know that you will be comparing how a firm in *each* of these market structures chooses its equilibrium price and equilibrium quantity. You will also be examining the firm's profit in the short run and long run. Putting this diagram on the board provides a good layout for the following chapters.

2. Once you discuss the characteristics that define perfect competition (many firms selling an identical product to many buyers, no restrictions on entry, established firms have no cost advantage over new firms, and sellers and buyers are well informed about prices) it is natural to give examples of perfectly competitive markets. The examples that *always* spring to mind are agricultural in nature. Often students, particularly those in urban areas, wonder why they will spend so much of their time studying agriculture. You need to combat the natural view that the model of perfect competition applies only to farms. Tell your students that although agriculture certainly meets all the requirements of perfect competition, a lot of other industries come close. If you have a mall near by, you can assign your students to walk through the mall and take note of the different types of businesses and list those that they think are closest to perfect competition. Businesses such as shoe stores, jewelry, toy stores, book stores, hair salons, and so forth are all commonly found in malls and are all relatively close to being in perfectly competitive markets. For instance, you can point out to the students that, of course, one jewelry store's products aren't identical to those of any other jewelry store, but they are very close substitutes. So, although the jewelry market does not exactly meet the definition of a perfectly competitive market, nonetheless it is likely close enough so that if we want to understand the forces that affect firms within this industry, perfect competition is a reasonable starting point.

■ Land Mines

1. Show what is meant by the term "price taker" by drawing the *market* supply and demand curves and the resulting equilibrium price (on the left side of the board) and then draw the *firm's* demand and marginal revenue curves on a separate graph (on the right side). Draw a dotted line across from the market graph to the firm graph. Really emphasize the fact that the market demand differs from the firm's demand because the firm is such a small part of the market. Students consistently confuse the difference between the market demand and the firm's demand, so the more time you spend clearly explaining this distinction, the better.

2. You will always have students asking why the firm bothers to produce the precise unit of output for which $MR = MC$. Indeed, it is simply amazing how many students "worry" about this one particular unit of output! Try the following: Draw the conventional upward sloping MC curve and horizontal MR curve. Make sure to draw these so that the firm will produce a good deal of output. Then, starting at 0, move a bit to the right along the horizontal axis and stop at a point. Tell the students that this point measures 1 unit of output and ask them if this unit should be produced. The answer ought to be yes, because you have arranged matters so $MR > MC$. Pick some numbers—say, $MR = \$10$ and $MC = \$1$. Ask your students what the profit is for this unit and what the firm's total profit is if it produces only 1 unit. The answers are $9 and $9. Below the x-axis, label two rows, one called "profit on the unit" and the other "total profit." Put $9 and $9 in each space under your 1 unit of output. Then move your finger a bit more along

the horizontal axis until you come to where you will define the second unit of output. Ask your students if this second unit should be produced. Again, the answer ought to be yes, because you have arranged matters so *MR* > *MC*. Pick another number for *MC*, say $2. Ask your students what the profit is on this unit and what the firm's total profit is if it produces 2 units. The answers are $8 and $17. *Stress* that the total profit is what interests the firm and the total profit equals the sum of the profit from the first *plus* the profit from the second unit. Pick a couple of more units and use numbers until you fell it is safe to generalize that the firm produces a unit of output as long as *MR* > *MC*. Then, slide your finger to the right, stopping at closer and closer intervals, asking the class if that particular unit should be produced. Always stress that the firm's total profit continues to increase, albeit more and more slowly. As you get closer to the magical *MR*-equal-to-*MC* point, make your stopping intervals even closer. Finally, when you reach *MR* = *MC*, tell the students that although this specific unit yields no profit, to have stopped *anywhere* before it means that the firm would have lost some profit. So, only by producing where *MR* = *MC* will the firm obtain the maximum total profit.

3. When explaining whether a firm exits, temporarily shuts down, or produces, draw the two possibilities and tell an intuitive story. First, compare average total cost, average variable cost, and price in side-by-side graphs. Then tell a story. I use Wally's Wiener World (WWW) hot dog cart. When price is greater than average variable cost (*P*>*AVC*), Wally can pay for his hot dogs, buns, and mustard, and he covers part of the cost of the cart (his fixed cost). I show these distances on the graph. I show that by operating, he at least can earn enough to pay part of his fixed cost, so he should stay open. But if *P* < *AVC*, Wally can't even afford to buy the dogs and buns, much less pay for the cart. In this circumstance, Wally is better off by shutting down.

■ ANSWERS TO CHECKPOINT EXERCISES

■ CHECKPOINT 12.1 A Firm's Profit-Maximizing Choices

a. Roy's total revenue = 40 × $25 = $1,000.

b. Roy is a perfect competitor, so his marginal revenue equals his price. Therefore Roy's marginal revenue = $25.

c. Roy is not maximizing profit because marginal cost ($20) is less than marginal revenue ($25). He should sell more bags until marginal cost rises to $25 because then his marginal cost equals his marginal revenue.

d. If the price is $18, Roy's marginal revenue is $18. Roy is maximizing profit by selling 25 bags because the marginal cost of the 25th bag is $18. Roy is incurring an economic loss because price is less than average total cost.

e. One point on Roy's supply curve is *P*= $18 and *q* = 25 bags.

■ **CHECKPOINT 12.2 Output, Price, and Profit in the Short Run**

1a. If the market price is $30 per lawn, the marginal revenue is $30 per lawn. Lisa mows 5 yards because the marginal cost of mowing the fifth yard is $30.

1b. Lisa's average total cost is $26 (= $130/5). Thus the economic profit per lawn is $4 (= $30 – $26), so Lisa's total profit is $20 (= $4 profit × 5 yards).

2a. If the market price is $20, marginal revenue is $20. Lisa mows 3 lawns because the marginal cost of mowing the third yard is $20.

2b. The average total cost is $25 (=$75/3). The economic "profit" per lawn is –$5 (= $20 – $25), that is, Lisa has an economic *loss* of $5 per lawn. Her total economic loss is –$15 (= $5 loss per yard× 3 yards).

3a. Lisa's shutdown point is at $10 per lawn and 1 lawn mowed. Mowing 1 yard has a marginal cost of $10, so when the price is $10, mowing 1 yard sets marginal cost equal to marginal revenue. Lisa' total variable cost at this level of output is $10 because her fixed cost (from when she mows 0 yards) is $30. Therefore when Lisa mows 1 yard, her average variable cost is $10 (= $10/1).

3b. When Lisa shuts down, her loss equals her fixed cost, $30.

■ **CHECKPOINT 12.3 Output, Price, and Profit in the Long Run**

a. If the market price is $30, marginal revenue equals $30. Lisa mows 5 lawns because that is the quantity for which marginal cost equals marginal revenue. The average total cost of cutting a lawn when 5 are cut is $26 so Lisa earns an economic profit of $4 per lawn. She cuts 5 lawns so her total economic profit is $4 × 5 = $20.

b. Because firms are earning an economic profit, new lawn-mowing firms enter the market.

c. In the long run, the price is $25, which is the minimum of average total cost and so is the price for which firms earn zero economic profit.

d. In the long run, Lisa cuts four lawns, where the marginal cost equals $25.

e. In the long run, Lisa's economic profit is $0.

ANSWERS TO CHAPTER CHECKPOINT EXERCISES

1a. Sugar's price is controlled by the government, so it is not a perfectly competitive market (even though it is an agricultural good). The market does not determine the price.

1b. Jeans are sold in a monopolistically competitive market. Different brands are similar and each firm controls its segment of the market, but there are many brands of jeans.

1c. The film market is an oligopoly. There are four major firms: Kodak, Fuji, Agfa, and Konica.

1d. The toothpaste market is monopolistically competitive with a large number of similar but not identical brands.

1e. The taxi rides are provided by a monopoly.

2. The firm cannot choose its price because it only produces a small portion of the entire market's output and its good has perfect substitutes. If the firm increases its production, it will have little, if any, impact on the market price. If the firm raises the price of its good above the market's price, no one will buy it, switching instead to cheaper, perfect substitutes. And, if the firm lowers its price below the market price, the firm will not maximize its profit because it will not pick up any sales beyond what it could have gained even if it did not lower its price. The firm's horizontal demand curve shows it can sell as much output as it wants at the market price.

3. Joe's Diner doesn't shut down because the price of service must be greater than average variable cost. By staying open, even though Joe does not have many customers, he has enough so that he can earn enough revenue to pay all of the variable costs of remaining open and help pay some of his fixed cost.

4. The profit-maximizing perfectly competitive firm's supply curve is only the portion above the minimum of average variable cost. Because the firm shuts down if price is less than the minimum average variable cost, at a price below the minimum average price the firm always produces 0 units of output. So, at these low prices, the firm's supply curve runs along the vertical axis.

5a. Other firms entered the post-it note market because 3-M was earning an economic profit.

5b. As years go by, fewer firms will enter the market because the economic profit evaporates.

5c. If the demand for post-it notes decreases, the price decreases and some firms will incur an economic loss. At some point, these firms will leave the market.

6. The profits of wood racquet producers decreased. As these (or other) firms used new technology and entered the graphite racquet market, the firms producing graphite racquets earned an economic profit. The economic losses for wood racquet producers and economic profits for graphite racquet producers has made wood racquets scarce because few firms produce them and graphite racquets common because many firms produce them.

7a. The wheat market is likely a perfectly competitive market because:
   • many farms sell an identical product to many buyers,
   • there are no restrictions on entry into (or exit from) the market,
   • established farms have no advantage over new farms, and
   • sellers and buyers are well informed about prices.

7b. The price increased through 1996 and then decreased relatively significantly after 1996.

7c. The quantity fluctuated around a falling trend through 1995, then it increased through 1997, after which it decreased.

7d. The main influences on demand have been rising incomes and rising population. Incomes increased particularly strongly after 1995 and so after 1995 this factor was likely the most important.

7e.   The main influences on supply have been advances in seed and fertilizer technology that have increased yields and the supply. The weather also has played a role and it has brought fluctuations in output.

7f.   Before 1997, if anything, there might have been some entry because of the (gently) rising prices. But, output was falling during these years, and so it is difficult to determine if there was any entry. Regardless, if there was entry (or exit) it was probably small. After 1997, with sharply falling prices and falling production, most likely exit has occurred.

8a.   A typical figure showing the cost and revenue curves is Figure 12.1. Before the fad began, the (few) scooter firms presumably were in long-run equilibrium, earning a normal profit. Figure 12.1 shows a typical firm, producing 40 scooters per day and selling them for $60 each. The firm's economic profit is $0 because P equals ATC.

FIGURE 12.1
Chapter Checkpoint Exercise 8a

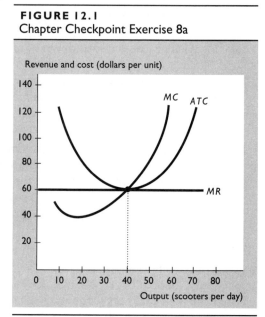

8b.   When the scooter fad is two years old, the scooter firms are likely earning an economic profit. A few new firms would have entered the market and other firms might be considering entry, but these firms would be considering entry only if the existing firms were earning an economic profit. Figure 12.2 illustrates a typical scooter firm that is earning an economic profit. The firm is producing 50 scooters per day and selling them for $80. The firm is earning an economic profit because $P > ATC$.

FIGURE 12.2
Chapter Checkpoint Exercise 8b

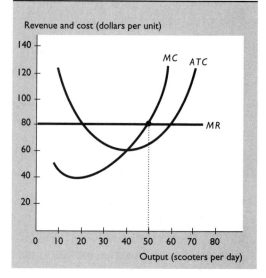

8c. After the scooter fad has faded, the price will return to its long-run equilibrium. Presuming that the costs of the (surviving) firms have not changed, the price returns to its initial level. The scooter firms earn only a normal profit. Figure 12.3 illustrates this outcome. In the figure, the firm is producing 40 scooters per day and selling them for $60 each. The firm is earning a normal profit because $P = ATC$.

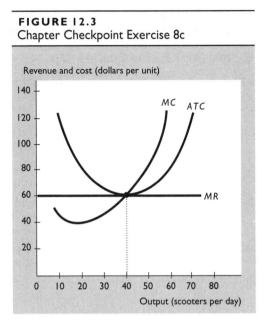

FIGURE 12.3
Chapter Checkpoint Exercise 8c

ADDITIONAL EXERCISES FOR ASSIGNMENT

■ Questions

1. A catfish farmer is operating in a perfectly competitive market. The market price of catfish is $5 per pound and each farmer produces 1,000 pounds per week. The average total cost is $7 per pound.
   a. What is a catfish farmer's profit in the short run?
   b. What happens to the total number of farms in the long run?
   c. If technology reduces the cost of catfish farming while the demand for catfish increases, what happens to price in the long run?

■ Answers

1a. Because the price is less than average total cost ($5 versus $7), each farmer incurs an economic loss of $2 per pound or a total economic loss of −$2,000.

1b. Because some firms are incurring an economic loss, they will exit the market. Supply decreases and the market price rises. In the long run, the number of farms declines.

c. Technology shifts cost curves downward. This effect alone would decrease the price in the long run. An increase in demand increases the price if there are external diseconomies. A combination of both events makes the change in the price unpredictable. If there are external economies, the price would fall. We would need to know more information about external economies or diseconomies to predict what happens to price.

ANSWERS TO ECONOMICS IN THE NEWS

■ Music Schools Scaling Up

1. The music education industry is certainly competitive because there are thousands of music schools nationwide. However, while competitive, music education is not strictly perfectly competitive. There are different teaching methods and some teachers are better than others. One teacher is not a perfect substitute for other teachers. But, all in all, the market likely is very close to being perfectly competitive.

2. The demand for music lessons has increased so the price of music lessons has risen. As a result, music schools are earning an economic profit, as Figure 12.4 indicates. In the figure, the price has increased to $40 per lesson. At this price, music schools are earning an economic profit. We know that the school illustrated in the figure is earning an economic profit because $P > ATC$.

3. Most likely firms are entering the music education business because the firms currently in the market are earning an economic profit. Assuming they can hire trained musicians, there are no barriers to keep new firms from entering the market and the lure of an economic profit will surely lead to entry!

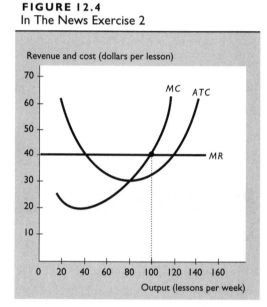

FIGURE 12.4
In The News Exercise 2

USING EYE ON THE U.S ECONOMY

■ Entry in Personal Computers; Exit in Farm Machines

The story provides good examples of economic profits motivating firms to enter a market (personal computers) and economic losses motivating a firm to exit a market (farm machines). For both of the stories, you can draw short-run and long-run scenarios.

   Use the PC market to discuss the transition from one firm (IBM) earning large economic profits in the short run to many firms eking out normal profits in the long run. You can note that the short run and IBM's economic profit lasted several years until the new firms could produce a reliable clone.

   The International Harvester portion of the article provides a good example of a firm exiting a market because of economic losses. As the structure of the agriculture industry changed (fewer family farms and more efficient, conglomerate farms), less equipment was needed. As a result, the demand for and hence the price of farm equipment decreased. The fall in price means firms incurred economic losses. While more firms than International Harvester were suffering losses, they chose not to exit. Navistar's decision allowed itself, and the surviving firms, the opportunity to earn a normal profit.

USING EYE ON THE GLOBAL ECONOMY

■ The North American Market in Maple Syrup

The article highlights the perfectly competitive wholesale maple syrup market. You can use this story to show short-run and long-run profit scenarios graphically. Show how technology led to some firms exiting the market while other, larger firms decided to adopt the technology. Also show how the demand curve shifted rightward as demand increased. If you want, you can use the story to address external economies.

Monopoly

Chapter 13

5. Explain how monopoly regulation influences output, price, economic profit, and efficiency.
    A. Gains from Monopoly
       1. Economies of Scale
       2. Incentives to Innovate
    B. Regulating Natural Monopoly

CHAPTER ROADMAP

■ Where We Are

In this chapter, we examine another market structure: monopoly. We discuss how monopoly arises and how a monopoly (single-price or price discriminating) chooses its profit-maximizing output and price. Recognizing that monopoly creates a deadweight loss, we discuss whether monopoly is efficient and fair. The concept of rent seeking is examined and reveals that rent seeking is likely to extract all of the economic profit earned by a monopoly. Finally, the benefits and regulation possibilities for monopolies are provided.

■ Where We've Been

The previous chapter studied perfectly competitive firms' demand and marginal revenue curves. We combined them with the cost curve analysis in Chapter 11 to determine perfectly competitive firms' profit-maximizing output and price decisions.

■ Where We're Going

After this chapter we examine two more market structures: monopolistic competition and oligopoly. Then, in Chapter 15, we move to a discussion of antitrust and regulation. Both of these chapters depend on the material presented in this chapter.

IN THE CLASSROOM

■ Class Time Needed

Because the students are familiar with firm behavior in perfect competition, this chapter is somewhat easier to present. You should spend between two to three class sessions on this material.

An estimate of the time per checkpoint is:

• 13.1 Monopoly and How It Arises—15 minutes

- 13.2 Single-Price Monopoly—25 to 45 minutes
- 13.3 Monopoly and Competition Compared—30 to 40 minutes
- 13.4 Price Discrimination—30 to 40 minutes
- 13.5 Monopoly Policy Issues—10 to 25 minutes

■ Extended Lecture Outline

13.1 Monopoly and How It Arises

A. A monopoly arises when:

1. a firm produces a product with no close substitutes, and
2. a barrier to entry protects a firm from new competitors. These barriers can be natural or legal.
   a. A **natural monopoly** arises when technology allows a firm to supply an entire market at a lower price than if two or more firms met the market demand.
   b. A **legal monopoly** arises when a firm owns all of a natural resource or when the government grants a firm a public franchise, government license, patent, or copyright.
   i. A *public franchise* is a firm's exclusive right to supply a product.
   ii. A *government license* is a license required to enter an industry.
   iii. A *patent* is an inventor's exclusive right to produce his or her product. Patents promote invention and innovation.
   iv. A *copyright* is an artist's exclusive right to publish his or her work.
3. Most monopolies are regulated by the government.

B. Monopoly Price-Setting Strategies

A monopoly has two price-setting options:

1. Setting a single price.
   A **single-price monopoly** sells each unit of its product for one price.
2. Charging different prices for different units
   A **price-discriminating monopoly** can sell its product for different prices. Price discrimination allows the monopoly to make a larger profit.

13.2 Single-Price Monopoly

A. Price and Marginal Revenue

1. Because the monopoly is the only producer in the industry, the market demand curve is the firm's demand curve.
2. The monopoly's marginal revenue curve is not its demand curve (as it was for the perfectly competitive firm) because to sell an additional unit of the good, the monopoly must lower the price of all units sold (not just of the extra unit). When the monopoly reduces the product's price to sell an extra unit, revenue is impacted in two directions:
   a. The monopoly loses revenue on the units that had been sold at the old, higher price.
   b. The monopoly gains revenue on the additional units sold at the lower price.

B. Marginal Revenue and Elasticity.

1. If demand is elastic, marginal revenue is positive.
2. If demand is inelastic, marginal revenue is negative.
3. A profit-maximizing monopoly will not operate on the inelastic portion of its demand.

C. Output and Price Decision
1. By comparing marginal revenue (*MR*) to marginal cost (*MC*), a monopoly determines its profit-maximizing level of output. If *MR* > *MC*, a monopoly increases its economic profit by increasing output. If *MC* > *MR*, a monopoly increases its economic profit by decreasing output. When *MC* = *MR*, a monopoly chooses this level of output to maximize economic profit.
2. To determine the profit-maximizing price, the monopoly charges the highest price (*P*) for the quantity produced. This price is determined from the demand curve.
3. A monopoly's profit is determined by computing the cost of producing each unit via the average total cost (*ATC*) curve. Economic profit equals profit per unit (*P* − *ATC*) times quantity. Equivalently, economic profit equals total revenue less total cost.
4. If a monopoly earns an economic profit, other firms have an incentive to enter, but barriers to entry prevent entry. As a result, a monopoly can earn an economic profit in the short run and the long run.

13.3 Monopoly and Competition Compared
A. Output and Price
1. Compared to a perfect competition, a monopoly produces a smaller output and charges a higher price.
B. Is Monopoly Efficient?
1. Perfect competition produces an efficient use of resources by producing a level of output for which marginal cost equals marginal benefit. A monopoly, which produces a level of output for which marginal benefit is greater than marginal cost, inefficiently uses resources.
2. The efficient use of resources in a perfectly competitive market maximizes the amount of consumer surplus and producer surplus enjoyed by society.
3. The monopoly reduces this surplus and creates a deadweight loss. The monopoly is inefficient.
C. Is Monopoly Fair?
1. In addition to creating a deadweight loss, the monopoly transfers part of consumer surplus to producer surplus.
2. Depending on certain conditions (under the fair results or fair rules standard), the monopoly might or might not be considered fair.
D. **Rent seeking** is the act of obtaining special treatment by the government to create economic profit or to divert consumer surplus or producer surplus away from others. A rent seeker can accomplish these tasks in two ways:
1. Buy a Monopoly
A firm (or person) that buys a monopoly for less than the monopoly's economic profit is rent seeking.
2. Create a Monopoly by Rent Seeking
A firm (or person) that lobbies the government to grant it exclusivity to supply a good or create entry barriers for its competitors is rent seeking.
3. Rent Seeking Equilibrium.
The cost of rent seeking, which is a fixed cost, extracts all economic profit from a monopoly. As a result, these monopolies earn a normal profit. Rent seeking alters the deadweight loss generated by a monopoly. The economic profit that had been earned by the monopoly becomes part of the deadweight loss. The act of rent seeking uses up resources, but this resource use provides no output.

13.4 Price Discrimination

Price discrimination is charging different prices for different units of a good. Its use is not limited to monopolies. Charging different prices is not always price discrimination because while two goods might appear to be the same, they might have different production costs. To be able to price discriminate, a monopoly must be able to
1. Identify and separate different buyer types.
2. Sell a product that cannot be resold.
A. Price Discrimination and Consumer Surplus
The monopoly's goal when it price discriminates is to gain as much consumer surplus as possible. This goal is accomplished by:
1. Discriminating Among Groups of Buyers.
   A firm charges different prices to different consumers.
2. Discriminating Among Units of a Good.
   A firm charges all of its customers the same price, but charges a lower price as a person buys additional units.
B. Profiting by Price Discriminating
By charging different prices or offering volume discounts, a firm is able to capture more of the consumer surplus than if it charges only one price. As a result, the firm increases its economic profit.
C. Perfect Price Discrimination
1. A firm extracts the entire consumer surplus if it can charge each consumer the maximum price the consumer is willing to pay.
2. As a result, the marginal revenue curve becomes the same as the demand curve for a perfect price discriminator.
3. A firm that practices perfect price discrimination chooses the same profit-maximizing level of output as does a perfectly competitive market. But the price discriminating firm captures all of the consumer surplus.
D. Price Discrimination Efficiency
1. Because the perfectly price-discriminating firm produces the same quantity of output as the perfectly competitive market, there is no deadweight loss. So while there is an efficient outcome in terms of production, the firm ends up with all of the producer and consumer surplus.
2. Rent seeking reduces the economic profit to zero.

13.5 Monopoly Policy Issues

A. Gains from Monopoly
Monopolies are allowed to operate because they offer benefits compared to alternate market structures.
1. Economies of Scale.
   A natural monopoly has economies of scale. It can provide enough output to meet the entire market demand at a lower price (and at a lower average cost) than two or more firms. When these economies of scale exist, it would be more costly to prevent the monopoly from operating.
2. Incentive to Innovate
   Monopolies have an incentive to innovate because they get to keep all of the economic profits.

B. Regulating Natural Monopoly

In order to promote a more efficient outcome, government can regulate natural monopolies. Two methods used to regulate monopolies are:

1. **Marginal cost pricing rule**

To generate an efficient use of resources, the regulator can require the monopoly to produce where price equals marginal cost (a perfectly competitive market outcome). This rule causes the monopoly to incur an economic loss. This rule is rarely used because of the negative effects on profit.

2. **Average cost pricing rule**

The regulator requires the monopoly to set price equal to average total cost. While this rule does not produce an efficient amount of output, the rule allows the firm to earn a normal profit.

■ Lecture Launchers

1. Did you ever set up a lemonade stand when you were a kid? Probably not, but you can bet your students have heard of this sort of endeavor and, depending on their circumstance, maybe even beseeched their parents to let them do so. And, even if they didn't, they can easily identify with this sort of small (!) business. Point out that if you were able to convince your folks to let you set up a lemonade stand, you probably ran a monopoly (at least for a day) as long as none of your friends set up a stand. Their parents provided the barrier to entry! You could determine your own price and sell a certain number of cups of lemonade. If you reduced your price, you could sell more. At the end of the day, you added up your revenues and found out you made money. By the next day (or weekend) after your friends saw your success, you lost your monopoly power as they opened competing stands. But for a little while, you were a monopolist! This easily understood story captures the essence of monopoly. Indeed, you can even embellish it to include price discrimination by pointing out how you might have charged your folks more—or less!—than other customers!

■ Land Mines

1. Marginal revenue can be a sticking point for many students. Students find it easier to see the difference between the monopoly's demand and marginal revenue curves if you take two steps. First develop a total revenue schedule using price and quantity data. Then add another column showing marginal revenue. As the text shows, place the marginal revenue values *between* the quantity values. In the next step, draw the demand and marginal revenue curves. Again, emphasize that marginal revenue is plotted *between* two quantity levels. By explicitly graphing the data, you also have the framework for showing that the price of the good is always less than marginal revenue for a monopoly.

2. Students differ in their learning styles. It is always wise to accommodate as many of these styles as possible. To more clearly show the deadweight loss, start with a numeric approach. Draw a figure, labeling points on the axes with prices and quantities. Use these values to make your point and explic-

itly calculate the deadweight loss. Then, realizing that some students learn better from a geometric approach, shade the appropriate areas.

3. To make it easier to compare the two regulation schemes, draw side-by-side matching graphs and label the axes with prices and quantities. By calculating the different prices, quantities, deadweight losses, and changes in consumer and producer surplus, the differences in the two schemes become more clear.

ANSWERS TO CHECKPOINT EXERCISES

■ CHECKPOINT 13.1 Monopoly and How It Arises

1a. The supermarket that stocks only the best-quality products is not a monopoly. The statement does not say that no other markets stock these products. If indeed it is the *only* supermarket in the area that stocks these high-quality products, it still is not a monopoly because there are no barriers to entry to prevent other supermarkets from also stocking the best-quality products.

1b. A supermarket that charges the highest prices is not a monopoly.

1c. The firm with the largest market share is not necessarily a monopoly.

1d. A truck stop in the middle of nowhere is a monopoly.

1e. A firm producing a good with perfectly inelastic demand could be a monopoly. Inelastic demand implies that there are no close substitutes for the good (like insulin), but does not imply that other firms are prevented from entering the market. Hence, by the definition, unless there is a barrier to entry, the firm is not a monopoly. But, more generally, simply because the demand for a product is inelastic does *not* mean that the producer is a monopoly.

1f. An airline with the only service on a route has monopoly power on that route.

2. The truck stop is a natural monopoly. If two truck stops supplied the market, costs would be higher. (The truck stop could have a legal monopoly if it has purchased all surrounding land or if it lobbied the government to allow it to have the only building permit for the area.) The airline might be a legal monopoly if it has been awarded sole landing rights at one of the airports.

■ CHECKPOINT 13.2 Single-Price Monopoly

a. The table showing Dolly's total revenue and marginal revenue schedules is to the right.

Price (dollars per caret)	Quantity (carets per day)	Total revenue (dollars)	Marginal revenue (dollars)
2,200	0	0	
2,000	1	2,000	2,000
1,800	2	3,600	1,600
1,600	3	4,800	1,200
1,400	4	5,600	800
1,200	5	6,000	400

b. Figure 13.1 illustrates Dolly's demand and marginal cost curves.

c. Dolly's marginal cost equals marginal revenue at 2 1/2 carats per day, where both equal $1,200. From the demand curve, the price charged is $1,700. Total cost of 2 1/2 carets per day is $3,200. Dolly's total revenue equals (2 1/2 carets) × ($1,700) = $4,250. Hence her total economic profit is $4,250 – $3,200 = $1,050.

d. As a result of the tax, Dolly's fixed cost changes, but her marginal cost does not. Her profit-maximizing level of output is still 2 1/2 carats and her price still equals $1,700. The tax eliminates all but $50 of Dolly's economic profit.

e. A $600 per carat tax increases Dolly's marginal cost by $600 at every level of output. With the increase in her marginal

FIGURE 13.1
Checkpoint 13.2 Exercise b

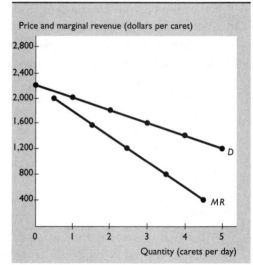

costs, Dolly now sells 1 1/2 carats per day because this is the level at which her new marginal cost equals her marginal revenue (both equal $1,600). From the demand curve, Dolly's sets a price of $1,900 a caret. Her total profit equals her total revenue minus her total cost. Her total revenue is (1 1/2 carets) × ($1,900) = $2,850. Her total cost is $2,100 plus the tax of $900, or $3,000. Hence her "profit" is $2,850 – $3,000 = –$150; that is, Dolly has an economic loss of $150.

■ CHECKPOINT 13.3 Monopoly and Competition Compared

Bobbie's barbershop is not efficient because she produces fewer haircuts than a perfectly competitive market would produce. The barbershop generates a deadweight loss of $3. The monopoly captures $6 of the consumer surplus. A rent seeker would be willing to pay $12, the amount of the economic profit.

■ CHECKPOINT 13.4 Price Discrimination

1. Price discrimination is a firm offering the same good for sale at different prices. Examples are a shoe store offering one pair of shoes for $50 and a second pair for half price. A restaurant that offers early bird specials for dinners before 6 pm or a movie theater that offers lower matinee ticket prices are engaging in price discrimination.

2. For a firm to price discriminate it must be able to identify specific consumers' willingness to pay different prices and must be able to prevent the resale of the product.

3a. The drug store is price discriminating.

3b. The airline is price discriminating.

3c. Domino's is price discriminating.

3d. Different interest rates reflect borrowers' different risks, which is a possible cost. Charging different interest rates is not price discriminating.

3e. The residents might not face price discrimination. There could be higher costs to transport the water to Los Angeles. If the different prices are based on volume use or if the different prices are based on different types of users, then there is price discrimination.

3f. If the price difference is based on different costs of mailing the letter versus the postcard, then there is no price discrimination.

■ CHECKPOINT 13.5 Monopoly Policy Issues

a. i) The price would fall to the price charged by a perfectly competitive firm where marginal cost equals marginal revenue.

ii) Assuming DeBeers is not a natural monopoly, DeBeers would make a normal profit. If DeBeers is a natural monopoly, it would incur an economic loss.

iii) The consumer surplus would increase because the regulation increases the output and lowers the price.

b. i) The price would fall compared to what the monopoly would charge, but would be higher than the price charged by a perfectly competitive market.

ii) The deadweight loss is less due to the regulation because DeBeers is required to increase output and lower the price.

iii) The consumer surplus would increase because the regulation increases the output and lowers the price.

ANSWERS TO CHAPTER CHECKPOINT EXERCISES

1a. Big Top's total revenue and marginal revenue schedules are in the table to the right.

1b. The circus will sell 350 tickets and charge $13 per ticket. Big Top's economic profit equals its total revenue, $4,550, minus its total cost, $4,100, for an economic profit of $450.

1c. Calculating the consumer surplus as the area of the consumer surplus triangle, consumer surplus equals $1,225. The producer surplus equals the area above the marginal cost curve and less than the

Price (dollars per ticket)	Quantity (hundreds of tickets per week)	Total revenue (dollars)	Marginal revenue (dollars)
20	0	0	
18	100	1,800	1,800
16	200	3,200	1,400
14	300	4,200	1,000
12	400	4,800	600
10	500	5,000	200
8	600	4,800	−200
6	700	4,200	−600
4	800	3,200	−1,000

price up to the quantity sold. The marginal cost curve is horizontal at $6.00. Therefore the producer surplus area is a rectangle and equals $2,450.

1d. The circus is not efficient because, compared to perfect competition, it decreases the number of shows and charges a higher price.

1e. The competitive equilibrium is 700 shows and $6 per ticket.

1f. If the circus offers a discount, producer surplus increases and consumer surplus decreases. The circus is practicing price discrimination. The practice reduces the deadweight loss and increases efficiency.

1g. If the government regulates the circus so that it makes a normal profit, the ticket price is $10 and 500 tickets are sold. The deadweight loss is a triangle whose area equals $400.

1h. If the circus is required to act efficiently, 700 tickets are sold at $6.00 each. The circus incurs a $2,000 economic loss, the difference between its total revenue, $4,200, and its total cost, $6,200.

2. The museum can offer discounts to senior citizens and students. If could offer free admission to children accompanied by adults to attract more visitors.

3. Although your students' answers will depend on the information they gather, what they will find is that the trips with the most restrictions generally have the lowest prices. And the restrictions are generally designed to separate vacation or leisure travelers from business travelers. The airline's goal is to charge the highest price a traveler is willing to pay and business travelers are almost always willing to pay higher prices than leisure travelers.

ADDITIONAL EXERCISES FOR ASSIGNMENT

■ Questions

1. The figure shows an industry. If the market is perfectly competitive, what is the equilibrium quantity that will be produced and the equilibrium price? If the market is a single-price monopoly, darken in the area of the deadweight loss.

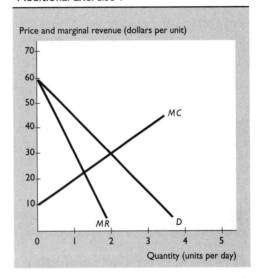

FIGURE 13.2
Additional Exercise 1

■ Answers

1. If the market is perfectly competitive, 2 units are produced and the price is $30. The deadweight loss is the darkened triangle.

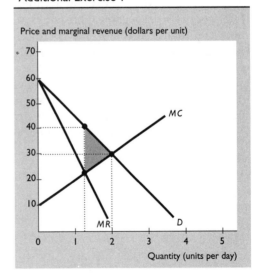

FIGURE 13.2
Additional Exercise 1

ANSWERS TO ECONOMICS IN THE NEWS

■ Drug Price Hikes

1. Drug companies have monopoly power for drugs for which they hold the patent. After the patent expires, they no longer have a monopoly for the drug. For instance, at one time Johnson and Johnson held the patent to produce Tylenol, which is acetametaphin. Once the patent expired, any company can produce acetametaphin, although only Johnson and Johnson can call it Tylenol.

2. Drug prices are rising because the cost of producing new drugs is increasing faster than average prices and because the demand is increasing for new drugs, which treat ailments previously untreatable.

3. Your students' answers will vary. Points they should keep in mind are the deadweight loss created by the patent versus the incentive effect to research new drugs, also created by the patent.

USING EYE ON THE U.S ECONOMY

■ Airline Price Discrimination

The story provides a good example of how airlines identify many buyer types. Charging different prices alone does not guarantee price discrimination. Airlines effectively price discriminate by requiring passengers to show identification. Before security scares, passengers could board a plane without showing identification so airlines could not prevent the resale of tickets. At that time, price discrimination was more difficult. You might see tickets advertised in the newspapers. There were businesses devoted to reselling low-priced tickets! For example, at that time, you could buy your grandmother's ticket for which she paid a reduced senior citizen fare. Today, even though there might be no security reasons for showing identification, airlines persist in requiring it. You can no longer resell tickets and so airlines can effectively price discriminate.

Monopolistic Competition and Oligopoly

Chapter 14

CHAPTER ROADMAP

■ Where We Are

In this chapter, we examine two more market structures, monopolistic competition and oligopoly. The profit-maximizing quantity and price are discussed for each structure. The chapter shows why firms in monopolist competition decide to advertise and develop new products. The last half of the chapter describes the range of output seen in oligopoly and develops the concept of game theory.

■ Where We've Been

The previous chapters studied perfectly competitive firms and monopoly firms. The material dealing with monopoly is used in this chapter because monopolistic competition is similar in some regards to monopoly.

■ Where We're Going

The next chapter covers how the government chooses to regulate monopolies and antitrust law. The material in Chapter 15 depends a bit on the subjects covered in this chapter, but primarily it uses results from Chapter 12, on perfect competition, and Chapter 13, on monopoly.

IN THE CLASSROOM

■ Class Time Needed

You can complete this chapter in two or perhaps more likely, three sessions. Probably most of the time will be spent on game theory because by this point the students will be familiar with the diagrams illustrating how firms in monopolistic competition select their profit-maximizing price and quantity, whereas game theory is a set of entirely new concepts.

An estimate of the time per checkpoint is:

- 14.1 Monopolistic Competition—40 to 50 minutes
- 14.2 Product Development and Marketing—10 to 15 minutes
- 14.3 Oligopoly—10 to 25 minutes
- 14.4 Game Theory—60 to 80 minutes

■ Extended Lecture Outline

14.1 Monopolistic Competition

Monopolistic competition is characterized by four factors: a large number of firms, product differentiation, competition, and easy entry.

A. A Large Number of Firms

The large number of firms implies
  1. each firm supplies a small portion of the market's total output.
  2. no single firm dominates the market nor can a single firm impact the market price.
  3. because there are so many firms, collusion to fix prices is not possible.

B. Product Differentiation

Product differentiation involves firms making their products slightly different from other firms' products. As a result there are no perfect substitutes and so the firm in monopolistic competition faces a downward-sloping demand curve. Differentiation also allows the firm to compete.

C. Competing on Quality, Price, and Marketing

A firm in monopolistic competition will compete on:
  1. Quality
     A firm promotes the idea that its product has better attributes than its competitors' products. These attributes could be design, reliability, etc.
  2. Price
     A downward-sloping demand curve implies that a firm can decrease the price of its good and increase the quantity sold.
  3. Marketing
     A firm uses advertising and packaging to publicize its product's uniqueness.

D. Entry and Exit

If firms in monopolistic competition earn an economic profit in the short run, new firms are motivated to enter the market. This increase in supply decreases each firm's demand and lowers the price until only normal profits are earned. If firms earn economic losses in the short run, some firms will exit the industry causing the price to rise until normal profits are earned by the remaining firms.

E. Identifying Monopolistic Competition.
  1. **Four-firm concentration ratio** is the percentage of sales captured by the top four firms in the market. If the ratio is greater than 40 percent, the market is considered concentrated. If the ratio is less than 40 percent, the market is considered be monopolistic competition.
  2. **Herfindahl-Hirschman Index (HHI)** is the sum of the squared percentage market shares of each of the 50 largest firms. This measure is used as a guideline by the Justice Department for decisions regarding whether to challenge mergers.
F. Output and Price in Monopolistic Competition
  Once a firm in monopolistic competition makes decisions about how to design, produce, and market its product, it must decide how much to produce and at what price to sell its product.
G. The Firm's Profit-Maximizing Decision
  1. Facing a downward-sloping demand curve, a firm in monopolistic competition chooses its profit-maximizing price and quantity as does a monopoly.
  2. The firm produces at the quantity that sets marginal revenue equal to marginal cost. The firm chooses the price by determining the maximum it can charge via the demand curve.
  3. Economic profit in the short run is possible and equals quantity × (price − average total cost).
H. Long Run: Zero Economic Profit
  1. Because there are no barriers to entry, other firms are motivated to enter the industry to capture part of any economic profit.
  2. As new firms enter and compete, an individual firm's demand and marginal revenue decrease. New firms enter until economic profits disappear and the remaining firms earn a normal profit.
I. Monopolistic Competition and Efficiency
  1. A firm in monopolistic competition chooses a profit-maximizing quantity where price is greater than marginal cost or, expressed differently, where marginal benefit exceeds marginal cost. This choice implies that the firm inefficiently uses resources. (Efficiency requires that price = marginal benefit = marginal cost).
  2. A benefit of monopolistic competition is that consumers enjoy product variety.
  3. A firm's capacity output occurs at the point where its average total cost is at a minimum. In the long run, a firm in monopolistic competition does not minimize average total cost and therefore has excess capacity. This excess capacity results from product differentiation.

14.2 Product Development and Marketing
Before deciding how much to produce, a firm must determine how its product will be designed (or redesigned) and marketed.
A. Innovation and Product Development
  A firm in monopolistic competition will continuously develop new products or improve the current one so that it can continue earning economic profits. If the firm does not innovate, new firms will enter the market and capture the existing firm's economic profits.
  1. To decide the degree to which it will innovate, a firm compares the marginal cost of innovation to the marginal benefit of innovation.
B. Marketing
  A firm uses marketing to convince consumers that its product differs from and is better than other products. These differences can be real or perceived.
  1. Marketing Expenditures
  The cost of marketing can represent a large portion of the price consumers pay for a product.

2. Marketing and advertising expenditures, which are fixed costs, increase total costs. Graphically, these expenditures mean the average total cost curve shifts upward. If these marketing expenditures can increase sales enough, the average total cost of the amount produced might decrease.

3. Advertising might increase demand for a firm's product (by taking away other firms' customers) or might decrease demand (as new firms enter the market trying to earn economic profits).

4. Whether monopolistic competition is efficient or not depends on comparing the benefits of product variety versus the cost of selling and unused capacity.

14.3 Oligopoly

A *natural oligopoly* exists when only a few firms can supply the market more cheaply than one firm (a monopoly) or many firms. This cost situation arises as a result of economies of scale. A *legal oligopoly* exists when a government grants production of a good or service to only a few firms. Because there are only a few firms, each firm can *influence* its own product's price, but it cannot control the market price. By being able to set its own price, the firm can attempt to maximize its profit, but it simultaneously impacts its competitors' profits and the market's profit.

A. Collusion

1. To maximize profit, firms in an oligopoly might choose to form a cartel.

   a. A **cartel** is a group of firms acting together (in collusion) to decrease output, increase price, and raise profits.

   b. Cartels are illegal in the United States.

2. To understand how an oligopoly operates, economists study **duopoly,** a market structure where there are only two firms.

B. Duopoly in Airplanes

1. A competitive outcome occurs in a duopoly when the firms produce the level of output determined by the intersection of the market supply and demand curves.

2. A monopoly outcome occurs when the firms produce the level of output determined by the intersection of the firm's marginal cost and marginal revenue curves and charge a price determined by the demand curve.

3. An oligopoly will produce a level of output ranging from the level produced by a perfectly competitive market and to that produced by a monopoly.

C. The Duopolists' Dilemma

When trying to increase its own profit (at the expense of its competitors' profits), a firm can set off retaliation by these competitors. As a result, the initiating firm might ultimately hurt its own economic profits.

14.4 Game Theory

Game theory is a tool used by economists to study the *strategic actions* of firms in an oligopoly.

A. What Is a Game?

A game is defined by its rules, strategies, and payoffs. The **prisoners' dilemma** game, played between two criminal suspects, shows the difficulty faced by parties (firms) trying to collude, even when it is mutually beneficial to do so.

B. The Prisoners' Dilemma

Two prisoners are caught committing a crime for which they must serve a 2-year sentence. The district attorney suspects they are the same criminals who committed an earlier crime. To get the criminals to confess to the earlier crime, the district attorney makes them play a game. The game is defined by the following:

1. Rules: If both prisoners confess, each will receive a 3-year sentence. If one prisoner confesses and his accomplice does not, the confessor receives 1 year while the accomplice receives a 10-year sentence. If neither confess, each gets a 2-year sentence.

2. **Strategies:** The possible actions of each player in a game. In the prisoners' dilemma, the strategies are that the prisoners can confess to the earlier crime or deny committing the crime.

3. Payoffs: A **payoff matrix** shows the outcomes facing the players for each of their possible actions in conjunction with possible decisions made by the other players. There are four possible payoffs in the prisoners' dilemma. If one prisoner (Art) confesses and the other prisoner (Bob) does not, Art serves 1 year and Bob serves 10 years. If Bob confesses and Art does not, Bob serves 1 year and Art serves 10 years. If both Art and Bob confess, each serves 3 years. If neither confesses, they only serve the 2 years for the crime for which they were caught red-handed.

4. Equilibrium:

   The game's equilibrium occurs when each prisoner chooses the best possible action given the action of his accomplice. This idea is also called a **Nash Equilibrium,** named after economist John Nash who proposed it. In the prisoner's dilemma, each convict chooses to confess.

5. Not the Best Outcome

   The equilibrium outcome is not the best for each prisoner. Without the ability to communicate and cooperate, the prisoners choose to confess. This choice produces a more severe sentence for each prisoner.

C. The Duopolists' Dilemma As a Game

   Airbus and Boeing play a game where each firm must choose how many airplanes to produce. They can produce 3 or 4 airplanes each week.

   1. The Payoff Matrix

      If they want to maximize the industry's profits ($72 million), each will collude and produce 3 planes per week. If Airbus cheats on the agreement to reduce output and produces 4 planes (while Boeing produces only 3 planes), Airbus makes $40 million and Boeing makes $30 million. If Boeing cheats on the agreement to reduce output and produces 4 planes (while Airbus produces only 3 planes), Boeing makes $40 million and Airbus makes $30 million. If both firms cheat on the agreement and make 4 planes, each firm makes $32 million.

   2. Equilibrium of the Duopolists' Dilemma

      The firms decide they are best off if each produces 4 airplanes per week.

D. Repeated Games

   1. By repeating the games, firms in a duopoly are more likely to cooperate and earn monopoly profits. If a firm knows that it can be punished in subsequent games with its competitors, it has an incentive not to cheat. This "tit for tat" strategy is likely to produce a monopoly outcome.

   2. The greater the number of firms and more difficult it is to detect cheating by other firms, the more likely it is for firms to cheat. This outcome produces a level of output that is closer to the perfectly competitive market's level of output.

■ Lecture Launchers

1. The prisoners' dilemma is a great way to start this lecture. Tell students they get to play a game and get two students to volunteer to be the "criminals." Give the entire class the story and rules. Don't use a payoff matrix at

this point, just write the options on the board. Then send one of your volunteers out of the room. Ask the remaining student what strategy he or she will take. Get your class to help. It usually takes a few minutes for everyone to agree that confessing is the best strategy. Send the first student from the room and then call in the second student. Ask this student what he or she will do. Because the class already knows what the first student has done, encourage them not to tell. Aid the students as they move toward choosing the equilibrium. Encourage students to remember this gaming strategy because it is the same material that you'll use to describe a firm's behavior.

2. John Nash's life makes for an interesting anecdote you can tell in class. He was an incredibly bright graduate student and assistant professor in the early 1950s. During this time he developed the concept of the Nash equilibrium. Tragically, he was taken severely ill with schizophrenia. Princeton, where he was employed, made a supremely human decision and kept him on the faculty even though he was totally disabled. He spent about the next three decades riding buses around Princeton and wandering the buildings at night. His wife divorced him but continued to care for him. Nash's condition has improved in recent years, but he still remains unable to teach. Princeton's gesture was repaid in 1994 when Nash won a Nobel Prize. Apparently the Nobel committee had heard of his improving condition and before they awarded him the prize, they called several of his friends to inquire if he would be able to accept the prize. Fortunately, he was and so the prize was awarded.

■ Land Mines

1. While students have gotten familiar with the demand, marginal revenue, and marginal cost curves over the past two chapters, still take the time to point out the curves as you draw them. Use actual numbers for quantity and price.

2. Some students have trouble remembering which structure (monopolistic competition or oligopoly) is the least competitive, or closer to the monopoly-end of the market structure spectrum. Students are familiar with the word "monopoly" because most have played the game, but the word "oligopoly" has no reference point. I like to add that "olig" is Latin for "few." This helps students place this market structure in the correct place along the spectrum of structures, closer to the monopoly end.

3. Determining the Nash equilibrium of a game is often difficult for students. I try to make the game more "practical" by pointing out to the students that in the real world, real firms are almost always doing "what if" analyses and that game theory is well designed for answering these sorts of what if questions. In the Airbus/Boeing game in the text, the two companies are trying to determine how many airplanes they should produce if their competitor produces 3 airplanes or if their competitor produces 4 airplanes. You can illustrate the equilibrium by starting with Airbus and stating that Airbus wants to determine what it should do if Boeing produces 4 airplanes. Then, after determining that Airbus will produce 4 airplanes, do the next

"what if" by looking what Airbus should do if Boeing produces 3 airplanes. In this case, Airbus (again) wants to produce 4 airplanes. Therefore Airbus' "what if" analysis has led to the conclusion that regardless of Boeing's decision, Airbus wants to produce 4 airplanes. You can conduct the same "what if" for Boeing's choices and determine that Boeing, too, will produce 4 airplanes regardless of Airbus' choice.

ANSWERS TO CHECKPOINT EXERCISES

■ CHECKPOINT 14.1 Monopolistic Competition

a. Lorie maximizes profits by producing 10 racquets. (Marginal cost is $15 per racquet. Marginal revenue between 0 and 10 racquets is $20 and between 10 and 20 racquets is $10, and so it equals $15 at 10 racquets.) She should charge $20. Lorie's average fixed costs are $100 ($1,000/10) and average variable costs (marginal costs) are $15 per racquet. Average total cost is $115 per racquet. Lorie has an economic loss of $20 − $115 or $95 per racquet. Therefore her economic "profit" equals −$950, that is, Lorie has an economic loss of $950.

b. Firms will not enter; indeed, firms will exit the restringing business.

c. In the long run, the demand for Lorie's restringing business will increase if she stays in the market.

d. In the long run, Lorie's economic profit will equal $0. Either she closes, in which case in the long run when her fixed costs are paid, her loss is $0, or if she remains open, the demand for her services increases as other firms leave and she winds up with a normal profit.

■ CHECKPOINT 14.2 Product Development and Marketing

a. The increase in demand will increase the number of cookies sold and most likely increase the price she charges. (The effect on the price depends on the precise manner in which the demand curve shifts, but most likely her price will rise.) Her economic profit will increase.

b. If additional advertising enables sales to increase so that total revenue increases more than total cost, she can increase economic profit.

■ CHECKPOINT 14.3 Oligopoly

1a. The price equals $6, the same as the price when only two firms were in the cartel. The profit-maximizing price does not depend on the number of firms in the cartel, though the more firms in the cartel, the lower is each firm's production quota.

1b. The price equals $0, once again the same price as before.

2a. The dilemma is that if each firm could trust the other to raise its price and cut its advertising, each firm's profit would increase. But each firm worries that if it alone hikes its price and cuts its advertising, its profit will fall drastically as its competitor's market share drastically increases.

2bi. Assuming the firms adhere to the cartel agreement to restrict output, the price of film will rise. To the extent that one or both firms cheat on the agreement, the price of film will be less than otherwise.

2bii. Once more, to the extent the firms comply with the cartel agreement, advertising expenditures as well as research and development expenditures will be cut.

■ CHECKPOINT 14.4 Game Theory

a. The payoff matrix is to the right with the entries in millions of dollars. In this matrix, if Bud and Wise both develop the drink, each earns a normal profit, which is $0 economic profit. If neither develops, both also have a return of $0, while if one develops and the other does not, the developer earns $2 million and the non-developer has an economic loss of –$1 million.

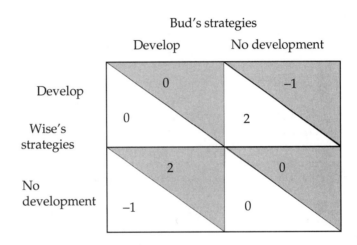

b. The game has the Nash equilibrium in which both develop the drink. Take Bud, for instance. If Wise develops, Bud wants to develop the drink because otherwise he loses $1 million. And if Wise does not develop the drink, Bud wants to develop the drink so that he can earn an economic profit of $2 million. Hence no matter what Wise does, Bud will develop the drink. Similar reasoning shows that Wise, too, will develop the drink.

c. There is little chance of cooperation because the game is essentially a winner-take-all arrangement. The only possibility of cooperation would be if one person developed the drink and the other did not, and then the developer paid the non-developer some amount more that $1 million to more than compensate the non-developer for his economic loss of $1 million. But this sort of payment between firms is exceedingly uncommon and surely illegal.

ANSWERS TO CHAPTER CHECKPOINT EXERCISES

1a. Bob's profit-maximizing quantity is 40 burgers and his profit-maximizing price is $2 per burger. He earns an economic profit of $0.75 per burger for a total economic profit of $30.

1b. Because Bob earns an economic profit, other firms will enter the market.

1c. Bob has excess capacity because the minimum of average total cost does not occur at 40 burgers. However, excess capacity is not certain in the short run for a firm in monopolistic competition. In the short run, the firm could produce at capacity, or at more than capacity. In the long run, however, the firm definitely will have excess capacity.

1d. As new firms enter the market, the demand for Bob's burgers will decrease.

1e. In the long run, Bob's economic profit equals $0.

1f. Bob has excess capacity because his is a firm in monopolistic competition. As a result, in the long run his price must equal his average total cost because he will earn only a normal profit. For this condition to occur, it must be that Bob produces where his demand curve just touches his *ATC* curve. But because Bob produces a differentiated product, his demand curve is downward sloping. As a result, his demand curve touches his *ATC* curve where the *ATC* curve is downward sloping. Where the *ATC* curve is downward sloping, the average total costs are not at their minimum and so Bob is not producing where his average total costs are minimized.

2a. The cruise market is monopolistic competition. There are many shipping lines offering cruises, and so the market is not an oligopoly. Cruises differ, so the market is not perfect competition. Many firms producing a differentiated product is the definition of monopolistic competition.

2b. Cruises are quite different. They go to different locations. They have different qualities of food. They cater to different age groups. They often have themes. They go for different lengths. They go at different times of the year.

2c. The price is determined from the demand for the different cruises. The quantity is determined by the intersection of the marginal cost and marginal revenue and then the price is set as the maximum price that sells the profit-maximizing number of cruises.

2d. The cruises probably are operating at less than capacity. If the industry has reached its long-run equilibrium, then definitely the cruises are operating at less than capacity. If the industry is approaching its long-run equilibrium, the closer it gets the more likely it is to have excess capacity.

2e. Entry has occurred because the demand for and hence the profit from cruises has increased during the last decade. The demand increased because the economy has been strong and because aging baby boomers want to take cruises. Firms enter an industry if they believe they will be able to earn an economic profit.

3a. The payoff matrix is to the right. Each entry is the economic profit in dollars. "Comply" means to comply with an agreement to act as a monopoly; "cheat" means to cheat on the agreement by producing more and charging a lower price. If they jointly behave as a monopoly, they will produce a total of 6 units a day and charge a price of $6 because this is the monopoly quantity and price. (See the solution to the Practice Problem 14.3 on page 352 or

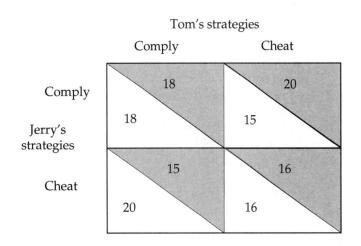

the Study Guide solution on page 226 for details.) To determine what happens if one cheats and the other complies, assume that Jerry complies so he behaves as a monopolist and produces 3 units. In this case, Tom will produce 4 or 5 units because those quantities maximize his profit. Why? If Jerry is producing 3 units, Tom can produce 4 units. As a result, 7 units will be produced and so the price is $5. Tom's profit equals $20. Jerry's profit equals $15. (Tom's profit is $20 and Jerry's is $12 if Tom produces 5 units. The payoff matrix assumes the "cheater" produces 4 units.) Now, what happens if both cheat? Start with the situation in which Jerry is not cheating and Tom is. As we just calculated, Jerry's profit is $15. Suppose Jerry produces 1 more unit for a total of 4. In this case, 8 units are produced, and so the price is $4. Jerry's profit is $16, higher than if he did nothing. (Tom's profit is also $16.) Hence Jerry will produce 1 more unit. But from this position, each producing 4 units, it pays neither Tom nor Jerry to produce another unit because by so doing they would decrease their economic profit. Therefore if both Tom and Jerry cheat, each has an economic profit of $16.

3b. The Nash equilibrium is for both Tom and Jerry to cheat, so each produces 4 units and has an economic profit of $16.

3c. If the game is played repeatedly, the firms will find a way to cooperate and maintain the cartel. Therefore each will produce 3 units and each will have an economic profit of $18.

4a. The payoff matrix is to the right. If Jenny and Joe both go to a movie, Jenny gets 100 + 100 = 200 and Joe gets −100 (from the movie) + 100 (from being with Jenny) = 0. If they both go to a game, Jenny has the payoff of 0 and Joe has the payoff of 200. If Jenny goes to a game and Joe to a movie, each has a payoff of −100. And if Jenny goes to a movie and Joe to a game, each has a payoff of 100.

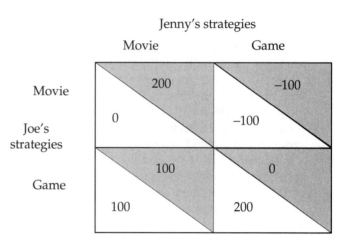

4b. The game is different from a prisoners' dilemma. For one point, the game has a slightly more complicated Nash equilibrium and the equilibrium will not be the worst outcome. Take Jenny's decision. If Joe is going to a movie, Jenny definitely wants to go to a movie. If Joe is going to a game, Jenny again goes to the movie. Hence Jenny will go to a movie regardless of Joe's choice. Similarly, Joe will always go to a game. So, the Nash equilibrium has Jenny going to the movie and Joe going to the game, so that each receives 100 as their payoff.

4c. The Nash equilibrium was explained in part (b) and has Jenny going to a movie and Joe to a game. If the game is played repeatedly, they might be able to settle upon both going to a game or both to a movie or alternate in some fashion, but if they alternate 50/50, there is no net gain in payoff to either.

ADDITIONAL EXERCISES FOR ASSIGNMENT

■ Questions

1. The equilibrium of a duopolist's game can have both firms acting as competitors, so that they get the "worst" outcome possible. From the social standpoint of efficiency, how does this outcome compare to their best outcome, when they jointly act as a monopoly?

2. Both AMD and Intel spend billions of dollars a year on research and development. Why can't they get together and jointly decide to decrease their spending?

■ Answers

1. The outcome where both act as competitors is definitely preferred to the outcome where they act as monopolists. If they act as monopolists, they

create a deadweight loss. If they act as perfect competitors, they will produce the efficient quantity and there will be no deadweight loss.

2. The problem faced by AMD and Intel is similar to any prisoners' dilemma game: Neither can trust the other to actually cut back on their research and development spending. And, if one firm did cut back and other did not, the one cutting back would run the risk of being driven from business.

ANSWERS TO ECONOMICS IN THE NEWS

■ Airlines Back Off Price Rise

1. The airline industry is an oligopoly.
2. Some airlines want to raise ticket prices to counter higher fuel prices.
3. By keeping its rates low, Northwest hopes to increase the number of tickets it sells at the expense of its competitors.
4. The airlines cannot collude to raise prices because it is against the law in the United States.
5. The firms cannot set and stick with a monopoly profit-maximizing quantity and price because one of the airlines is likely to cheat.

USING EYE ON THE U.S ECONOMY

■ Examples of Monopolistic Competition

You can list several of the industries listed in the figure on the board. Ask students to list them in order of competitiveness. You also can these data to promote discussion on calculating the four-firm concentration ratio and the Herfindahl-Hirschman Index.

■ The Selling Cost of a Pair of Running Shoes

This is a great example to use in class. First, students are very familiar with running shoes. Second, each student usually has particular likes and dislikes regarding specific brands and they each *believe* in the sales pitches of these companies. Once they see this breakdown of costs, students have to admit that the majority of the price they pay is due to selling costs. You can introduce discussion on whether the differences are real or if the advertising is worth the added expense.

USING EYE ON THE GLOBAL ECONOMY

■ Duopoly in Computer CPUs

This story provides a good example of a monopoly-controlled market and how other firms have entered to try to capture economic profits. It also shows how firms decide to advertise and innovate. You can also highlight the competition on price and quality. Let students speculate on how the firms will continue to compete.

Regulation and Antitrust Law

Chapter 15

CHAPTER ROADMAP

■ Where We Are

Chapter 15 is the last chapter devoted to studying industry structure. In this chapter, we investigate different types of regulation imposed by the government. We also review the history of antitrust law and current topics in antitrust cases.

■ Where We've Been
In the previous three chapters we've reviewed four types of market structure and studied how firms in each market structure selected their profit-maximizing output and price. We've compared the efficiency of the outcomes generated by each market structure. This chapter builds on the previous work because those chapters explained why competition is desirable, which is the thrust of the antitrust laws. In addition, Chapter 13 examined natural monopolies, a topic re-examined in this chapter.

■ Where We're Going
The next chapter leaves behind the industry structure and the output side of firms to begin a three-chapter unit studying input markets and the distribution of income. Chapter 16 leads off by examining the different types of factors (labor, capital, land, and entrepreneurship) and discussing, as well as analyzing, the markets in which these factors are traded.

IN THE CLASSROOM

■ Class Time Needed
You can complete this chapter in one session. If you want to spend more time, you can bring in current events, such as the situation in the California electricity market or perhaps some on-going regulation or deregulation issue from your state.

An estimate of the time per checkpoint is:

- 15.1 Regulation—20 to 30 minutes
- 15.2 Antitrust Law—20 to 30 minutes

■ Extended Lecture Outline

15.1 Regulation
A. Economic Theory of Regulation

Regulation is the government's administration of rules designed to determine prices, product standards, and types. Regulation can also include the conditions under which new firms can enter a market. The government also deregulates industries by removing restrictions on price, product development, and market entry.

1. Public Interest Theory

Public interest theory proposes that regulation attempts to produce the efficient use of resources and eliminate deadweight loss.

2. Capture Theory

Capture theory asserts that regulation attempts to maximize the profits of producers. It assumes that the cost of regulation is high, and as a result, regulation will increase the surplus of small, easily identifiable groups with low organizational costs.

B. The Scope of Regulation

Regulation has evolved over the past 115 years in the United States.

   1. The Interstate Commerce Commission, the first federal regulatory agency, was organized in 1887 to regulate interstate railroads. It now regulates several other industries, including oil pipelines and water carriers.

   2. Since the 1930s, the number of regulatory agencies greatly increased (at both the state and federal levels). By the 1970s, almost one quarter of all industry was regulated. In the last 20 years, there has been a tendency for deregulation.

C. The Regulatory Process

   1. Regulatory agencies have certain characteristics including:

      a. Governmental appointment of bureaucrats to manage the agencies.

      b. Government funding of the agencies.

      c. Adoption of operating practices for controlling prices and other regulated aspects of the firm.

   2. Regulatory agencies allow firms to choose production technology but do not allow the firms to set prices, output, or markets served. Agencies regulate natural monopolies and cartels in different ways.

D. Natural Monopoly

   1. A natural monopoly is an industry in which one firm can supply the market at a lower cost than can two or more firms.

   2. Natural monopolies tend to have large fixed costs and marginal costs that are low and increase slowly. The average fixed costs decline as they are spread over larger amounts of output, so the average total cost curve is sloping downward when it intersects the demand curve.

E. Regulation in the Public Interest

   1. Public interest theory asserts that regulation serves to produce an efficient use of resources (where marginal cost equals marginal benefit).

      a. A **marginal-cost pricing rule** sets price equal to marginal cost. This regulation results in an efficient use of resources, but causes the regulated firm to suffer an economic loss. If the firm cannot find a way to earn a profit (perhaps by using a *two-part tariff* or perhaps by price discrimination), the government has to decide whether or not to subsidize the firm. If the government levies a tax to fund the subsidy, society experiences a deadweight loss. The regulator must determine which deadweight loss is greater: the one created by taxation or the one created by the inefficient use of resources.

      b. An **average-cost pricing rule** sets price equal to average total cost. This rule ensures that firms cover their total costs, but it generates a deadweight loss. This outcome is considered efficient if the deadweight loss is less than the subsidy's necessary cost using a marginal-cost pricing rule.

   2. Capture theory concludes that regulation serves to maximize firms' profits.

      a. **Rate of return regulation** sets a price that enables the firm to earn a specific rate of return on capital. If costs are correctly assessed, the regulated price will equal average total cost.

b. With rate of return regulation, firms have the incentive to exaggerate their costs because higher costs are passed on to consumers as higher prices. Thus rate of return regulation can generate an inefficient outcome.

3. Because rate of return regulation has weaknesses, a regulator may choose to use incentive regulation. **Incentive regulation** encourages firms to operate efficiently and control costs. The two main types of incentive regulation are earnings-sharing regulation and price caps.

b. *Earnings-sharing regulation* allows firms to return to customers only part of any economic profits they earn, so the firm can retain some part of any economic profit.

a. *Price cap regulation* sets a maximum price that a firm can charge. Firms have the incentive to reduce costs in order to earn economic profits over the time of the price cap because they can keep any or all (depending on the specifics of the regulation) of an economic profit.

F. Oligopoly Regulation

A cartel, which can occur in oligopolistic markets, engages in illegal activity to reduce output, raise price, and earn economic profits.

1. According to public interest theory, the oligopoly is regulated so that a competitive outcome occurs and resources are efficiently used.

2. According to capture theory, the cartel will influences the regulator so that output is restricted to its monopoly level.

15.2 Antitrust Law

Antitrust law, enacted by Congress and enforced by the judicial system, is the body of law that is used by regulators to restrict monopolistic behavior.

A. The Antitrust Laws

1. The Sherman Act, passed in 1890, was the first U.S. antitrust law. Section 1 of the Sherman Act outlaws "contracts, … or conspiracy in restraint of trade." Section 2 makes illegal "attempts to monopolize."

2. The Clayton Act, passed, in 1914, along with its two amendments, the Robinson-Patman Act (1936) and the Celler-Kefauver Act (1950), prohibit specific business practices "only if they substantially lessen competition or create monopoly." The practices are:

a. Price discrimination.

b. Tying arrangements.

c. Requirements contracts.

d. Exclusive dealing.

e. Territorial confinement.

f. Acquiring a competitor's shares or assets

g. Becoming a director of a competing firm.

B. Landmark Antitrust Cases

1. Any price fixing action is *per se* illegal; that is, once proven it is always illegal because there is no admissible defense for price fixing.

2. Convicting a firm of "attempts to monopolize" is not as clear. The "Rule of Reason" stated that actions must generate an unreasonable restraint of trade for them to be illegal.

C. Today's Showcase: The United States Versus Microsoft

1. The Case against Microsoft. The government has charged Microsoft with the following:

a. Possessing monopoly power in the PC operating system market.

b. Using predatory pricing and tying arrangements to harm its competitors in the market for Web browsers.

c. Using other anticompetitive practices to restrict competition.

2. Microsoft has challenged these charges and claims that it is just trying to innovate and offer consumers value.

D. Mergers Rules

The Department of Justice uses guidelines based on the Herfindahl-Hirschman index (HHI) to help decide whether or not to challenge mergers within a market.

1. An HHI between 1,000 and 1,800 shows a market is moderately concentrated. The Department of Justice challenges any merger in this range that will raise the HHI by more than 100 points.

2. An HHI greater than 1,800 shows a highly concentrated market. The Department of Justice challenges a merger in this range if the merger will raise the HHI by 50 points.

■ Lecture Launchers

1. Most students are familiar with the government's case against Microsoft or, if not with the details, with the fact that the government has filed suit. Encourage a brief discussion on student perceptions of the lawsuit. Do they think Microsoft is restricting output? Do they think innovation has been harmed by Microsoft's alleged monopoly practices? Do they think Microsoft's requiring customers to buy their Web browser is illegal? Ask students if they have been following Microsoft's introduction of Window's XP system. Microsoft plans to "require" customers to buy Microsoft's new media player along with Windows XP. Explain that these types of concerns are what antitrust law addresses, and economists are concerned with how efficiently these markets operate. I usually ask students what kind of expert witnesses were called at Microsoft's trial. Of course, each side brought its own *economists*...some of whom were paid over $1,000 an hour!

■ Land Mines

1. To help present the differences between marginal-cost pricing and average-cost pricing, draw matching graphs side-by-side. Show students the prices that will be allowed by regulators. Ask students which regulation is "better." Be sure to show your students that marginal-cost pricing generates an economic loss even though output is at the competitive level.

2. A large percentage of students read the Clayton Act as *always* prohibiting the activities listed, such as price discrimination or exclusive deals. Ask your students why airlines and movie theaters can price discriminate even though it is outlawed by the Clayton Act? Ask them why Coke and McDonald's are allowed to have an exclusive deal so that only Coke products can be purchased at McDonald's while Pepsi and KFC have similar exclusive deal? The objective is to force the students to understand that the business practices mentioned in the Clayton Act are illegal *only if* they substantially lessen competition or create monopoly. You can state this qualifying phrase as often as you like (indeed, you *should* state it often) but real-life, specific examples are necessary to hammer the point home!

ANSWERS TO CHECKPOINT EXERCISES

■ CHECKPOINT 15.1 Regulation

a. The firm will produce 400,000 cans, which is where its marginal cost equals its marginal revenue.

b. The firm will charge $0.60 per can, which, as the demand curve shows, is the maximum price the company can charge and sell the 400,000 cans produced.

c. If the monopoly can capture the regulator, the firm gets the regulator to allow it to maximize its economic profits. This outcome occurs when 400,000 cans are produced.

d. The monopoly's goal is to produce 400,000 cans. When it is producing 400,000 cans, its price will be $0.60 a can. Now, when 400,000 cans are produced, the company's average fixed cost is $0.30 a can and its average variable cost is equal to its marginal cost, $0.20 a can. Therefore its "legitimate" average total cost is $0.50 a can, and so the maximum excess average total cost the company would claim is an additional $0.10 per can.

e. Only if the regulated monopoly produces 800,000 cans (where demand equals marginal cost) does it produce an efficient outcome.

■ CHECKPOINT 15.2 Antitrust Law

1. From the FTC, BP Amoco PLC and ARCO were required to divest:
   (1) all of ARCO's assets and interests related to and primarily used with or in connection with ARCO's Alaska businesses;
   (2) all of ARCO's assets related to its Cushing, Oklahoma crude oil business.

   In particular, the FTC said "Proposed Respondents will divest all of ARCO's Alaska assets to Phillips Petroleum Company ("Phillips"), an approved up-front buyer. The vast majority of these assets must be divested to Phillips within 30-days of the signing of the Proposed Consent Order. Some of the ARCO Alaska assets require third-party or governmental approvals and Proposed Respondents have up to six (6) months to divest those particular assets. Proposed Respondents will divest the Cushing assets to an acquirer or acquirers that receive the prior approval of the Commission and in a manner approved by the Commission. They must divest the Cushing assets within four (4) months of signing the Proposed Consent Order."

2. The Standard Oil Company was broken up years ago because the courts believed that it was restraining trade to an unreasonable level. In recent years, some of these individual firms have merged. These actions are a result of the market changing. This outcome would be analogous to the government allowing fragmented portions of the old AT&T to merge. The communications market has changed and new types of competitors have developed. In the petroleum industry, the government has decided that the

merged firms now represent a *more* efficient operation and that they face sufficient competition to restrain their behavior.

ANSWERS TO CHAPTER CHECKPOINT EXERCISES

1a. If the firms behave as a cartel, they will select the monopoly quantity, where $MR = MC$, and set the monopoly price. The monopoly quantity is 250 calls and the price will be 17.5¢ per call.

1b. If regulated in the public interest, 500 calls will be made and the price will be 5¢ per call.

1c. If the companies capture the regulator, the output and price will be the monopoly output and price, 250 calls and a price of 17.5¢ per call.

1d. The deadweight loss generated by the regulation is the area of the deadweight loss rectangle, which equals $1/2 \times$ (250 calls) $\times$ (12.5¢ per call) = $15.63.

1e. Marginal-cost pricing would lead to efficient use of resources.

2a. From the Web site, in 1998 "The FTC alleged that Intel illegally used its market power when it denied three of its customers continuing access to technical information necessary to develop computer systems based on Intel microprocessors, and took other steps to punish them for refusing to license key patents on Intel's terms. ... Over the years, Intel has promoted and marketed its microprocessors by providing customers with technical information in advance of the official commercial release of new microprocessor products. This makes it possible for computer makers to have computers based on new Intel microprocessors ready to sell at the time of the official commercial release of the microprocessors, or shortly afterwards. ... This is part of the mutually beneficial relationship between Intel and its customers. Intel benefits because its customers—computer systems manufacturers—commit resources to designing new computer products that incorporate the new Intel microprocessors. The customers benefit because they are able to introduce "leading edge" computer products with the latest microprocessor technology on a timely basis, the complaint states. The FTC alleged that on at least three occasions, Intel has terminated or threatened to terminate its mutually beneficial relationships in a selective, targeted fashion to retaliate against the firms that sought to protect or assert patent rights in rival microprocessor technologies or that refused to license such rights to Intel. This retaliation has primarily taken the form of cutting off access to technical information needed to design computer systems based on soon-to-be-released Intel microprocessors. By its actions, Intel sought to injure the customer until that customer surrendered the patent licenses Intel desired."

2b. Again from the Web site, "The proposed order would prohibit Intel from withholding or threatening to withhold certain advance technical information from a customer or taking other specified actions with respect to such information for reasons related to an intellectual property dispute with that customer. The order also would prohibit Intel from refusing or threatening to refuse to sell microprocessors to a customer for reasons related to an intellectual property dispute with that customer. According to the Commission, these provisions are designed to prevent Intel from restricting access to microprocessor products, or advance technical information relating to such products, as leverage in an intellectual property dispute against a customer that is receiving the information from Intel at the time the dispute arises."

2c. Intel essentially agreed to make its chips more widely available and to allow other companies to enforce their patents. This agreement will increase the quantity of chips, and thereby lower the price and increase consumer surplus.

3a. Your students' answers will vary. One issue they might discuss concerns the point that there would be a massive public outcry if the government tries to regulate the Internet. In addition, it is not obvious that price and quantity regulation are needed for the Internet because, at least currently, the Internet appears competitive with relatively easy entry into many aspects of it. However, if a few firms such as AOL grow "too large" the government in the future might consider some sorts of economic regulation.

3b. Again, your students' answers will vary. Some points they might mention include the fact that there are many special interest groups strongly opposed to taxing e-commerce, such as firms engaged in e-commerce and consumers who are heavy buyers of products sold by e-commerce. In addition, imposing the tax would be difficult, at least at the state level. If one state moved to tax e-commerce sales from firms located within that state, the firm could easily move to another state.

3c. Your students' answers will vary. But there seem to be no specially difficult aspects of antitrust law when it comes to the Internet. Attempts to monopolize will remain as difficult as always to prove. The Clayton Act prohibition of acquiring a competing firm if it substantially lessens competition will also remain equally difficult to prove.

4a. Before 1996, electric utilities in California were regulated as they had been for many previous years. Prices were set by the state and the companies owned their own generating plants as well as their transmission and distribution networks.

4b. The 1996 deregulation required that the transmission lines be transferred to a non-profit organization, the Independent System Operator. Utilities continued to own the distribution networks but they were required to sell their generating plants to independent, unregulated private firms. As a result, the wholesale price of electricity was deregulated, though the retail price remained regulated by the state. Further, the utilities were not allowed to sign long-term contracts with the private power producers. Rather the utilities were required to buy power each day.

4c. The retail price of electricity has remained regulated; the electric utility companies have not been allowed to sign long-term contracts with private power producers; the electric utilities have no been allowed to own their own generating plants.

4d. When the equilibrium price would exceed the price cap, the price cap becomes binding. The quantity of electricity generated and offered for sale is less with the price cap than if the price were allowed to reach its equilibrium. Shortages of electricity are the result.

4e. If the state had used an earnings-sharing plan, at first consumers would have been pleased because initially the policy created profits for the electricity utility companies. But after 2000 consumers would have been "shocked" by rapidly rising prices. Quite likely there would be fewer rolling blackouts, but the price of electricity would be higher.

5a. From the Web page, "Judge Jackson is being asked to agree to the splitting of Microsoft into two businesses, in what is referred to as a 'reorganization'. … Microsoft is required to separate its operating systems business from its applications business, with Internet Explorer going to the application business. … There are conduct remedies that ban exclusive dealing, essentially meaning that Microsoft would not be allowed to require a licensee to avoid using non-Microsoft software, or to promote Microsoft software exclusively, or to sabotage the running of the performance of any Microsoft-competitive software… "

5b. Microsoft's competitors almost certainly will gain. The effect on Microsoft's consumers is more difficult to determine. If Microsoft's assertions, that by integrating products, Microsoft was making usage easier for the typical user, then customers might well be harmed. However if the government's contention that Microsoft stifled competition and kept prices higher than otherwise is correct, then Microsoft's customers might benefit.

5c. Your students' answers will vary. If they assert that breaking up Microsoft is a movement toward greater efficiency, they must also assert that Microsoft has significant market power. If they assert that breaking up Microsoft will create a deadweight loss, they must point to factors such as integration as being a major benefit to consumers.

ADDITIONAL EXERCISES FOR ASSIGNMENT

■ Questions

1. Two recently proposed mergers were WorldCom and MCI and Alcoa and Reynolds Aluminum. The WorldCom/MCI merger would have raised the Herfindahl-Hirschman Index (HHI) from 1,850 to 3,000 and the Alcoa/Reynolds Aluminum merger would have raised the HHI from 1,270 to 1,800. What do you think the Department of Justice's stance was on these mergers?

■ Answers

1. The Department of Justice challenged both mergers. The outcome was that neither merger occurred. The WorldCom/MCI decision was particularly bitter for the companies because the merger had already been approved by a few other countries!

ANSWERS TO ECONOMICS IN THE NEWS

■ The California Power Quagmire

1. The problems with California's electricity supply industry are two-fold. First, there is inadequate supply. New plants have not been built for years. With the increase in demand and no change in supply, the price of electricity was destined to rise. Second, the partial deregulation was a disaster. The existing companies were required to sell much of their power generating capacity. Then, wholesale prices were deregulated but retail prices were kept regulated. When wholesale prices soared in 2000, the companies were paying much more for electricity from independent producers than they were allowed to charge their customers. As a result, the companies rather quickly lost billions of dollars!

2. Though your students' answers will vary, many economists think that the problems stem from retaining some regulation while eliminating other regulation. Of course, it must be noted that the companies acquiesced to the partial deregulation that later did them severe harm.

USING EYE ON THE U.S ECONOMY

■ Regulating Electricity in California

Quite likely the mess in California will continue for years. If you are fortunate enough (?) to live in California, this Eye on the U.S. Economy can immediately serve as a springboard to what likely will become heated (no pun intended) discussion. Indeed, if you live virtually anywhere in the West or the East, this Eye can serve as a fascinating case study in the hazards of partial deregulation.

■ Regulatory Roller Coaster

This story clearly shows how markets change and cause regulators to view competition and efficient outcomes differently over time. You can have students discuss why prices have risen. Is it lack of regulation or demand for more channels? What kind of innovations can produce effective competition for cable firms? Why haven't satellite dish systems produced this kind of competition?

USING EYE ON THE GLOBAL ECONOMY

■ The AOL Time Warner Merger

This story highlights a merger that required approval from the Federal Trade Commission and the Federal Communications Commission. The Department of Justice did not participate in the merger decision. Even though rivals (Disney) lobbied against the merger, the FTC and FCC disagreed and allowed the merger to occur with conditions. As the story reports, part of the agreement required the new firm to make concessions guaranteeing consumer access to the Internet. Ask your students their opinions: Would they have approved this merger? Be sure to ask them to explain their answers.

Demand and Supply in Factor Markets

Chapter

16

CHAPTER OUTLINE

5. Explain how rents and natural resource prices are determined.
   A. The Market for Land (Renewable Natural Resources)
   B. Economic Rent and Opportunity Cost
   C. The Supply of a Nonrenewable Natural Resource

CHAPTER ROADMAP

■ Where We Are

In this chapter, we examine how demanders (firms) and suppliers (households) interact in competitive factor markets to determine the quantity of resources to employ. We also examine how the prices (wages, rents, interest rates) are determined in these markets.

■ Where We've Been

In previous chapters we have studied supply and demand. This chapter applies supply and demand and the model of a competitive market to factor markets.

■ Where We're Going

This chapter is the first of three that concentrate on incomes. We'll look at the labor market in more detail in Chapter 17. Then in Chapter 18, we explore economic inequality and poverty.

IN THE CLASSROOM

■ Class Time Needed

You can complete this chapter in about two sessions. Most of the material reviews concepts presented in earlier chapters and will not require a great deal of time. Two topics, the value of marginal product and economic rent, are new concepts that should take more of your time.

An estimate of the time per checkpoint is:

- 16.1 The Anatomy of Factor Markets—10 to 15 minutes
- 16.2 The Demand for a Factor of Production—25 to 40 minutes
- 16.3 Wages and Employment—20 to 35 minutes
- 16.4 Financial Markets—15 to 25 minutes
- 16.5 Land and Natural Resource Markets—20 to 30 minutes

■ Extended Lecture Outline

16.1 The Anatomy of Factor Markets

Three factors of production (labor, capital and land) are traded in **factor markets,** which are markets where the equilibrium quantities and prices (**factor prices**) are determined. A fourth factor of production, entrepreneurship, creates firms and hires the other factors.

A. Labor Markets
   1. Labor is the work effort of people.
   2. Employers and potential employees interact in the **labor market** to trade labor services. Some labor is traded on a daily basis (casual labor) but most is traded using a long-term contract, called a **job.**
   3. Human capital is an individual's skills gained through education and experience.
   4. The price of labor is the wage rate.

B. Financial Markets
   1. Capital includes buildings, machines, tools and other constructed items used to help produce goods and services.
   2. **Financial capital** is the funds used to buy and operate capital.
   3. In the **financial markets** firms are the demanders and households are the suppliers. Borrowing and lending, that is, the trading of financial capital, occurs in the financial market. The price of financial capital is expressed as an interest rate. There are two kinds of financial markets:
      a. A **stock market** is the market where stocks of companies are traded. A stock represents the owner's entitlement to a company's profits.
      b. A **bond market** is the market in which bonds issued by firms or governments are traded. A **bond** is a promise made by firms or governments that they will pay certain sums of money on specific dates.

C. Land Markets
   Land consists of all the gifts of nature including metal ores, oil, and natural gas. The price of land is called rent.
   1. **Commodity markets** are the markets in which raw materials are traded.

D. Competitive Factor Markets
   Most markets in which factors are traded are competitive, that is, there are many buyers and sellers. In other factor markets, there is an element of monopoly power.

16.2 The Demand for a Factor of Production

The demand for a factor of production is a **derived demand** because the factor's demand depends on consumer demand for the product that the factor produces.

A. Value of Marginal Product
   1. **Value of marginal product** is the value to a firm of hiring one more unit of a factor of production. The value of the marginal product equals the price of a unit of output multiplied by the factor's marginal product.
   2. The value of marginal product curve is graphed with the number of workers on the x-axis and the value of marginal product on the y-axis. The curve is downward sloping because the value of the marginal product decreases as employment increases.

B. A Firm's Demand for Labor
   1. The value of the marginal product and the wage rate determine the quantity of labor a firm demands.

     a. The value of marginal product reflects the additional revenue earned by the firm by hiring one more worker and the wage rate is the additional cost the firm incurs by hiring the additional worker.

     b. To maximize profits, a firm hires up to the point where the value of marginal product equals the wage rate.

  2. A Firm's Demand for Labor Curve

     a. A firm's demand for labor curve is also its value of marginal product curve.

     b. As the wage rate rises, a firm hires fewer workers and as the wage rate decreases, a firm hires more workers. That is, as the wage rate changes there is a change in the quantity demanded of labor or a movement along the demand curve.

  3. Changes in the Demand for Labor. The demand for labor depends on three factors. Changes in these factors will shift the demand for labor curve.

  4. The price of the firm's output. As the price of the firm's product increases, the firm demands more labor because an increase in the product's price increases the value of the marginal product. The demand curve for labor shifts rightward.

  5. The prices of other factors of production.

     a. If the price of capital increases relative to the wage rate, a firm substitutes capital for labor. The firm's demand for labor curve shifts leftward.

     b. If the decrease in the price of capital leads to a large enough increase in the scale of production, a firm might buy additional capital and hire more labor, thereby increasing the demand for labor. This change occurs in the long run.

  6. Technology. Depending on the type of technology, the demand for labor might increase or decrease. An increase in technology might decrease the demand for labor in that industry but increase the demand for labor in the industry that produces and maintains the technology.

16.3 Wages and Employment

A. The Supply of Labor

  1. A person supplies labor in order to earn an income. While the wage rate is a key factor in the amount of labor a person supplies, there are other factors as well.

  2. An individual's labor supply curve is upward sloping at lower wage rates, but eventually bends backward at high wage rates.

  3. The market labor supply curve is the summation of all labor supplied at various wage rates. The market labor supply curves for individual industries slope upward.

B. Influences on the Supply of Labor

The supply of labor depends on several factors:

  1. The Adult Population. An increase in the adult population increases the supply of labor.

  2. Preferences. As more women have chosen to work, the supply of labor has increased.

  3. Time in School and Training. As more people enroll in higher education, the supply of high-skilled labor increases and the supply of low-skilled labor decreases.

C. Labor Market Equilibrium

The labor market equilibrium determines the wage rate and the level of employment.

  1. If the wage rate exceeds the equilibrium wage rate, there is a surplus of labor and the wage rate will decrease.

  2. If the wage rate is less than the equilibrium wage rate, there is a shortage of labor and the wage rate will rise.

16.4 Financial Markets
A. The Demand for Financial Capital
   1. A firm's demand for financial capital depends on its demand for capital (goods). The quantity of capital demanded by a firm depends on the interest rate.
   2. The higher the interest rate, the smaller the quantity of capital demanded.
   3. The demand for financial capital depends on two main factors:
      a. Population growth. As the population grows, more people demand goods and services, so the demand for capital increases.
      b. Technological change. As technology advances, the demand for some types of capital increases and the demand for other types decreases (the outmoded types).
B. The Supply of Financial Capital
   People's saving is the source of the supply of financial capital.
   1. The higher the interest rate, the more people save and the greater the quantity of financial capital supplied.
   2. The supply of financial capital depends on three main factors:
      a. Population growth. As the population grows, the number of savers increases as does the supply of saving.
      b. Average income. The higher a person's income, the more he or she saves.
      c. Expected future income. If a household's expected future income is low, its saving is high. If a household's expected future income is high, its saving is low.
C. Financial Market Equilibrium and the Interest Rate
   The intersection of the demand for financial capital curve and the supply of financial capital curve determines the equilibrium interest rate and the quantity of capital.
   1. Over time, both the demand for, and supply of, capital increase, which leads to fluctuations in the interest rate.

16.5 Land and Natural Resource Markets
All natural resources, called "land," fall into two categories: renewable and nonrenewable. A **renewable natural resource** is one that can be used repeatedly. A **nonrenewable natural resource** can be used only once.
A. The Market for Land (Renewable Natural Resources)
   1. The higher the rent, the lower the quantity of land demanded.
   2. The quantity of land is fixed, so regardless of the rent, the supply of land does not change. Thus the supply of land is perfectly inelastic.
B. Economic Rent and Opportunity Cost
   1. Some human resources are so unique (like a movie star) that they also are in fixed supply.
   2. **Economic rent** is the income received by any factor of production over and above the amount required to induce its supply.
   3. Opportunity cost, as measured by the supply curve, is the amount of money required to induce a factor to be supplied.
C. The Supply of a Nonrenewable Natural Resource
   1. Over time, the quantity of a nonrenewable resource decreases, but its *known* quantity might increase as technology enables us to find more of it.
   2. Using a nonrenewable resource reduces its supply and increases its price, but as technology reveals new supply, the resource's price can fall. Recently, this latter factor has outweighed the former and resource prices have decreased.

■ Lecture Launchers

1. The bet between Julian Simon and Paul Ehrlich (presented in "Eye on the Global Economy") can be a great attention-getter. Review the theories on which each economist based his ideas. Ehrlich's contention follows Malthus' prediction that unchecked population growth would place so much pressure on the demand for nonrenewable natural resources, that prices of these resources would rise. Ehrlich has suggested that government limit population growth and resource use. Simon, on the other hand, contended that people would meet the challenge by developing more efficient ways to use these resources. He predicted that the prices of these resources would fall. To prove their points, Simon offered a bet in 1980 that the prices of five metals (copper, chrome, nickel, tin and tungsten) would fall in that decade.

   Ask your students who they think won the bet. You can make an overhead of the graph provided in the text. Reveal only the data from 1970 to 1980. Ask students which side of the bet they would take. Of course, these data show that prices are rising. Then, slowly uncover the years showing the early 1980s. All of those students supporting a decrease in prices believe they are correct! Then continue uncovering up the data through 1985 though 1989 that show prices rising. Ask students if any want to change their minds now! Finish your introduction by revealing the rest of the data and showing that while prices have changed, overall they have declined. Simon was correct and won his bet. Ehrlich refused to renew the bet for the decade of the 1990s.

■ Land Mines

1. It has been several chapters since the difference between a movement along a curve and a shift in a curve was discussed. Take the time to re-emphasize that a change in the variable on the vertical axis causes a movement along the curve but other factors will shift a curve. Point out these differences when explaining the labor, capital, and land markets.

2. The idea of economic rent versus opportunity cost can be clarified by drawing the supply curve and reminding students that the supply curve represents the (opportunity) cost of inducing a factor of production into employment. Any price paid above that cost (above the supply curve up to the market price) represents an economic rent.

ANSWERS TO CHECKPOINT EXERCISES

■ CHECKPOINT 16.1 The Anatomy of Factor Markets

The committee is using all the different types of factors. First, the committee itself is the entrepreneurship. Then, it is using labor (organizers, ticket sellers, officials, dormitory staff, cooks, builders); land (ski slopes, stadium property); and capital (stadiums, dormitories, computers, kitchen equipment).

■ CHECKPOINT 16.2 The Demand for a Factor of Production

a. The marginal product of the third worker is 16 wraps.

b. The value of the marginal product of the third worker is $64 (16 wraps × $4 per wrap).

c. Happy Joe's will hire 6 workers because the value of the marginal product of the sixth worker, $40 (= 10 wraps × $4 per wrap), equals the wage rate.

d. When Happy Joe's hires 6 workers, 90 wraps are produced.

e. If the wage rate rises to $48, Happy Joe's (who is now somewhat less happy) hires 5 workers. The value of the marginal product of the fifth worker is $48, which equals the new wage rate.

f. With the changes in productivity and the price of a wrap, Happy Joe's now hires 7 workers. The value of the marginal product of the seventh worker is equal to the marginal product, which is now 16 wraps, times the price of a wrap, which is now $3. Hence the value of the marginal product of the seventh worker is (16 wraps) × ($3 per wrap) = $48, which is equal to the wage rate.

■ CHECKPOINT 16.3 Wages and Employment

1a. If beach holidays become less popular, the demand for lifeguards will decrease and wage rates would fall.

1b. If new equipment prevents people from drowning, the demand for lifeguards would dive downward and the wage rate would similarly dive.

2. The demand for sales clerks in stores will decrease as more transactions take place via the Internet. As a result, wage rates will decrease.

3. Your students answers will vary because they likely will list different occupations. However, as a sample answer, as more people use the Internet, the sales of computers will increase. These computers will break and need repair. The demand for PC producers and repairers will increase. As more firms enter the Internet market, they will hire Web-page designers. The demand for Web-page designers will also increase. The demand for other types of workers will decrease. As more people use the Internet for news, fewer newspapers will be demanded so newspapers will lay off people. If more sales are transacted via the Internet, fewer sales clerks will be needed. Fewer customer service representatives will be needed as people use the Internet to get product information.

4. As more people go to college, the supply of low-skilled labor will decrease. If this is the only change, wages for low-skilled labor will increase. For example, garbage collectors or bus drivers might command higher wages. As the supply of high-skilled workers increases, their wages will decrease.

■ CHECKPOINT 16.4 Financial Markets

a. Lou's cost of capital is $100,000 × 0.03 = $3,000.

b. Lou needs financial capital for his equipment ($100,000) and to pay his workers. For his workers, Lou needs 50 weeks × 100 hours per week × $8 per hour = $40,000. Thus, in total, Lou needs $140,000 of financial capital.

c. With the new technology, Joe will not need the $40,000 to pay workers but will need to borrow $10,000 to buy the additional equipment. Lou now needs $110,000 of financial capital.

■ CHECKPOINT 16.5 Land and Natural Resource Markets

1. The discovery of oil off Newfoundland increased the supply of oil and has kept oil prices from rising higher than they have. The people benefiting from the discovery are the owners of the oil fields and the firms selling this oil. In addition, consumers benefit because the price of oil is lower.

2. With the increased supply, the price of water will fall in Arizona and California. Water is a renewable resource in Canada so it will not run out.

3. The increased demand for bottled water has encouraged land owners to sell the spring water produced on their land. Springs are renewable resources and will not run dry.

4. Farmers sell their land for development because they believe their return from selling the land is greater than they will receive from farming. The price offered for the land is high because the demand for land to use for development is high.

ANSWERS TO CHAPTER CHECKPOINT EXERCISES

1a. If the demand for college graduates does not increase, wages for college graduates will fall and the number employed will increase. This outcome is shown in Figure 16.1 in which the wage rate falls from W_1 to W_2 and the number employed increases from L_1 to L_2.

1b. The demand for college professors will increase. Salaries for college professors will increase as will the number of college professors.

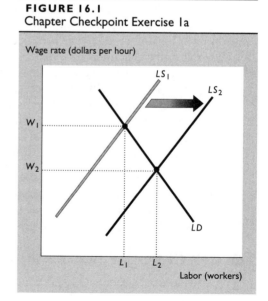

FIGURE 16.1
Chapter Checkpoint Exercise 1a

1c. The supply of high-school graduates will decrease and the supply curve will shift leftward. The wage rate will rise and the number employed will decrease, as shown in Figure 16.2 in which the wage rate rises from W_1 to W_2 and the number employed decreases from L_1 to L_2.

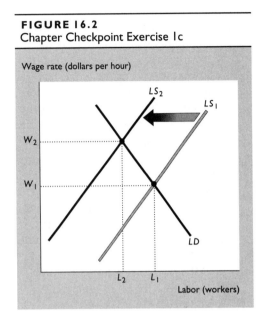

FIGURE 16.2
Chapter Checkpoint Exercise 1c

2. The demand for information technology workers will increase. If fewer classrooms, dormitories, and apartments are needed, the demand for this type of capital and land will decrease. The demand for capital that relates to the delivery of classes, such as computers, will increase.

3a. When Palm Island decides to build an airport, the demand for financial capital and land increases. The government needs the land to build the airport and needs financial capital to fund the construction. The supply of financial capital does not change nor does the supply of land.

3b. If Palm Island's population doubles, the demand for capital and land increases. People will need capital and land to build homes, and land owners will need capital to build shopping centers, hospitals, etc. The government will need more land for building roads, schools, and other new infrastructure, so its demand for financial capital will increase in order to pay for the new infrastructure. There will be an increase in the supply of financial capital as the population increases. The supply of land will not change.

3c. If the price of coconuts increases, the demand for land and financial capital increases. If people believe they can earn a higher return by growing coconuts, they will demand more land that is lying fallow or being used in a different way. In starting new farms, these people will need to borrow financial capital to fund their operations. The supply of land will not change. The supply of capital likely decreases because high prices for coconuts translate into high expected future incomes for Palm Island residents.

3d. As Palm Island encourages entrepreneurs to immigrate, the supply of, and the demand for, financial capital increases. As this is an increase in population, the demand for land increases. The supply of land does not change.

4a. The statement is probably correct. As growers substitute capital for labor, the demand for farmhands decreases. With the decrease in demand comes lower wages. The only way the statement might be incorrect would be if lower priced capital led to growers increasing the scale of their operations enough so that the demand for farmhands increased. However, it is unlikely that a lower price for tomatoes will encourage consumers to eat so many additional tomatoes that the increases in the growers' scale offsets the initial decrease in demand for pickers.

4b. The statement is false. The decrease in the demand for basketball means that the demand for basketball players will decrease. As a result, the salaries paid to basketball players will decrease.

4c. This statement is correct. The new diamond discovery in Canada reduces world diamond prices and profit opportunities for South African miners. South African mine owners will decrease mining activity and demand fewer workers because the lower price for diamonds means that the value of the marginal product of diamond workers has fallen.

4d. Assuming that fuel efficiency is the only influence changing, the statement is correct.

5. The rent in Hong Kong is higher than the rent in Chicago. The population of Hong Kong is greater than in Chicago and there is a less land available. If the price of space is too high in Hong Kong, firms have few options for substitute locations. If the price of space in Chicago rises, firms have many options for relocating. The demand for newer buildings is greater in Hong Kong than in Chicago because of population growth in Hong Kong and increases in demand for commercial space.

6. The statement is false on a couple of grounds. First, as more people buy Internet service, the price of the service will rise. (It would fall only if the supply of the service increases more than the demand increases and no change in the supply was mentioned in the question.) Second, as more people surf the Internet, businesses will increase their demand for Web pages and thereby increase their demand for Web-page designers. The increase in demand for Web-page designers will increase their wage rate, not decrease it.

ADDITIONAL EXERCISES FOR ASSIGNMENT

■ Questions

1. Have students choose a labor market with which they are familiar. They should come up with different events that affect both supply and demand. Have them draw a supply and demand diagram to show what happens to employment and wages as a result.

■ Answers

1.   Your students' answers will depend on the market they select and the events they analyze. One point to be careful about is to be sure that the students shift the correct curve for each event. In other words, if a student is analyzing an influence that changes the demand, be certain that the student shifts the demand curve and not the supply curve.

ANSWERS TO ECONOMICS IN THE NEWS

■ Expanding Nanny Industry

1.   The nanny industry is expanding because there are more households in which both parents are working. The source of expansion is mainly due to demand. There are new companies that have recognized this change and have started to offer services of training nannies or importing nannies from other countries. This entry reflects an increase in supply.

2.   Nannys' wage rates have increased because the increase in demand has outstripped any increase in supply.

3.   Becky Kavanagh believes that the demand curve has shifted rightward and that the wage rate has not increased enough to reach its new equilibrium. As a result, there is a shortage of nannies. In Figure 16.3, the demand curve has shifted rightward and the new equilibrium wage rate is W_2. If the wage rate has not increased to W_2, there will be a shortage of nannies. Although Ms. Kavanagh is in a position to know whether nanny services are able to provide enough nannies to meet demand, she might be misinterpreting the rising of the wage rate as evidence of a shortage of nannies.

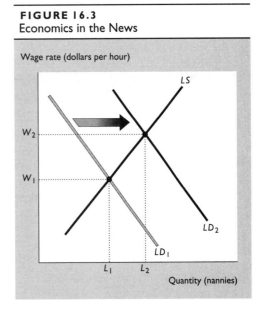

FIGURE 16.3
Economics in the News

4.   The provision of payroll services is increasing because households realize the large amount of paperwork that must be completed when a nanny is employed. In previous years, the payment of nannies occurred under the table. These nannies and their employers did not pay any Social Security taxes. As the nanny industry has gained more prominence and people formally choose to be a nanny as a profession, employers and nannies are behaving more like actual firms. As a result, households and nannies must complete all the forms that firms and employees complete. Payroll services provide this professional service.

5.   As long as the trend of two-wage earner families continues, the use of nannies and payroll services will increase.

USING EYE ON THE U.S ECONOMY

■ Reallocating Labor

You can use this story to draw labor markets for the different industries. You can draw the labor markets for several industries (say coal mining and computers) and have the student give you their opinions as to what has occurred in these labor markets. Once you have completed the graphs, use the data from the table to show whether students have correctly described what has happened in the labor market for coal miners (employment has decreased) and computers (employment has increased).

■ Interest Rate Fluctuations

This story provides information on the behavior of interest rates over the past 40 years. Make sure to explain the meaning of real interest rates. I like to remind students that if they open a savings account, the bank pays them a "nominal interest rate," say of 7 percent. Ask students how valuable their account will be at the end of the year if prices rose by 7 percent. Most students realize that they are left with no "real" gain. Explain that this difference, nominal interest rate – inflation rate, is the "real interest rate." You also can use this "Eye" to discuss the different average returns in the stock market versus the bond market as well as the different variability of these returns.

USING EYE ON THE GLOBAL ECONOMY

■ Natural Resource Prices

This story provides an interesting account of how resource markets operate. It also shows that people will respond to resources being used up because people create new technologies. The bet between Simon and Ehrlich is a fun teaching tool; see the lecture launcher for a suggestion about how you can use it in class!

Earnings Differences

Chapter 17

CHAPTER OUTLINE

CHAPTER ROADMAP

■ Where We Are

In this chapter we examine the labor market in more detail. We explore factors such as skill levels, union power, and discrimination that can account for why wages differ. We also study monopsony and comparable-worth laws.

■ Where We've Been

Chapter 16 looked at competitive factor markets and explained why the demand for a factor, say the demand for labor, is the same as the value of the marginal product. This chapter focuses on the labor marker and uses supply and demand to study it. In this chapter we use the result that the demand for labor is the same as the value of the marginal product.

■ Where We're Going

This chapter is the second of three that concentrate on incomes. Chapter 16 studied factor markets in general and this chapter focuses on the labor market. In Chapter 18 we use what we have seen in Chapters 16 and 17 to explore economic inequality and poverty.

IN THE CLASSROOM

■ Class Time Needed

This chapter's material is relatively straightforward and so you can complete it in one session. The one technical topic, monopsony, likely will require the greatest care in presentation.

An estimate of the time per checkpoint is:

- 17.1 Skill Differentials—15 to 20 minutes

- 17.2 Union-Nonunion Wage Differentials—20 to 25 minutes

- 17.3 Sex and Race Wage Differentials—15 to 20 minutes

■ Extended Lecture Outline

17.1 Skill Differentials

Differences in skills, a result of education and on-the-job training, lead to large differences in earnings. By studying a competitive labor market with two types of labor (high-skilled and low-skilled) the differences in earnings can be explained.

A. The Demand for High-Skilled and Low-Skilled Labor

　　1. High-skilled labor has a higher value of marginal product than low-skilled labor. As a result, the demand curve for high-skilled labor lies above the demand curve of low-skilled labor.

　　2. The gap between the two curves represents the value of marginal product of skill.

B. The Supply of High-Skilled and Low-Skilled Labor
   1. The acquisition of skill is considered an investment in human capital. Human capital is the accumulated skill and knowledge of people.
   2. The opportunity cost of acquiring human capital includes actual expenditures (tuition) and forgone opportunities (reduced income while attending school).
   3. Some people earn skills while working. This process is called on-the-job training. A person undergoing training usually earns a lower wage rate than a person performing a comparable job who is not training. The difference in wage rates is the cost of acquiring the skill.
   4. The high-skilled labor supply curve lies above the low-skilled labor supply curve. The vertical distance between the two curves measures the cost of acquiring the skill.
C. Wage Rates of High-Skilled and Low-Skilled Labor
   1. The wage rate for high-skilled labor is higher than the wage rate for low-skilled labor. High-skilled labor is paid a higher wage rate because:
      a. it has a higher value of marginal product than does low-skilled labor. Therefore at any given wage rate, the demand for high-skilled labor is greater than demand for low-skilled labor.
      b. skills are costly to acquire. Therefore at any given wage rate, the supply of high-skilled labor is less than the supply of low-skilled labor.
   2. The higher the value of marginal product of the skill, the larger is the vertical distance between the demand curves for high-skilled and low-skilled labor. The more costly it is to acquire skills, the larger is the vertical distance between the supply curves for high-skilled and low-skilled labor. The larger these two differences, the larger the wage differentials between high-skilled and low-skilled labor.

17.2 Union-Nonunion Wage Differentials

A. A **labor union** is an organized group of workers whose purpose it is to increase the wage rate and improve working conditions on the job.
   1. There are two types of unions:
      a. Craft unions. A craft union is a group of workers who have similar skills but work in different industries and regions.
      b. Industrial unions. An industrial union is a group of workers who have a variety of skills but work for the same company or in the same industry.
   2. Unions are organized into subunits called locals. Locals can be organized into three forms:
      a. Open shop. An open shop is an arrangement in which workers can be employed without joining the union.
      b. Closed shop. A closed shop is an arrangement in which only union members can be employed by a firm. Closed shops are illegal under the Taft-Hartley Act.
      c. Union shop. A union shop is an arrangement in which a firm can hire nonunion workers, but the workers must join the union to keep the job. Right-to-work laws, which cover 20 states, prohibit union shops and allow employees to work without joining a union.
   3. Unions engage in **collective bargaining** with firms to negotiate wages and working conditions. The union and the employer use several tools when undergoing the collective bargaining process.
      a. Strikes: a group decision to refuse to work under prevailing conditions.
      b. Lockouts: the firm's refusal to operate its plants to employ workers.

    c. Binding arbitration: When firms and unions cannot agree on wage rates or other working conditions, they can submit their disagreement to a third party that settles the disagreement.

  4. Professional associations, organized groups of professionals such as doctors, accountants and lawyers, act like unions by controlling the standards of their members and restricting entry into the professions.

B. Union's Objectives and Constraints

  1. A union aims to achieve three objectives:

    a. Increase compensation. This compensation includes wage rates, fringe benefits, retirement pay, and vacation time.

    b. Improve working conditions. A union tries to secure occupational health and safety as well as environmental safety.

    c. Expand job opportunities. To expand opportunities, the union attempts to increase its members' job security and create additional jobs.

  2. Unions face constraints on both the supply and demand side of the labor market.

    a. On the supply side, the union faces competition from nonunion workers. The greater the union's presence in the market, the easier it is for the union to achieve its objectives.

    b. On the demand side, the union faces the law of demand when it tries to increase wages. The downward-sloping demand curve shows that at higher wages, the quantity demanded of labor decreases.

C. Unions in a Competitive Labor Market.

Unions try to increase wages and increase employment by affecting supply and demand in the labor market.

  1. Unions Change the Supply of Labor

    a. Unions try to shift the labor supply curve leftward by restricting the number of workers receiving on-the-job training.

    b. By restricting supply, the union generates higher wages but decreases the quantity of labor demanded and thereby decreases employment.

  2. Unions Change the Demand for Labor

    a. Unions try to make the demand for labor less elastic. If they succeed, an increase in wages has a lesser impact on employment.

    b. Unions also attempt to increase the demand for labor by using several methods:

      i. Increasing the marginal product of union members. Unions do so by providing training and certifying workers.

      ii. Encouraging restrictions on imports. Unions encourage the government to restrict the importation of products that compete with comparable union-made goods.

      iii. Supporting minimum wage laws. By supporting minimum wage laws, unions aim to encourage firms to substitute high-skilled union labor for the low-skilled workers paid by the minimum wage.

      iv. Supporting immigration restrictions. By restricting the amount of low-skilled immigrant labor, unions act to increase the demand for its members.

      v. Increasing the demand for union-produced goods. If unions can increase the demand for these goods, firms producing these goods will employ more union members.

D. The Scale of Union-Nonunion Wage Differentials
  1. Overall, union wages are 30 percent higher than nonunion wage rates.
  2. In some cases, union wages are higher because union members perform jobs requiring higher skills.
  3. Allowing for differences in skill requirements, on the average union wages are 10 to 25 percent higher than nonunion wages.
E. Monopsony
  1. A **monopsony** is a market in which there is only one buyer, such as a labor market with only one employer. This employer unilaterally decides how much labor to hire and the wage rate. A monopsony earns a higher profit than if it had to compete with other firms for labor.
  2. A monopsony does not have a demand curve but faces a downward-sloping value of marginal product curve. To choose the profit-maximizing amount of labor, the monopsony equates the marginal cost of labor to the value of marginal product. At this quantity of labor, the monopsony pays the wage rate determined by the labor supply curve.
  3. If the monopsony didn't have its market power, it would hire more labor and pay a higher wage rate as determined by the intersection of the labor supply curve and the value of marginal product curve.
  4. The more elastic the supply of labor, the less power the monopsony has to lower the wage rate and employment. The monopsony's economic profits are also reduced.
  5. There are few monopsonies today, but there are some dominant firms in isolated communities.
  6. When a monopsony is on the demand side and a union is on the supply side of a labor market, a **bilateral monopoly** exists. The wage and employment outcome depends on which party has greater power.
F. Monopsony and the Minimum Wage
  1. In a competitive labor market, a minimum wage higher than the equilibrium wage reduces employment. In a monopsony labor market, a minimum wage can increase employment and the wage.

17.3 Sex and Race Wage Differentials

Women and minorities earn less per hour than white men. There are four possible explanations for these differences.

A. Men and women perform different jobs, and the jobs men do pay a higher wage. Data show though, that women and minorities earn lower wages than white men when they do the *same* job.
B. Discrimination is reflected in the value of marginal product.
  1. Discrimination against women and minorities results in a leftward shift in the value of marginal product curve and hence lower wage rates as well as lower employment.
  2. Discrimination in favor of white men results in a rightward shift in the value of marginal product curve leading to higher wage rates as well as increased employment.
  3. One line of economic reasoning suggests that discriminating firms operate at an economic disadvantage and therefore, firms are unlikely to discriminate. The theory suggests that by discriminating, a firm faces higher costs than those firms that do not discriminate. Higher costs are a disincentive to discriminating because the discriminating firm's profits are decreased.
C. Differences in human capital generate wage differences. Those people with more human capital (as measured by years of schooling, years of work experience, and job interruptions) earn higher

wages. White men tend to have more education and fewer job interruptions, and hence earn higher wages than women and minorities.

D. By allocating their time towards certain tasks, people acquire a degree of specialization. Those people specializing in acquiring job-related human capital earn higher wages than those people specializing in household tasks.

E. Comparable-worth laws have been passed to require equal pay for equal work.

  1. **Comparable worth** is paying the same wage for different jobs that have been judged to be comparable.

  2. Comparable-worth laws can eliminate wage differences.

  3. Comparable-worth laws result in unemployment in the industry whose wages have been raised and a shortage of labor in the industry whose wages have been lowered.

F. The most effective wage policy is one that encourages education and the accumulation of human capital.

■ Lecture Launchers

1. Students are always interested in wages and income. Play off this interest by launching your lecture using an overhead of the graph in "Eye on the U.S. Economy: Do Education and Training Pay?" Note the earnings of those people with little education and lower skills. Note the value of a college education. You can always add that success in your economics class will play a major role in these earnings! Also note how these earnings vary over age and where they peak.

   You can also mention that the text covers the most important factors that affect wages, but there are many other factors that play minor roles. For example, new research shows that "attractive people" earn more than "unattractive people." Depending on your sense of confidence (and presumably on your appearance) you can proclaim yourself to be the best paid economics professor in the state!

■ Land Mines

1. Note that the differences in the high-skilled and low-skilled labor supply and demand curves are *vertical* distances. These distances represent the value of skill and the cost of acquiring skills, respectively. That is, these are dollar values that are measured along the vertical axis. They are *not* areas nor are they horizontal distances

2. When explaining the monopsony labor market, draw on the students' intuition about monopoly. Draw the market faced by a monopoly with demand, marginal revenue, and marginal cost curves. Remind the students that the firm chooses quantity at the intersection of the marginal cost and marginal revenue curves, but sets a higher price by using the demand curve. Then tell them that the monopsony operates in a similar fashion, but on the *supply* side of the market. Because the monopsony has market power, it faces a cost of labor higher than the wage rate if it hires more labor. Why? For the analogous reason a single price monopoly's marginal revenue is less than its price. If a single-price monopoly wants to sell an

additional unit of output, it must lower the price on *all* the units of output it sells. Similarly, if a monopsony wants to hire another unit of labor, it must raise the wage it pays on *all* the labor it hires. Therefore, just as the single-price monopoly's marginal revenue curve lies below its demand curve, the monopsony's marginal cost of labor curve lies above its supply of labor curve. Then, once the monopsony chooses the profit-maximizing level of employment by equating the wage rate to the marginal cost of labor, it chooses to pay the lowest wage possible by using the labor supply curve.

3. Many students want to see how unemployment is shown in the labor market graphs. It's helpful to explain that the equilibrium wage would generate zero unemployment if there was no job search and if firms and workers had perfect information. The labor market framework does not show the dynamic nature of the market. Students tend to buy this explanation until comparable-worth laws are examined. At this point, the labor market framework *is* used to show unemployment. Remind students that this is more of a snapshot of the effects of comparable-worth laws. The "unemployment" and "shortage" shown in the graphs reflect differences in the value of marginal product and supply induced by the law. There is still additional underlying unemployment in the market due to job search, and so forth. Thus the unemployment created by comparable-worth laws can be fruitfully thought of as "extra" unemployment!

ANSWERS TO CHECKPOINT EXERCISES

■ CHECKPOINT 17.1 Skill Differentials

1a. The value of the marginal product for protective services and hence the demand for labor for protective services exceeds that of machine operators. Likely the supply of labor for protective services is less than that for machine operators. As a result of the higher demand and lower supply, people working in protective services are paid more than people working as machine operators.

1b. If the demand for labor for protective services is only slightly greater than the demand for machine operators and the supply of labor for protective services is much less than the supply of labor for machine operators, then the equilibrium quantity of machine operators will exceed that of people working in protective services.

2. The difference in pay is a result of the fact that managerial skills are in much smaller supply in Hong Kong and Malaysia. There are many low-skilled factory floor workers in Hong Kong and Malaysia. There are few high-skilled managers. As a result, the equilibrium wage rate paid the (scarce) high-skilled managers in Hong Kong and Malaysia is many times greater than the wage rate paid the (abundant) low-skilled factory floor workers.

■ CHECKPOINT 17.2 Union-Nonunion Wage Differentials

1a. If high school graduates did not have to apply for jobs through the unions, the union would have less of an opportunity to restrict the supply of labor. The supply of elevator installers and repairers would increase and their wages would decrease.

1b. If the elevator companies provided training, there definitely would be a greater supply of workers. The wage rate would fall and the number of workers employed would increase.

2. If the union succeeds in having a minimum wage of $6 being imposed, then for up to 6 workers the firm's marginal cost of labor equals $6. After 6 workers, the firm's marginal cost of labor jumps higher. But with the decrease in the marginal cost of labor for the first 6 workers, the firm will employ 6 workers. If it wants to employ more than 6 workers, it must pay a higher wage.

■ CHECKPOINT 17.3 Sex and Race Wage Differentials

a. Women golfers are not discriminated against because more people prefer to watch male golfers. Male golf tournaments draw more spectators than women's tournaments and also have higher television ratings. Male golfers hit the ball harder and farther than female golfers. Maybe spectators prefer this difference in skills. If one compares the women's tour to minor men's events (like the Nike Tour), the women's events attract more sponsorship, more spectators, higher television ratings, and higher prize money. This set of facts likely reflects the fact that female golfers have more skills than second-tier male golfers and that people prefer to watch women golfers rather than the second-tier men golfers.

b. The difference in prize money could be the result of two reasons. First, the amount of money available for prizes is a function of sponsorship fees and television revenue. Because the men's tour attracts greater sums of money, it can pay higher prize money. Second, the U.S. Open tennis tournament occurs at the same time and place for the men and women. Because of negative publicity, the tournament agreed to pay the same prize money. If the U.S. Open tennis tournament took place at different venues and times, it is likely that the prize money would not be the same. Except for the four "grand slam" events, the two tours rarely meet at the same tournament and the prize money for these separate events differs. Of the four "grand slam" events, only the U.S. Open and the Australian Open pay the same prize money. Wimbledon and the French Open pay the men more prize money.

c. If a comparable-worth law required the same prize money for only the U.S. Open, there would be little effect on the number of women golfers. Women have to qualify for the tournament and there is a specific number of spots available. If the comparable-worth law required equal prize money for *all* tournament events on the ladies' tour, there likely would be more women striving to earn a qualifying spot. And the tour would have to find sponsors willing to supply more money. As it stands now, many of these events already have trouble attracting sponsors.

ANSWERS TO CHAPTER CHECKPOINT EXERCISES

1a. The wage rate for low-skilled labor is $5 per hour and 5,000 hours of labor are employed. The amount is determined by the intersection of the labor supply and demand curves.

1b. The demand and supply curves for high-skilled workers is in Figure 17.1. The figure illustrates that the equilibrium wage rate paid high-skilled workers is $8 an hour and the quantity of employment is 6,000 hours.

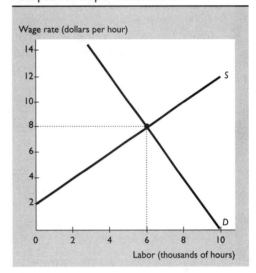

FIGURE 17.1
Chapter Checkpoint Exercise 1b

2a. If workers become unionized and limit the number of high-skilled workers to 5,000, the wage rate is $10 an hour.

2b. The wage differential between high-skilled and low-skilled workers is $5. High-skilled workers earn $10 and low-skilled workers earn $5.

3a. When the mine is a monopsony, it hires 2 workers because that is the quantity of workers that sets the marginal cost of labor equal to the value of the marginal product. The labor supply curve shows that the firm pays the workers $6.50 day.

3b. The monopsony hires 2 workers.

3c. The two workers produce 38 bags of gold.

3d. With the minimum wage of $7.50, the mine hires 3 workers. The minimum wage has increased both the wage rate paid the workers and the number of workers employed.

4. The effects depends on how the comparable-worth laws affect the wage rates in the markets. The wage rates will be equalized. It is highly unlikely that the wage rate of elevator installers and repairers will be lowered to equal that of aircraft mechanics and service technicians, but if it is there is no change in the market for airline mechanics and service technicians but there is a shortage in the market for elevator installers and repairers. If the wage rate of aircraft mechanics and service technicians is raised to equal

that of elevator installers and repairers, there is no change in the market for elevator installers and repairers but there is a surplus in the market for aircraft mechanics and service technicians. Finally, if the comparable-worth wage rate for both markets is set between the current wage rates, there will be a shortage in the market for elevator installers and repairers (because their wage rate is lowered) and a surplus in the market for aircraft mechanics and service technicians (because their wage rate is raised).

5. Your students answers will depend on the company they select. As of May, 2001, there were 17 companies on this list. Most of the companies were placed on the list for refusing to recognize a union or for refusing to pay the wage rate the union demanded. A boycott aimed at having a union recognized will increase union membership and a boycott aimed at having a contract approved will increase union members' wage rates.

6a. Your students' answers will depend on when you assign this question. A point to keep in mind when viewing these data is the state of the economy, that is, whether the economy is in, say a recession or a strong expansion.

6b. Once again, your students' answers will depend on when you assign this question. When you check their answers to this question, make sure that they are consistent with the data reported for exercise 6a. For instance, if in part (a) a student reports that the wage rate rose and employment increased, then the answer here must be that an increase in the demand for labor dominated any sort of change in supply.

7. The nations that would be the biggest suppliers of immigrants likely would be the nations in which people faced the poorest future but had sufficient funds to purchase the fare to move to other countries. These nations presumably would include a lot of Eastern Europe and nations such as India. Residents of Africa might not have the funds necessary to actually move. Many of the Central American nations would be large sources of immigrants. The nations that would attract the largest number of immigrants would be the advanced Western European nations (from Eastern Europe) and the North American nations of the United States and Canada (from Central and South America). Immigrants increase the supply of labor in the nation to which they go and decrease the supply of labor in the nation from which they leave. This effect means that wage rates in the advanced nations would tend to decrease and wage rates in the less advanced nations would tend to increase. However, some immigrants also bring capital with them, which would increase the demand for labor in the advanced nations and decrease it in the less advanced nations. This effect mitigates the first because it tends to increase the wage rates in the advanced nations and decrease them in the less advanced nations.

ADDITIONAL EXERCISES FOR ASSIGNMENT

■ Questions

1. Suppose two people graduate from medical school and residency with similar skills and abilities. One doctor takes a job in Hawaii while the other takes a job in Frozen Tundra, North Dakota. Can you use the labor supply and demand model to explain why the doctor in Hawaii earns $100,000 per year while the doctor in Frozen Tundra earns $150,000?

■ Answers

1. Looking at the supply and demand of doctors, the most likely difference is on the supply side. Very few doctors (or humans!) want to live in Frozen Tundra. But many doctors (and other people) want to live in Hawaii. Hence the supply of physician services in Hawaii is greater than the supply in Frozen Tundra. As a result, the wage rate of physicians in Hawaii will be lower than that of physicians in Frozen Tundra.

ANSWERS TO ECONOMICS IN THE NEWS

■ Wal-Mart Fights a Union

1. The wage rate for meat workers after joining the union would rise. The union could shift the supply for labor curve leftward by requiring training and thereby restricting the supply of labor.

2. Wal-Mart would be making a rational decision to close the meat department if union wages rise high enough so that Wal-Mart incurs a loss. Wal-Mart might also be closing the meat department to prevent the drive for unionization from spreading, a process that could create significantly lower profits for Wal-Mart.

3. If the workers had not joined a union and Wal-Mart was earning at least a normal profit in the meat department, it would not close the department. However, if the department was incurring an economic lose anyway, then it would be a rational decision to close the meat department.

4. Unions, similar to all monopolies, create economic inefficiency. Hence if the meat department at Wal-Mart becomes unionized, a deadweight loss will result.

5. Students will have different opinions regarding a law that prevent actions like Wal-Mart. It might be interesting, particularly if your class has some older students, to ask the students if they currently or ever have belonged to a union and then correlate their union membership with the answers to this question.

USING EYE ON THE U.S ECONOMY

■ Do Education and Training Pay?

The story provides evidence supporting how education and age are major factors in wage differences. You can also point out that people with lower levels of education not only earn lower pay initially but throughout their lifetimes. In addition, point out that, on the average, after only five years a person with a college degree will be earning more than a person with a high school degree *ever* earns! Ask your students what high school graduates will be facing upon retirement. You can remark that these data are a great inspiration for doing well in your class!

■ Union Membership

The table provides data on a variety of unions. You can review the different types of unions (craft versus industry). You also can note that unions representing service employees (state, county and municipal employees, service employees, food and commerce workers, and teachers) have a high percentage of union total membership. Does this reflect a change in the composition of output in the economy?

■ Sex and Race Earnings Differences

This chart provides data that can easily start a heated discussion in class! Make sure you point out that this data reflects a *positive* approach to wage differences as opposed to a *normative* one. You can use the graph as an introduction for this section by saying that you will be discussing reasons for these differences. After covering the material, you can elicit more discussion by asking students how well they feel economic theory explains the differences.

Inequality, Poverty, and Redistribution

Chapter 18

CHAPTER ROADMAP

■ Where We Are
In this chapter we examine economic inequality, how it is measured, and the factors that create this inequality. The government's attempts to modify the inequality by redistributing income also are reviewed.

■ Where We've Been
The last two chapters studied factor markets in general (Chapter 16) and the labor market in detail (Chapter 17). This chapter builds on those two by examining the "results" of those two chapters, that is, examining the distribution of income.

■ Where We're Going
This chapter is the last of three that concentrate on incomes. The next chapters move to international trade, international finance, and the economics of farms and cities. None of the material used in this chapter is necessary for the next three chapters, which are the concluding three in the book.

IN THE CLASSROOM

■ Class Time Needed
You can complete this chapter in one session. You might spend a little longer if you get student questions about issues such as welfare or changes in the distribution of income, but in the absence of that, likely one class session is appropriate. The single hardest issue in the chapter is the Lorenz curve, so be sure to spend adequate time discussing its construction.

An estimate of the time per checkpoint is:

- 18.1 Inequality in the United States—15 to 25 minutes
- 18.2 How Inequality Arises—10 to 15 minutes
- 18.3 Income Redistribution—15 to 20 minutes

■ Extended Lecture Outline

18.1 Inequality in the United States
A. Income and Wealth Distributions
   1. In the United States, the poorest 20 percent of the population earns 3.6 of total income while the richest 20 percent earns 49.4 percent of total income.
   2. In terms of cumulative percentages, the poorest 60 percent of households earned 27.4 of total income.

3. In terms of average incomes, the poorest 20 percent earns an average income of $9,940 and the richest 20 percent of the population earns an average of $125,401 annually.

4. Wealth is distributed more unequally than is income. The poorest 90 of households owned 29.1 of total wealth while the richest 1 percent owned 38.1 percent.

5. In terms of average wealth, the poorest 40 percent of households had an average wealth of $1,100 while the richest 1 percent had an average wealth of $10,204,000.

B. Lorenz Curves

A **Lorenz curve** plots the cumulative percentage of income (or wealth) on the y-axis in relation to the cumulative percentage of households on the x-axis.

1. If income (or wealth) is equally distributed across households, a Lorenz curve would fall along a straight line called the "line of equality." The closer the Lorenz Curve is to this line, the more equally income (or wealth) is distributed.

2. Income is distributed more equally than is wealth, so its Lorenz Curve is closer to the line of equality than is the Lorenz Curve for wealth.

C. Inequality over Time

The distribution of wealth and income has become more unequal over time.

1. Change in Income Distribution
   a. Technological change, which has increased the return to education, has enabled the richest households to make greater gains relative to the gains made by lower income groups.

2. Change in Wealth Distribution
   a. In the past 20 years, the richest 1 percent of households have increased their wealth from 34 percent to 38 percent of total wealth.
   b. This change in wealth is due, in part, to the fact that the richest households hold a larger proportion of their wealth in the stock market and the stock market's extraordinary performance until the last couple of years boosted their wealth.

D. Who Are the Rich and the Poor?

1. Education is the single largest factor in determining a household's income.

2. Other factors determining income are household size, marital status, age, race, and region of residence.

3. The lowest-income household is likely to be a black woman over 65 living alone in the South with fewer than 9 years of schooling. The richest-income household is likely to be a college-educated white married couple between 45 and 54 years old with two children living in the West.

E. Poverty

1. **Poverty** is a condition in which a household's income is too low to provide the necessary amount of food, shelter, and clothing.

2. The Social Security Administration defines the poverty level for a four-person household in 1999 to be an income of $17,029 or less.

3. Poverty rates, which vary by race, are falling for all groups in the U.S.

F. Comparing Like with Like

To compare economic status across households, a variety of standards can be used:

1. Wealth Versus Income

The distribution of wealth is more unequal than is income because wealth data include only tangible assets while income data include both tangible assets and human capital.

2. Annual or Lifetime Income and Wealth?
   a. A typical household's income changes over time. Income is low at younger ages, rises to a maximum at retirement age, and then declines.
   b. Because measures of inequality do not account for the fact that households are at different stages in their lifetimes, the degree of inequality is overstated.

18.2 How Inequality Arises

A household's income depends on three things:

A. Resource Prices

While the labor market is the largest source of income for most people, differences in wages account for only part of economic inequality.

B. Resource Endowments
   1. Differences in capital endowments account for a portion of inequality
   2. Differences in physical and mental abilities are a source of inequality.

C. Individuals' choices make the distribution of income more skewed than the distribution of abilities.
   1. Wages and the Supply of Labor
      a. As the wage rate increases, people supply more labor. This behavior causes the distribution of income to become more skewed than hourly wage rates.
      b. There are a large number of people with incomes below the average income (earning a low hourly wage rate and working a few hours) and a smaller number of people earning large incomes (earning a high hourly wage rate and working many hours).
   2. Saving and bequests can work to increase or decrease inequality. But two features of bequests raise the level of inequality:
      a. Because debts cannot be bequeathed, most people inherit a small amount of money (or nothing) and only a few households inherit large sums of money.
      b. Because people tend to marry within the same socioeconomic class, inherited wealth tends to be concentrated in a small number of households. As a result, the wealth distribution becomes more unequal.

18.3 Income Redistribution

The government redistributes income in three main ways:

A. Income Taxes

Income taxes can be progressive, regressive, or proportional.
   1. A *progressive* income tax is one that taxes incomes at a higher average rate as income increases.
   2. A *regressive* income tax taxes incomes at a lower average rate as income increases.
   3. A *proportional* income tax imposes a constant tax rate regardless of income levels.

B. Income Maintenance Programs

Three types of income maintenance programs:
   1. Social Security is a public insurance program. It requires payroll taxes be paid by both employers and employees and redistributes these payments to retired or disabled workers and their surviving spouses and children. Medicare, also funded via Social Security, provides medical care for the elderly and the poor.
   2. Unemployment compensation is paid to unemployed workers.
   3. Welfare programs are provided for people who do not qualify for Social Security or unemployment compensation.

C. Subsidized Services

The government also provides subsidized services.

1. These are services provided by the government for less than the services' costs.
2. Recipients, who might or might not be taxpayers, consume these transfers in kind from other taxpayers, who do not consume the services.
3. Examples include public education and Medicaid.

D. The Scale of Income Redistribution

The impact of these government programs can be determined by examining the Lorenz curves before and after redistribution.

1. A household's **market income** is the income earned by employing factors of production in the absence of government redistribution. A household's **money income** is market income plus money benefits received from the government.
2. Lorenz curves show money income is more equally distributed than market income.
3. The scale of distribution also can be seen in the portion of income received by households as a result of government redistribution. The poorest 20 percent of households receive 70 of their income from the government. The richest 20 percent of households receive almost nothing from the government.

E. The Big Tradeoff

Because redistribution uses scarce resources, society faces the big tradeoff between efficiency and equity.

1. Redistribution creates inefficiency because one dollar received from taxpayers results in less than one dollar being paid out to recipients due to the cost of administering the program. Additionally, taxing productive activities generates a deadweight loss.
2. Benefit recipients also face weaker incentives to work.

F. A Major Welfare Challenge

Welfare faces the challenge of promoting the long-term goal (which is to acquire human capital) without providing disincentives in the short term.

G. The **negative income tax** is a tax and redistribution scheme that guarantees each household a minimum annual income and taxes all income above this minimum amount at a fixed marginal tax rate.

1. A negative income tax provides more incentives for low-income households to work, but does not eliminate the deadweight loss generated by taxation.
2. To enact a negative income tax, the tax rate would need to be high. This large cost is one of the negative income tax's drawbacks.

■ Lecture Launchers

1. You can use the example of college tuition and subsidized services to show how the redistribution of income works. If you're teaching at a public institution, ask students what their in-state tuition is. Also ask for an out-of-state student to provide an estimate of his or her tuition fees. Ask students why the state sets up this fee structure. You can also ask students why the state is particular when deciding if a student qualifies as a state resident. By asking these questions, see if your students come around to the fact that the state is redistributing income. You can also remind students that by attending a public institution, their parents are recouping a portion of the state taxes they have paid

If you are teaching at a private institution, you can use the same exercise, but you will probably need to provide the data. You can also point out that because there is no distinction made between in-state and out-of-state fees at private schools, there is no obvious redistribution of income. (Though in many cases, the federal government provides funding to private schools and it also provides student loans.)

■ Land Mines

1. The Lorenz curve presents students with another graph to understand. Carefully go over the framework for the Lorenz curve, explaining what is meant by "cumulative percentage" and pointing out the variables on the axes. (Remind your students that unlike most of the graphs they have studied, there are no price or quantity variables on these axes.) You can select 5 class members, assign them incomes, and then calculate the Lorenz curve for these 5 members. When I do this exercise, I always make sure that my incomes add to a nice "round" number. For instance, incomes of $20,000, $30,000, $40,000, $50,000, and $60,000 give a total income of $200,000 so that it is easy to calculate both the percentage of the total each "20 percentile" group earns (10 percent, 15 percent, 20 percent, 25 percent, and 30 percent) as well as the cumulative percentages (10 percent, 25 percent, 45 percent, 70 percent, and 100 percent).

   I draw the Lorenz curve first and then point out to the students that as beautiful as it might be, we really need some sort of reference. Draw the "line of equality" by asking students questions such as "If the 'poorest' 20 percent of families (pointing at the x-axis) earned 20 percent of income (pointing at the y-axis), where would this point be plotted?" After completing this exercise for the other percentages, the students should understand the "line of equality" serving as a reference line. Point out how the actual Lorenz curve compares to the line of equality.

ANSWERS TO CHECKPOINT EXERCISES

■ CHECKPOINT 18.1 Inequality in the United States

a. Lorenz curves are in Figure 18.1.
b. Income is distributed more unequally in the United Kingdom than in the United States because the Lorenz curve for the United Kingdom is farther from the line of equality than the Lorenz curve for the United States.
c. The distribution of income is more equal in Canada than in the United Kingdom. The Canadian Lorenz is closer to the line of equality than is the Lorenz curve for the United Kingdom.

FIGURE 18.1
Checkpoint 18.1 Exercise a

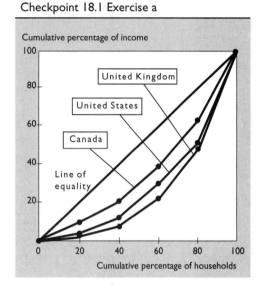

■ CHECKPOINT 18.2 How Inequality Arises

The first step in answering these questions is to calculate each worker's income by multiplying their wage rate by the hours they work per day. The results are in the table to the right.

a. The total income of all 10 workers is $2,320 so the mean daily income is $232.
b. The ratio of highest to the lowest daily income is 5 to 1 ($500 to $100).
c. The median income is $210.
d. The mode income is $210.
e. The mean exceeds the median and mode, which are equal to each other.

Name	Income (dollars per day)
Alan	100
Bill	120
Carol	120
Denise	210
Ed	210
Frank	210
Gina	210
Hal	320
Ira	320
Jen	500

f. The distribution of income is in Figure 18.2.

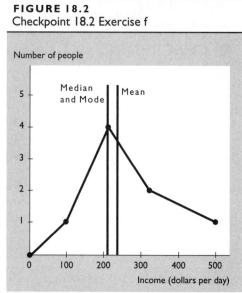

FIGURE 18.2
Checkpoint 18.2 Exercise f

Practice Problem		Exercise	
Households	**Income (percentage)**	**Households**	**Income (percentage)**
Lowest 20 percent	7.5	Lowest 20 percent	9.5
Second 20 percent	14.5	Second 20 percent	14.2
Third 20 percent	18.5	Third 20 percent	18.1
Fourth 20 percent	23.3	Fourth 20 percent	22.8
Highest 20 percent	36.1	Highest 20 percent	35.3

g. For the Lorenz curves, the above table shows the percentage of the total income earned by each 20 percentile group (which is a group of 2 workers). The cumulative percentages of income are calculated by summing the percentages in the table. The resulting Lorenz curves are plotted in Figure 18.3.

h. The distribution of income is more equal in this Exercise than in the Practice Problem. This result is immediately visible because the only difference between the two questions is that in this Exercise the lowest income individual, Alan, chose to work more than he did in the Practice Problem. Therefore Alan's income is higher in this Exercise than in the Practice Problem.

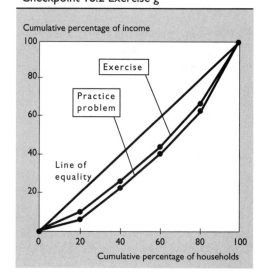

FIGURE 18.3
Checkpoint 18.2 Exercise g

■ CHECKPOINT 18.3 Income Redistribution

Households	Market income (millions of dollars)	Received from government (millions of dollars)	Tax paid (millions of dollars)	Income after negative income tax (millions of dollars)	Income (percentage)
Lowest 20 percent	5.0	4.0	1.0	8.0	8.0
Second 20 percent	10.0	4.0	2.0	12.0	12.0
Third 20 percent	18.0	4.0	3.6	18.4	18.4
Fourth 20 percent	28.0	4.0	5.6	26.4	26.4
Highest 20 percent	39.0	4.0	7.8	35.2	35.2

a. The total income for the 5 percentile groups is $100 million, so the average income is $20 million. Hence each group will receive 20 percent of the average, or $4 million. Each group pays 20 percent of its (market) income as tax. The table above shows the calculations necessary to determine each group's percentage share of the income.

b. Figure 18.4 has the Lorenz curves, both before and after the negative income tax.

c. It is likely that the negative income tax scheme has higher average income. First, the maximum marginal tax rate with the negative income tax is much lower than in the Practice Problem, which should increase high-income people's incentives to work. Second, to the extent that the negative income tax is easy to administer, so not many resources are lost in applying it, the negative income tax scheme again leads to higher average income. And, to the extent to that the benefit scheme in the Practice Problem has strong disincentives to work, once again the negative income tax likely has weaker disincentives to work and so the negative income tax (again) leads to higher average income.

d. Income is distributed more equally in the exercise than in the real U.S. economy.

FIGURE 18.4
Checkpoint 18.3 Exercise b

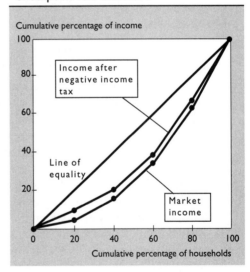

ANSWERS TO CHAPTER CHECKPOINT EXERCISES

1a. The Lorenz curve is in Figure 18.5.

1b. Income is distributed more equally in the United States. The lowest 20 percent of households have a greater percentage of the total income in the United States and the top 20 percent have a smaller percentage of total income in the United States.

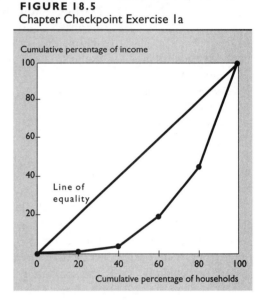

FIGURE 18.5
Chapter Checkpoint Exercise 1a

2. In this economy, each person earns $1,050,000 in lifetime earnings. They live for 70 years, so each person spends $15,000 each year.

2a. At age 45, each person earns $30,000 so income distribution is equal across all ten individuals. Because each has worked 31 years, each person has earned a cumulated income of $930,000 and has spent a cumulated total of $675,000. Therefore each person's wealth is $255,000 (= $930,000 − $675,000), so wealth is also equally distributed

2b. In terms of income, the 25, 35, and 45 year-old persons each have $30,000 incomes while the 55 and 65 year olds do not earn an income. In terms of wealth, the 25-year-old has earned income totaling $330,000 and has spent $375,000. This person has a negative wealth, −$45,000. The 35 year old has earned $630,000 and spent $525,000 and so has a wealth of $105,000. The 45-year-old has earned $930,000 and spent $675,000 and has a wealth of $255,000. The 55-year-old has earned $1,050,000 and spent $825,000 and has wealth of $225,000. The 65-year-old has also earned $1,050,000 but has spent $975,000 so has wealth equaling $75,000. Wealth is unequally distributed.

Case (a) has greater apparent equality than Case (b), but that is because in case (b) the individuals are at different stages of their life. Over their lifetimes, the individuals will be identical.

3a. From the Web page: "A living wage ordinance requires employers to pay wages that are above federal or state minimum wage levels. Only a specific set of workers are covered by living wage ordinances, usually those employed by businesses that have a contract with a city or county government or those who receive economic development subsidies from the locality. The living wage level is usually the wage a full-time worker would need to earn to support a family above the federal poverty line, ranging from 100 percent to 130 percent of the poverty measurement."

3b. The concept of a living wage is related to the concept of poverty. The living wage is an attempt to set what is essentially a minimum wage that is high enough so that the recipients' incomes exceed the poverty level.

3c. The living wage is basically a high minimum wage that applies to only a certain set of workers, in particular, workers whose employers have a connection to the government.

3d. Similar to any minimum wage, the living wage will create unemployment. It is probably not a good solution to the problem of low income because it will clearly harm some (already) low income workers who lose their jobs.

4a. The main element in President Bush's proposal is to lower federal marginal income tax rates across the board. There also are proposals to decrease the marriage tax penalty and increase the child credit. Outside of the federal income tax proposal, President Bush also proposes to (slowly) repeal the estate tax. All of the President's proposals phase in over eight years, that is, the full reduction in marginal tax rates and the repeal of the estate tax are proposed to be accomplished in 2010.

4b. The Center on Budget and Policy Priorities asserts that the majority of the tax cut will go to high income households. From their Web page, "The best estimate is that just under 39 percent of the tax cut would go to the one percent of Americans with the highest incomes. … the bottom 80 percent of the population would receive 29 percent of the tax cut." Assuming this analysis is correct (for which, keep in mind that the Center on Budget and Policy Priorities is a generally liberal think tank), the nation's after-tax income would be distributed less equally. The after-tax Lorenz curve would shift farther away from the line of equality as the after-tax income of the rich rose relative to the after-tax income of the poor.

5a. According to Dr. Siems, "Social Security is in trouble because of its basic structure and maturity as a PAYGO program." By this statement, Dr. Siems is referring to the point that Social Security is a "pay-as-you-go" program, which means that the taxes collected from workers are immediately paid to recipients and the surplus is placed into government securities. In the future, there will be far fewer workers per recipient, which creates a major problem of collecting enough tax revenue to pay promised benefits.

5b. He suggests that rather than being a pay-as-you-go program, funds collected by Social Security be invested in areas such as the stock market so that the benefits are "prefunded." Individuals would own their accounts so that Social Security would be similar to a pension plan that allows its members to invest their funds in various assets.

5c. According to Dr. Siems, the return on funds given to Social Security currently are low and going lower. It is primarily poorer retired people who rely heavily on Social Security. If investing funds in the stock market results in a higher average return and hence higher benefits, then the income of primarily poorer households would increase relative to richer households (who already are probably heavily invested in the stock market).

ADDITIONAL EXERCISES FOR ASSIGNMENT

■ Questions

Country 1		Country 2	
Households	**Income (percentage)**	**Households**	**Income (percentage)**
Lowest 20 percent	7	Lowest 20 percent	1
Second 20 percent	12	Second 20 percent	6
Third 20 percent	16	Third 20 percent	19
Fourth 20 percent	30	Fourth 20 percent	34
Highest 20 percent	35	Highest 20 percent	40

1. Based on the table above, draw Lorenz curves for the two countries. Which country exhibits greater income inequality? Why?

■ Answers

1. The Lorenz curves are in Figure 18.6. Country 1's income is more equally distributed. We can tell that Country 1's income is distributed more equally because its Lorenz curve is closer to the line of equality

FIGURE 18.6
Additional Exercise 1

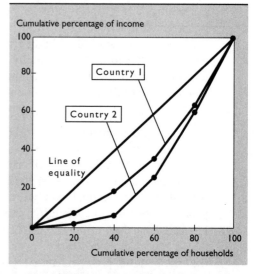

ANSWERS TO ECONOMICS IN THE NEWS

■ Income Gap of Richest and Poorest Widens

1. From the Center on Budget and Policy Priorities Web page, after-tax income of the top 1 percent of taxpayers grew 40.4 percent from 1989 to 1998 and after-tax income of the bottom 90 percent of taxpayers grew 5.2 per-

cent. One point to keep in mind when analyzing these data is that the income data include capital gains, and the soaring stock market of the late 1990s, which contributed large amounts of taxable capital gains to the richer taxpayers.

2. The report is controversial because the issue is controversial. (It is also controversial because the report is relatively polemic in nature.) Advocates for poorer Americans seize upon these reports as evidence that the government must redistribute more income toward poorer families. Other analysts assert that the report is misleading because it mixes and matches earned income and capital gains and uses IRS data that might not be as accurate as other data. Any inaccuracy might be particularly troublesome at the lower end of the income scale because many low-income Americans do not file tax returns.

3. There are at least two major problems. First, wealth comparisons omit measures of human capital, which for many workers is a large component of their wealth. Second, no measure of income or wealth inequality takes account of the fact that different families are at different positions in their life cycles.

4. According to the Center on Budget and Policy Priorities, "Over the 1990s, the average real income of high-income families grew by 15 percent, while average income remained the same for the lowest-income families and grew by less than two percent for middle-income families—not enough to make up for the decline in income during the previous decade. In two-thirds of the states, the gap in incomes between the lowest-income and the highest-income families grew over the last decade. The gap between low- and high-income families declined significantly in only three states— Alaska, Louisiana, and Tennessee."

5. Your students' answers will depend on when you assign the problem and your state.

6. To quote from the Center on Budget and Policy Priorities Web page: "The findings in this analysis provide an important context for assessing how the nation should choose to take advantage of the extraordinary opportunity that the emergence of the budget surplus offers. The Bush Administration has proposed a large tax cut package which, as other Center reports have shown, is likely to consume most if not all of the surplus that is available independent of the Social Security and Medicare trust funds. This plan would confer about 40 percent of its tax-cut benefits on the top one percent of the population and about half on the top five percent of the population. Since the top one percent receives significantly less than 40 percent of the national after-tax income, the tax package would further increase the share of after-tax income the top one percent of taxpayers receive, thereby further exacerbating income disparities."

USING EYE ON THE U.S ECONOMY

■ Consumption Inequality

This article makes a wonderful springboard to a discussion of what we are really trying to measure with our inequality measures. Ask the students what inequality measures attempt to measure. Most likely we are interested in income inequality because it leads to inequality in utility. Ask your students if perhaps inequality of consumption is a better measure of inequality of income because consumption is more directly related to utility that income. There is no single "right" answer, but the discussion should help them think more deeply about Lorenz curve measures of income and wealth inequality.

International Trade

Chapter 19

B. Nontariff Barriers
   1. How a Quota Works
   2. Health, Safety, and Other Nontariff Barriers
4. **Explain the arguments used to justify trade barriers and show why they are incorrect but also why some barriers are hard to remove.**
   A. Three Arguments for Protection
      1. The National Security Argument
      2. The Infant-Industry Argument
      3. The Dumping Argument
   B. Fatally Flawed Arguments for Protection
      1. Saves Jobs
      2. Allows Us to Compete with Cheap Foreign Labor
      3. Brings Diversity and Stability
      4. Penalizes Lax Environmental Standards
      5. Protects National Culture
      6. Prevents Rich Countries from Exploiting Developing Countries
   C. Why Is International Trade Restricted?
      1. Tariff Revenue
      2. Rent Seeking
      3. Compensating Losers

CHAPTER ROADMAP

■ Where We Are

Chapter 19 studies international trade. It answers basic questions, such as why nations engage in international trade and the role played by comparative advantage. It also studies the effects of trade barriers, tells why arguments for protectionism are flawed, and then explains why governments are motivated to impose trade barriers.

■ Where We've Been

This chapter is completely different from the last. This chapter uses the supply and demand model, developed in Chapter 4, and the production possibilities frontier, developed in Chapter 3. It also uses the idea of comparative advantage, first encountered in Chapter 3.

■ Where We're Going

The material in this chapter is used only sparingly in the international finance chapter. Essentially this chapter serves as a background for that chapter because the international finance chapter takes the presence of international trade as given.

IN THE CLASSROOM

■ Class Time Needed

The material in this chapter is not overly challenging but often students find it fascinating. International trade can lead to interesting class discussions depending on the views of your class. If you have little or no discussion, you can probably cover it in one and one half class periods. But if you have students who want to discuss some of the various reasons given for protection, it is worthwhile to spend more time, say up to two periods.

An estimate of the time per checklist topic is:

- 19.1 Trade Patterns and Trends—10 minutes
- 19.2 The Gains from International Trade—25 to 35 minutes
- 19.3 International Trade Restrictions—20 to 35 minutes
- 19.4 The Case Against Protection—20 to 40 minutes

■ Extended Lecture Outline

19.1 Trade Patterns and Trends

A. Trade in Goods
   1. Manufactured goods are 50 percent of U.S. exports and 60 percent of U.S. imports.
   2. Industrial materials are 17 percent of U.S. exports and 20 percent of U.S. imports.
   3. Agricultural products are 7 percent of U.S. exports and 3 percent of U.S. imports.

B. Trade in Services
   Vacations abroad, hotel stays, and restaurant meals in a foreign country, as well as shipping services, are among a few examples of trade in services.

C. Trends in the Volume of Trade
   In 1960, we exported around 5 percent of total output and imported around 5 percent of the goods and services we bought. In 1998, we exported 11 percent and imported 13 percent.

D. Trading Partners and Trading Blocs
   1. U.S. Trading Partners. Canada is our biggest trading partner, with Mexico and Japan being almost as large.
   2. Trading Blocs. The United States belongs to the North American Free Trade Agreement (NAFTA) and Asia-Pacific Economic Cooperation (APEC).

E. Balance of Trade and International Borrowing
   The **balance of trade** is the value of exports minus the value of imports.

19.2 The Gains from International Trade

A. Why the United States Exports Airplanes
   1. No Trade.
      With no trade, the equilibrium position is where the domestic quantity demanded is equal to the domestic quantity supplied.
   2. Trade.
      With international trade, if the world price is greater than the domestic price, U.S. manufacturers sell to foreigners and airplanes are exported.

3. Comparative Advantage

The United States has a comparative advantage because it can produce airplanes at a lower opportunity cost than can other nations.

B. Why the United States Imports T-Shirts

1. No Trade

Again the equilibrium position is where the domestic quantity demanded is equal to the domestic quantity supplied.

2. Trade

If the world price is less than the domestic price, U.S. consumers will buy from foreign producers and T-shirts are imported into the United States.

3. Comparative Advantage

The rest of the world has a comparative advantage in T-shirts because it produces them at a lower opportunity cost than they can be produced in the United States.

C. Gains from Trade and the PPF

1. Production Possibilities in the United States and China

Suppose the United States and China produce only satellites and sports shoes. Further, assume that the U.S. opportunity cost of producing 1 satellite is 10 million pairs of shoes and the Chinese opportunity cost of producing 1 satellite is 50 million pairs of shoes.

2. No Trade

With no trade, we assume the United States produces 5 satellites and 50 million shoes and China produces no shoes and 2 satellites.

3. Comparative Advantage

The United States has a comparative advantage in satellites because its opportunity cost is lower than China's opportunity cost. China has a comparative advantage in producing shoes.

4. Achieving the Gains from Trade

The United States and China can achieve the gains from trade if the United States specializes in producing satellites, China specializes in producing shoes, and the two countries trade. In this way, *both* countries can gain because *both* countries can have more satellites and more shoes.

5. Dynamic Comparative Advantage

Dynamic comparative advantage is comparative advantage that arises from learning-by-doing.

19.3 International Trade Restrictions

A. Tariffs

A **tariff** is a tax that is imposed by the importing country when an imported good crosses its international boundary. Imposing a tariff on an imported good, such as T-shirts, results in:

1. Rise in Price of a T-Shirt
2. Decrease in Purchases

The higher price results in domestic consumers decreasing the quantity they demand.

3. Increase in Domestic Production

The higher price also results in domestic producers increasing the quantity they supply.

4. Decrease in Imports

Imports decrease because consumers decrease the quantity they demand and domestic producers increase the quantity they supply.

5. Tariff Revenue

The government gains tariff revenue on the imported goods.

6. U.S. Consumers Lose

Consumers lose because they pay more than the opportunity cost and the tariff deprives them of items they are willing to buy at a price that exceeds the opportunity cost.

B. Nontariff Barriers

1. How a Quota Works

A quota is a specified maximum amount of the good that may be imported in a given period of time.

2. Health, Safety, and Other Nontariff Barriers

Detailed health, safety, and other regulations also restrict international trade.

19.4 The Case Against Protection

A. Three Arguments for Protection

1. The National Security Argument

a. A country must protect industries that produce defense equipment and armaments as well as those on which the defense industries rely for their raw materials and other intermediate inputs.

b. The problem with the argument is that it would include virtually any industry.

2. The Infant-Industry Argument

a. The **infant-industry argument** is that it is necessary to protect a new industry to enable it to grow into a mature industry that can compete in world markets.

b. However, the argument is only valid if the benefits of learning-by-doing not only accrue to the owners and workers of the firm but also spill over to other industries. Even in this case it is more efficient to help the industry by granting a subsidy to the firms in the industry.

3. The Dumping Argument

a. **Dumping** occurs when a foreign firm sells its exports at a lower price than its costs of production.

b. It is virtually impossible to detect dumping because it is hard to determine a firm's cost. And it is hard to think of a good that is produced by a natural global monopoly. Finally, if a good or service were a truly global natural monopoly, the best way to deal with it would be by regulation.

B. Fatally Flawed Arguments for Protection

1. Saves Jobs

a. The argument is that when we buy from abroad, it costs domestic jobs.

b. Free trade does cost some jobs, but it also creates other jobs because imports create jobs. And although protection does save some particular jobs, it does so at inordinate cost.

2. Allows Us to Compete with Cheap Foreign Labor

a. The argument is that protection allows domestic firms to compete with cheaper foreign labor.

b. The defect of this argument is that it ignores the fact that wages and productivity are tied together.

3. Brings Diversity and Stability

a. The analogy is made to an investment portfolio, with the idea that diversification provides stability.

b. However, the argument against it is that even economies like Saudi Arabia, which are not diversified, can benefit from specializing in the activity at which it has a comparative advantage and then investing in a wide range of other countries to bring greater stability to its income and consumption.

4. Penalizes Lax Environmental Standards
   a. Many poorer countries, such as Mexico, do not have the same environmental policies that we have and because they are willing to pollute and we are not, we cannot compete with them without tariffs.
   b. Not all poorer countries have significantly lower environmental standards than the United States. And a poor country cannot afford to be as concerned about its environment as can a rich country.

5. Protects National Culture
   a. Free trade in books, magazines, movies, and television programs would mean U.S. domination of culture.
   b. This argument is rent-seeking on the part of suppliers of books, magazines, movies, and television. Many Hollywood producers are citizens of other countries.

6. Prevents Rich Countries from Exploiting Developing Countries
   a. Free trade will mean that citizens of rich nations exploit the people in poorer nations.
   b. Free trade increases the demand for products from poorer nations and thereby increases the income of workers in those nations.

C. Why is International Trade Restricted?
   1. Tariff Revenue
      The government gains revenue from the tariffs it imposes.
   2. Rent Seeking
      Rent seekers, people attempting to profit from trade barriers, will lobby intensively to impose trade barriers.
   3. Compensating Losers
      Although the gains from trade outweigh the losses, not all the losers from free trade are compensated.

■ Lecture Launchers

1. It is easy to get caught up in all the latest trade agreements and accords like NAFTA, the WTO, and debates over fast-track negotiating authority and lose some of the most basic arguments that have been offered up for free trade. The quote that I like to recite in class is from the master himself, Adam Smith. In *The Wealth of Nations,* he had no need for fancy rhetoric and sophistry. He got right to the heart of the matter. "It is the maximum of every prudent master of a family never to make at home what it will cost him more to make than to buy . . . If a foreign country can supply us with a commodity cheaper than we ourselves can make it, better buy it of them." Presenting this Adam Smith quotation in class is important for a couple of reasons. One it forces students to understand that trade is not some abstract principle that only applies to people who live inside the beltway in Washington. It applies to the household, the business leader, and the person on the street. In addition, it allows us to focus on the true meaning of the word economics. The word economics comes from the Greek word *economicus,* which means the affairs of the household. If the economizing nature of one leading a household is virtuous then by logical extension it should apply to

neighborhoods, states, nations, and regions. And, although perhaps not every student in your class will be excited by the derivation of the word "economics," every student in your class should realize that free international trade benefits the nation.

2. I have a long-standing thought experiment that I like to present to my students when I start talking about international trade. At the beginning of class I ask them to imagine the following hypothetical situation. Assume that each student in the class is free to trade any personal belonging that he or she has brought to class. It can consist of notebooks, calculators, folders, backpacks, electronic organizers, plastic coffee mugs, or just about anything. Usually I will pick a student and ask if he or she would like to trade his or her economics textbook for my Palm Pilot or anything else of value I happen to bring to class that day. There is usually no shortage of volunteers given that most of the students in my class are there against their will (economics being part of the social science core). I ask my class not to be concerned about the market prices of the respective items but rather to focus on why the trade might take place at all. Someone will invariably point out that it has to do with the values that each person places on the trade. I'll ask the class what value the student placed on the textbook and the Palm Pilot. They will not have to respond with numbers or prices. They will simply say that the student valued the Palm Pilot more than the textbook. What about me I ask? The response is the same, only in reverse. I value the textbook more than I value the Palm Pilot. My final question is this: would the trade have taken place if either condition did not hold? The answer is a resolute no. Both parties to the trade did so because it made each better off than they were before the trade. This is fundamental to all trading arrangements. No one trades to make oneself worse off. In fact, you could argue that no one trades to make oneself just as well off as before the trade. What would be the point? Now I come in with the grand finale. I announce that when all trades are over, the classroom is better off then it was before. In fact it is wealthier than before. This usually draws a few snickers and a few "you must be kidding" remarks. I explain that society becomes better off (wealthier) whenever there is a way to rearrange the distribution of goods such that those who most highly value them are in possession of them. This observation can lead to a whole host of other discussions as well. For instance, you could ask your class if everyone in the room benefited by the same amount. The answer is no. However, you should remind the class that what is important is that on net the classroom is better off. Sum up by telling your class that this is true of international trade as well, that is, the net benefits are not equally distributed. Remind your class that this is not one of the promises of free trade. However, increasing world wealth is one of the promises and it is fulfilled.

3. In the United States, independence is one of those virtues that we just take for granted like mom, baseball, and apple pie. However, being independent has its costs. Let's take a look at two completely different nations, India and Hong Kong. Following World War II, both would have been ranked as members of the world's poorest countries. We certainly can't make the

statement now. Hong Kong has long surpassed India in economic prowess by any measurement you wish to use. Why? For many decades India isolated itself from the rest of the world (particularly following its independence from Great Britain). For sociological and political reasons, India had decided that it was going to go it alone. But going it alone exacts tremendous costs. It means that India had to produce things for itself that its neighbor might have been able to produce for half the cost or less. This also means that in the meantime it gives up the ability to specialize. Spending so much time trying to do everything makes it difficult to become good at any one task. Ironically, the act of trying to be self-sufficient and independent actually makes one worse off.

■ Land Mines

1. You might have a student (or students) in class who claim to favor not free trade but "fair trade." This phrase is not only a common refrain from those who favor free trade but it is also a common remark made by those who secretly are against free trade. You should tackle this head on in class because some students find the argument that trade should only be free if it can be fair compelling. In fact, many politicians say that the United States will bring down its tariffs, quotas, and other barriers as soon as our trading partners do. Upon closer scrutiny, it can be seen that this argument does not hold up. If you are engaging in an activity that is making you worse off, why would you want to make sure that someone else stops doing the very same thing before you will stop? It's like the person who defends high speeding on the freeway by saying "I'll stop speeding as soon as the rest of these nuts stop speeding." But if slowing down is a good thing on its own (saves lives, saves fuel, etc.), then you don't have to wait for someone else to slow down before you are able to enjoy the benefits. Free trade is no different. If one of our trading partners is able to sell products and services in our country free of trade restrictions then our consumers will be the beneficiaries. If that same country does not want to allow its own consumers to enjoy the same benefit, this refusal should have no bearing on our decision to keep the barriers down. In other words, this is an argument for unilateral free trade. The moral of the story: "beware of the wolf in sheep's clothing." The "free trade but fair trade" argument is simply a pretext for no trade.

2. Related to the above issue, another that might confront you in class is the idea that the effectiveness of free trade agreements is based on whether or not our country will be able to increase its exports. If it can't or won't then the agreement is judged a failure. But let's hold on a moment. Americans can't eat wheat we export to France, we can't enjoy personal computers we send to Singapore, and we don't get the benefits of a pharmaceutical that is sent half way around the world to South Africa! Imports on the other hand are the goods and services that our trading partner sells to us. We directly consume French wine and wear bathing suits made in Singapore and give our loved ones diamond jewelry that came from the mines of South Africa. The bottom line is that we export so that we can import, not the other way around.

ANSWERS TO CHECKPOINT EXERCISES

■ CHECKPOINT 19.1 Trade Patterns and Trends

a. In 1990, Mexico exported 14.8 percent of its total production to the United States. In 1990, Mexico imported from the United States 14.4 percent of the goods and services its citizens purchased.

b. In 1998, Mexico exported 27.4 percent of its total production to the United States. In 1998, Mexico imported from the United States 24.3 percent of the goods and services its citizens purchased.

■ CHECKPOINT 19.2 The Gains From International Trade

a. In the United States, the opportunity cost of 1 unit of food is 2 units of manufactured goods.

b. In Cuba, the opportunity cost of 1 unit of food is 2/5 of a unit of manufactured goods.

c. Cuba had a comparative advantage in producing food because it had the lower opportunity cost. As a result, Cuba can produce food by forgoing fewer manufactured goods than can the United States.

d. The United States would import from Cuba the good in which Cuba has a comparative advantage, so the United States would import food.

e. The United States will gain from this trade because it can wind up with more food and more manufactured goods. Essentially the United States will be able to buy food less expensively than it must pay to produce the food domestically and the United States will be able to sell manufactured goods for a higher price than it can receive domestically.

f. Cuba also will gain from the trade. Cuba will be able to sell food for a higher price and buy manufactured goods for a lower price.

■ CHECKPOINT 19.3 International Trade Restrictions

1a. Higher tariffs would increase the price U.S. consumers pay for toys imported from China.

1b. Because the price of Chinese imported toys rises, the quantity imported would decrease.

1c. The quantity of toys produced in the United States would increase.

1d. The U.S. government's tariff revenue likely would increase. The precise change on U.S. tariff revenue depends on the magnitude of the tariff before the change (if it was zero, tariff revenue definitely increases as long as some trade occurs) and the elasticity of demand for imported goods.

1e. The U.S. and Chinese gains from trade would definitely decrease.

2a. In restricting the amount of beef imported into the United States, the quota raises the price of beef to U.S. consumers.

2b. The quantity of beef produced in the United States increases.

2c. The U.S. and Australian gains from trade are reduced by the U.S. quota.

■ CHECKPOINT 19.4 The Case Against Protection

1. Perot's argument against the North American Free Trade Agreement was that Americans could not compete against cheap Mexican labor. What is wrong with his argument is that he failed to see that wages are tied to productivity. It is not enough for a nation to simply have lower wages. In order to compete, the nation must have lower average labor costs per unit. Perot saw American workers as being the principle losers under the agreement.

2. President Bush's argument is no different than the one proposed to support NAFTA in its original form. Extending NAFTA is a way of spreading the gains from free trade ever wider. The losers under such an arrangement would be the inefficient industries (and, in the short term, the workers within these industries) in each member country, that is those industries without a comparative advantage.

3. Hong Kong has one of the most successful economies in the world as a result of adopting unilateral free trade. Both its exports and imports increased a result. There really isn't any argument for restricted free trade that might have benefited Hong Kong.

ANSWERS TO CHAPTER CHECKPOINT EXERCISES

1a. From the U.S. *PPF,* the opportunity cost of 1 bag of coffee is 10 cars.

1b. From the Brazilian *PPF,* the opportunity cost of 1 bag of coffee is 1/50 of a car.

1c. Brazil has the comparative advantage in producing coffee because it produces coffee at a (much!) lower opportunity cost.

1d. The United States has a comparative advantage in producing cars because the United States produces cars at a lower opportunity cost. In the United States, the opportunity cost of a car is 1/10 bag of coffee and in Brazil it is 50 bags of coffee.

1e. With free trade, the United States will import coffee from Brazil and Brazil will import cars from the United States.

1f. Brazil gains from trade with the United States because now it will be able to consume at a point beyond its production possibilities frontier.

2a. Brazil produces 300 million bags of coffee per year. Half of the coffee is traded to the United States, so Brazil consumes 150 million bags of coffee. The world price of a bag of coffee is 1/25 of a car, so the world price of a car is 25 bags of coffee. Hence with the 150 million bags of coffee traded to the United States, Brazil buys 6 million cars. Figure 19.1 shows that Brazil's consumption changes from point *A* to point *B*, where Brazil consumes 150 million bags of coffee and 6 million cars. Brazil's consumption of cars *and* coffee have both increased.

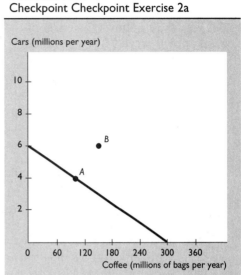

FIGURE 19.1
Checkpoint Checkpoint Exercise 2a

2b. The United States will specialize in producing cars so the United States produces 200 million cars. The United States imports 150 million bags of coffee from Brazil, so the United States will consume 150 million bags of coffee. For this coffee the United States pays Brazil 6 million cars by exporting 6 million cars to Brazil. Therefore the United States consumes 194 million cars (= 200 million produced minus 6 million exported). Figure 19.2 illustrates that the quantities of the goods the United States consumes change from point *A′* to point *B′*.

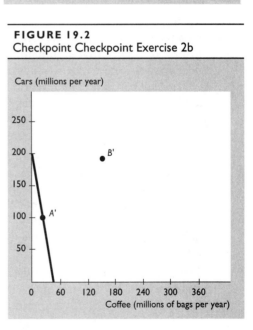

FIGURE 19.2
Checkpoint Checkpoint Exercise 2b

3a. The price of a car in Brazil will be $12,000.

3b. The quantity of cars imported into Brazil will be 20 million. At the price of $12,000, Brazilian firms will produce 60 million cars but at this price Brazilian consumers will buy 80 million cars. The difference is the number of cars imported.

3c. The quantity of cars produced in Brazil is 60 million.

3d. The government's tariff is $2,000 per car. The total tariff revenue the government collects is the number of cars imported multiplied by the $2,000 per car tariff. Therefore the government will collect ($2,000 × 20 million) = $40 billion.

4. Figure 19.3 shows the effect of the quota. The supply curve of cars becomes the curve labeled *S + quota*.

4a. As Figure 19.3 shows, the price of a car will be $11,000.

4b. The quantity of cars imported into Brazil will be the amount specified by the quota, 50 million cars per year.

4c. At the price of $11,000 a car, Figure 19.3 shows that the quantity of cars Brazilians will purchase is 90 million. Of this 90 million, 50 million are imported. Thus the remaining 40 million are produced in Brazil. The 40 million cars produced in Brazil is labeled in the figure as 40 million and is determined from the supply curve at the $11,000 price per car.

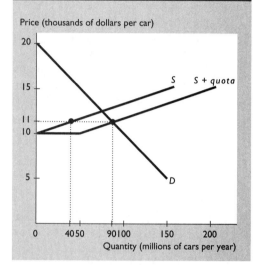

FIGURE 19.3
Checkpoint Checkpoint Exercise 4

5. Most likely the argument in favor of the tariff was the infant-industry argument. According to proponents of this argument, protection is necessary to a new industry in order to enable it to grow into a mature industry that can compete in world markets. Protection is not the best way to achieve the goal. A more efficient way to do so would be to subsidize the firms in the industry. Also note that it took the car industry approximately 50 years to grow beyond the infant stage!

6. The Canadian argument is that free trade in books, magazines, movies, and television programs means U.S. domination and the end of local culture. The argument is faulty because many of the creators of American cultural products are not Americans, but the talented citizens of other countries, ensuring the survival of their national cultural identities. The ones that really gain from the protectionism are the writers, publishers, and broadcasters in Canada.

7. The argument put forward by the New Zealand and Australian governments would be that the quota is impeding free trade. The argument put forward by the U.S. government is that it must protect its domestic industry. The U.S. government's argument is the true example of rent seeking. The beneficiaries of this quota are likely to be small in number but the benefits they receive might be quite large. However, the costs are likely to be quite diffuse as they will be spread over many more consumers.

ADDITIONAL EXERCISES FOR ASSIGNMENT

■ Questions

1. Why is it that some economists are suspicious that some of those who claim they are for "free trade but fair trade" are not really championing the cause of free trade?

2. Evaluate the following statement. "If we trade with Japan and they acquire an absolute advantage in everything because of their superior technology, then we run the risk of exporting all of our jobs."

■ Answers

1. Economists realize that those who argue for free trade but only if it is fair are, in a sense, engaged in a stall tactic. The advantages of free trade are strong enough that we have no need to wait for our trading partners to embrace it. We can lead by example and enjoy the benefits ourselves.

2. The statement ignores the fact that even if a country were to gain an absolute advantage in everything (a pretty unlikely scenario but possible) the country still would not have a comparative advantage in everything. In other words, the United States would still benefit from trade because it would still command a comparative advantage in some areas, even if by some chance it was at an absolute disadvantage in all areas.

ANSWERS TO ECONOMICS IN THE NEWS

■ At Loggerheads

1. The benefits of free trade between Canada and the United States will be increased production and lower prices. Without protection, the countries will have to face their comparative advantage. The one with the lower opportunity cost in the production of lumber, presumably Canada, will be the more successful producer.

2. American producers want to limit Canadian imports to decrease the supply of lumber. As a result, the price of lumber increases and American producers earn higher profits.

3. The American lumber producers benefit from the limits. They earn higher profits because they gain monopoly power and can raise the price of their product. The losers are the Canadian producers who are unable to sell their product and American consumers. Output of lumber has been reduced, and as a result, the consumers must pay a higher price.

USING EYE ON THE PAST

■   The History of the U.S. Tariff

The story presents an interesting history of tariff rates in the U.S. Start off by reviewing what is meant by the "average tariff rate." Note that the Smoot-Hawley tariff did not tax imports at 100 percent, but somewhere between 50 percent to 60 percent. It is interesting to note that the Smoot-Hawley tariff (the first tariff shown) and the latest trade meetings (organized by the WTO) both generated controversy!

Economists still disagree over the role the Smoot-Hawley tariff played in the depression. Some claim the tariff caused it, others say it exacerbated it, while others contend it played little if any role. Today, people from around the world greet any meeting of the WTO with solid protests. But for different reasons than those against Smoot-Hawley. Can you imagine people in the 1930s protesting human rights or the environment?

USING EYE ON THE GLOBAL ECONOMY

■   The Major Items That We Trade with Other Nations

Similar to the previous "Eye on the Global Economy," this "eye" clearly highlights U.S. trade behavior. You can make an overhead of the graph and block out the categories on the left-hand side. Have students guess what they think these large categories are. Will their first guess be oil or cars? Have them pick out the goods in which the U.S. has a trade surplus.

You can also discuss the role that services play in the trade volume. Ask them what they think has happened to the trade in services over the last few years. Point out that until the last decade, services were not even counted in these calculations. The WTO has discussed the problems faced when trying to calculate the volume of trade in services. One interesting item is "royalties and licensing fees." This fee represents payments to firms for use of their intellectual property including trademarks, technologies, and entertainment.

■   The Major U.S. Trading Partners and Volumes of Trade

The information here is a real jewel. Before I even ask my students to read the international trade chapter, I will often ask them to write their own list of the top three trading partners. When we are through, I ask them to open their texts and take a look at the actual list. What is most surprising to students is that China ranks only fourth on the list. In fact, China is not even one of our most important trading partners when it comes to sheer volume of exports. There are ten other countries to whom we export more than to China. Explain to your students that China has receives a disproportionate share of media attention when it comes to free trade and free trade agreements.

■ Competing with Low-Wage Nations

You can ask students why would New Balance continue to make shoes in the United States? In fact, New Balance challenged the Federal Trade Commission (and lost) for the right to place "Made in the U.S.A." labels in their shoes. The FTC ruled against New Balance because about 30 percent of the materials in the shoe are produced overseas. The very fact that New Balance is able to survive in the industry at all in spite of the cost differential between their processes and those of China suggest that something else is going on. Ask your students if New Balance has some form of hidden comparative advantage that is not immediately apparent. You can also ask your students how much more they would be willing to pay for shoes "that save U.S. jobs."

Chapter 20

Farms and Cities

3. **Explain why cities grow and evaluate tolls as a way of achieving an efficient use of roads.**
   A. Basics
      1. External Production Benefits
      2. External Consumption Benefits
   B. Urban Sprawl
      1. A Model of a City: The Basic Idea
      2. The Demand for Urban Land
      3. The Supply of Urban Land
      4. The Equilibrium Size of the City
      5. Why Cities Grow
      6. Qualifications and Modifications to the Basic Model
      7. Environmental Externalities and City Size
   C. Traffic Congestion
      1. Using Tolls to Achieve Efficient Road Use

CHAPTER ROADMAP

■ Where We Are

This chapter studies issues facing farmers and U.S. farm programs as well as issues facing urban city dwellers. Essentially this chapter applies to farms and cities aspects of the microeconomic theory that has been presented in the previous sections of the book.

■ Where We've Been

Chapter 20 does looks at a topic very different that the immediate predecessor, which studied international trade. But, as in the previous chapter, supply and demand continues to pay an important role in the analysis. In addition, this chapter also relies upon two other topics from previous chapters. The first is elasticity, which was examined in Chapter 5. The second is the theory of costs and how costs influence competitive firms' behavior, which were presented in Chapters 11 and 12.

■ Where We're Going

The next chapter returns to the area of international economics by studying international finance. It uses nothing from this chapter. Chapter 21 takes the fact that nations trade as a given, so it relies upon little from Chapter 19. The main tool of analysis used from previous chapters is the supply and demand model.

IN THE CLASSROOM

■ Class Time Needed

You can complete this chapter in one and one half to two and one half class sessions.

An estimate of the time per checkpoint is:

- 20.1 Incomes and Prices of Farm Products—30 to 45 minutes
- 20.2 Government Policy in Agriculture—30 to 45 minutes
- 20.3 The Economics of Cities—30 to 50 minutes

■ Extended Lecture Outline

20.1 Incomes and Prices of Farm Products

Changes in the supply and demand of agricultural products, combined with inelastic supply and inelastic demand, contribute to fluctuations in farm income and prices.

A. Output Fluctuations in an Agricultural Market

The supply of farm products is inelastic because once harvested, the crop's supply cannot be changed. As a result, as demand changes, total revenue changes drastically.

1. Normal Harvest.

a. Under normal conditions, farmers earn a normal profit that allows farmers to cover their opportunity cost.

2. Poor Harvest

a. If there is a poor harvest, supply decreases and the supply curve shifts leftward. The result is a higher price and an *increase* in total revenue.

b. Farmers who did not lose their crop earn an economic profit (total revenue exceeds opportunity cost). Farmers who lost their crops incur an economic loss.

3. Bumper Harvest

a. If there is a large harvest, supply increases and the supply curve shifts rightward. The result is a lower price and a *decrease* in total revenue.

b. Farmers' total revenue decreases and they incur an economic loss (total revenue is less than opportunity cost).

B. Inelastic Demand

1. The fact that farm revenue increases when supply decreases and farm revenue decreases when supply increases reflects the *total revenue test* and is the outcome of the inelastic demand for farm products.

2. The elasticity of demand for agricultural products ranges from 0.2 to 0.4. Demand is inelastic because there are few substitutes for food. As a result, when the prices of agricultural products change, demand responds very little.

C. Demand Fluctuations in an Agricultural Market

1. Normal Year

a. During a normal year, farmers earn a normal profit. Total revenue covers the opportunity cost of production.

2. Low Demand

a. If the economy slows and incomes fall, demand for agricultural products decreases and the demand curve shifts leftward. The price decreases.

      b. Total revenue decreases and farmers incur an economic loss (total revenue is less than opportunity cost).

  3. High Demand

      a. If the economy expands and incomes increase, demand for agricultural products increases and the demand curve shifts rightward. The price increases.

      b. Total revenue increases and farmers earn an economic profit (total revenue exceeds opportunity cost).

D. Inelastic Demand and Inelastic Supply

  1. A change in demand causes a large change in price because demand is inelastic and supply is perfectly inelastic (once a crop is harvested).

  2. Specifically, when demand changes, the price must change by a large amount to bring about market equilibrium (because supply cannot change). As a result, total revenue also changes by a large amount.

E. Falling Prices of Farm Products

Prices of farm products have decreased while farm output has increased over the last 50 years as a result of:

  1. Increase in Demand

      a. Population Growth: Both the U.S. and world populations have risen, which leads to an increase in the demand for farm products. Population growth increases the demand for food by about 1 percent per year.

      b. Both U.S. and world incomes have increased. The income elasticity for food is positive, which means that as incomes increase, people's demand for food increases. Income growth increases the demand for food by about 1.4 percent per year.

      c. Combined, increases in population and income have doubled the demand for food in the last 50 years.

  2. An Even Greater Increase in Supply

      a. The supply of farm products has increased as a result of improved technology and productivity growth. These improvements include seed, fertilizers, and equipment.

      b. Supply has increased by about 360 percent in the last 50 years.

  3. Supply, Demand, Price, and Quantity

      a. The increases in supply and demand have generated large increases in output while prices have dropped dramatically since 1950.

      b. The number of individual farms have fallen by about 50 percent. Output on the remaining farms has increased.

F. Down on the Farm

  1. Technology has increased the amount of farm output for a given amount of inputs.

  2. Increases in capital intensity have lowered average total cost at high output levels, encouraging the survival of large farms.

20.2 Government Policy in Agriculture

The U.S. government attempts to stabilize farm income using two practices: price supports and production flexibility contracts.

A. How Price Supports Work

  1. The **price support system** is a system in which the government sets a price for a good and then buys any surplus product a farmer can't sell in the market at the support price.

2. The price set by the government is higher than the equilibrium price. As a result, the profit-maximizing level of output produced by farmers exceeds the quantity demanded. The price support generates a surplus that must be purchased by the government.

3. Farm incomes increase because farmers receive a higher price per unit and produce a higher level of output.

4. Consumers lose because they pay a higher price for a lower quantity of output.

B. Inefficiency of Price Supports

1. Price supports create inefficiency because farmers overproduce (compared to the competitive equilibrium), and the marginal cost of production exceeds the marginal benefit.

2. The inefficiency's cost can be divided into three parts:

   a. The farmers' gain in revenue from increased output can only occur with increased costs.

   b. Consumers and taxpayers lose because their expenditures on food and their taxes increase. They consume less food.

   c. Society loses because the gain to farmers is less than the loss to consumers. This difference (a *deadweight loss*) equals the increase in farms' total costs. This deadweight loss is greater than the typical deadweight loss of overproduction, because with price supports, no one gets to consume the overproduction.

C. Production Flexibility Contracts

1. **Production flexibility contracts** provides farmers with a support payment from the government based on the acreage covered by the contract and not on the amount of production. These contracts are part of the 1996 Federal Agriculture Improvement and Reform Act. They replaced price supports for most farm products except dairy products, peanuts, and sugar.

2. Production flexibility contracts provide farmers with increased income without affecting efficient levels of price and quantity.

3. The contracts do not generate the social losses created by price supports.

D. Farm Subsidies and International Trade

1. Because they subsidize farms, most countries contribute to depressed farm prices and inefficient world trade.

2. By restricting imports of lower-priced products (through quotas), the governments can maintain their price supports.

3. Additionally, these quotas (which increase domestic production and surpluses) cause an increase in exports, thereby lowering prices and farm incomes in other countries.

4. Overall, worldwide farm subsidies inefficiently allocate food production, lower world prices, and produce an oversupply of food.

20.3 The Economics of Cities

A. Basics

People live in cities because city living provides two things:

1. External Production Benefits. By living in densely populated areas, people are more productive and generate group output that is greater than the sum of the individual outputs if people lived farther apart.

2. External Consumption Benefits. Large cities, with their bigger markets, can provide services that smaller cities cannot. Firms that could not earn a profit in smaller towns can do so in large cities.

3. Cities also generate economic problems: urban sprawl and traffic congestion.

B. Urban Sprawl

City sizes are limited by natural physical features (oceans, rivers, mountains), adequate water supply, and economic factors (supply and demand).

1. A Model of a City: The Basic Idea
   a. Edwin Mills, a distinguished economist, uses supply and demand to explain a city's geographical spread and its land prices.
   a. By modeling a city as a circle, land values and rents depend *only* on the distance from the city's center.
   b. The highest valued land lies at the center. Moving farther away, rents and land values decrease.

2. The Demand for Urban Land
   a. Mill's circular model of the city creates a diagram that places the distance from the city center on the *x*-axis and the price of land on the *y*-axis.
   b. The model produces a downward-sloping demand curve for land because as the land is further away from the city center, people are willing to pay less for the land. The increasing cost of transportation moving farther from the center is the main reason for the decrease in land's value.

3. The Supply of Urban Land
   a. The supply of land is perfectly inelastic because the quantity is fixed at each distance from the city center.
   b. Land can be used either for the city or for farmland. The value of land used for farming is a constant amount that does not depend on its distance from the city center.

4. The Equilibrium Size of the City
   a. Land is allocated to its highest valued use. Land that is more highly valued as farmland is used for farming. Land that is more highly valued in urban use is used as part of the city.
   b. City size is determined by the intersection of the supply and demand curves (where the land has the same value whether it is used for farming or for urban use).

5. Why Cities Grow
   a. Technological change (cheaper cars, improved freeways, public transit) spurs cities' growth by allowing people to move further from the city center. This change means that the demand curve for urban land shifts rightward.
   b. Technological change also decreases the value of farmland and so the size of the city increases.

6. Qualifications and Modifications to the Basic Model
   a. Realism can be added to the model by adding highways, rail lines, suburban centers, and satellite cities.

7. Environmental Externalities and City Size
   a. If left unchecked, market forces might allow cities to grow too large so that inefficiencies occur. These inefficiencies include pollution, too little recreational land, and traffic congestion.
   b. To counter these inefficiencies, cities enact land use regulations and zoning laws.

C. Traffic Congestion
   1. Roads become congested because people do not account for the congestion they add to roads when they decide to drive.

2. As individuals, people decide whether to drive by equating the marginal benefit of taking a trip to the marginal private cost (*MC*) of taking the trip.
3. There are additional costs generated by a single driver taking to the road: The greater the number of drivers, the more congestion and the longer a trip takes, so the higher the costs.
4. The marginal social cost (*MSC*) curve reflects these additional costs and lies above the *MC* curve. The efficient use of roads is determined by the intersection of the *MSC* curve and the marginal benefit curve.
5. Because the *MC* does not reflect the total effect of an individual's driving, roads are overused. Congestion occurs and generates a deadweight loss.
6. To achieve efficient road use, people must take into account the cost their trips impose on society.
   a. Governments can impose tolls to produce the efficient number of vehicle trips.
   b. The toll increases the marginal private cost and reduces congestion to the efficient level, that is, the toll reduces but does not eliminate congestion.

■ Lecture Launchers

1. Unless you live in a rural community, most people rarely think of farmers and farming. You can use this fact to point out how efficiently the food distribution systems work in the United States. Food is vital to life—people can live without electricity, without entertainment, and without fancy clothing, but no one can live without food. Mention to your class that one might presume that because food is so vital the government heavily intervenes in the food distribution systems to insure that everyone gets adequate high-quality food. But in reality, government intervention in food distribution is not significantly heavier than in other markets and, indeed, is much less than in some markets such as health care. Clearly the government does intervene in the food industry—the text covers farm programs, and there are other government programs designed to inspect food as well as the food stamp program designed to help people buy food. But the amount of government involvement in the distribution of food is not especially heavy, particularly when compared to the distribution of health care and education! The fact that food finds its way to the shelves and then to our stomachs without immense government involvement is a compelling real-world example of how the price system works.

■ Land Mines

1. It has been several chapters since elasticity was discussed. When showing how farm prices and revenue change, review why an inelastic demand generates large changes in equilibrium price and total revenue. An easy method to use is to draw a relatively steep demand curve and let the supply curve shift rightward. Use explicit numbers for the price and quantities so that you can calculate the total revenue. By using the total revenue test, you can show that with this steep demand curve, a price increase leads to an increase in total revenue.
2. As part of the review of elasticity, it is important to review *why* the supply and demand are inelastic. For the supply, explain that once a crop is har-

vested, the supply is fixed regardless of how high the price rises. You can emphasize this point by drawing a vertical supply curve and asking your students how much corn (or whatever good you use) the farmer sells when the price is $10 per bushel. Then move your finger up the supply curve. Now ask how much corn the farmer supplies when the price reaches $20 per bushel (and so on). The point is that the supply does not change. The farmer cannot supply any more corn no matter how high the price rises.

You can do a similar exercise to explain demand. Remind students that because there are few substitutes for food, the demand is inelastic.

3. The chapter also provides a good chance to review cost curves and how technology reduces costs and shifts the cost curves downward. Because these technology advances increased capital intensity and fixed costs (with smaller changes in labor costs), today's farms must be larger than they were 50 years ago in order for farmers to earn normal profits. Because many students have never lived on farms, they are unaware of the technological improvements impacting farms. Harvesting machines can now pick most crops without any use of labor beyond a driver. Fertilizers and drought resistant crops have greatly improved the productivity of land. Global positioning satellite systems have improved land use and crop rotation.

4. You can finish the chapter by discussing how the government deals with congestion by imposing tolls. Students should be able to determine that an efficient toll will generate an efficient number of vehicles. They should be able to see that this toll shifts the MC curve upward so that the curve goes through the efficient quantity equilibrium. If you're in a city with bad traffic congestion or you have students from these cities, you can ask students how much they would be willing to pay to be able to freely drive to campus or work.

ANSWERS TO CHECKPOINT EXERCISES

■ CHECKPOINT 20.1 Incomes and Prices of Farm Products

a. The equilibrium price in a normal year is $7 per ton, so farm total revenue is $700 million.

b. With a bumper crop of 104 million tons, price falls to $5 per ton and farm total revenue falls to $520 million.

c. With a poor crop of 96 million tons, price rises to $9 per ton and farm total revenue rises to $864 million.

d. With a boom in demand and normal supply, price rises to $9 per ton and farm total revenue rises to $900 million.

e. With a slump in demand and normal supply, price falls to $5 per ton and farm total revenue falls to $500 million.

■ CHECKPOINT 20.2 Government Policy in Agriculture

1a. The quantity of rice produced is 36 tons and the quantity of rice consumed is 30 tons.

1b. The government buys 6 tons of rice.

1c. The consumer-taxpayer spends $180 million for 30 million tons compared to $136 million for 34 million.

1d. There is a deadweight loss created by the price support system because farmers use resources to produce rice that consumers don't want to buy. There is rice produced for which the marginal benefit is less than the marginal cost.

2. There is not enough information to determine if farmers prefer the flexible production contract. With the price supports, farmers' total revenue is $180 million for producing 36 tons of rice. With the flexible production contract, farmers' total revenue is $162 million for producing 34 tons of rice. Presuming that the marginal 2 tons of rice beyond 34 tons aren't extremely costly, farmers would prefer the flexible production contract, but this preference is based upon an assumption about the marginal cost. (Consumer-taxpayers definitely prefer the flexible production contract because they pay less to consume more rice.)

■ CHECKPOINT 20.3 The Economics of Cities

1a. Figure 20.1 shows the new demand curve. Based on the figure, the limits of Concentric City extend 35 miles.

1b. The price of an acre at the city's center is $14,000 per acre.

1c. Once again based on Figure 20.1, the price of an acre 5 miles from the city's center is $11,000 per acre.

2a. The problems confronting the city include congestion and pollution. The city's limits need to expand but the surrounding land has great value left in its natural state because it attracts hikers, campers and tourists.

2b. The city can impose pollution limits to keep the environment clean. To limit congestion and encroachment on natural areas, the city can enact a building moratorium or charge impact fees (extra fees developers must pay in order to develop land for building). These impact fees could try to capture the value of the land when it used for recreational use and thereby effectively increase the price of farm land and thus decrease the equilibrium size of the city. In some cities that want to preserve natural areas, urban planners are hired to develop a comprehensive land plan that integrates all of the community's needs.

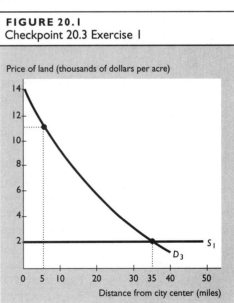

FIGURE 20.1
Checkpoint 20.3 Exercise 1

ANSWERS TO CHAPTER CHECKPOINT EXERCISES

1a. A small change in supply creates a large (and opposite) change in price and total revenue because demand is inelastic. Demand is inelastic because there are few substitutes for most food items. As a result, when the price of a food product increases, consumers do not decrease the quantity they demand very much. As a result, farmers' total revenues increase.

This situation is illustrated in Figure 20.2. In it, the small decrease in supply from S_0 to S_1 results in a price hike from $3.00 per bushel to $5.00 per bushel and farmers' total revenue increases from $150 billion to $200 billion. The supply has shifted because there has been a change (a decrease) in supply. However, the demand has not changed. Instead, there has been a change in the quantity demanded, which is reflected in a movement along the demand curve in Figure 20.2.

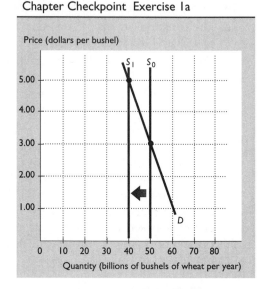

FIGURE 20.2
Chapter Checkpoint Exercise 1a

1b. A small change in demand creates a large change in price and total revenue because supply is perfectly inelastic. Once a crop is harvested, supply is fixed. As a result, if the demand for a product increases (which means the demand curve shifts rightward), there is no increase in the quantity supplied (there is a movement upward along the supply curve but because the supply curve is vertical, the quantity supplied does not change) and total revenue increases because the price rises, though the quantity does not change.

This situation is illustrated in Figure 20.3. In this figure, demand increases so the demand curve shifts rightward from D_0 to D_1. The supply is perfectly inelastic, so the price soars from $3.00 a bushel to $5.00 a bushel. The farmers' total revenue skyrockets from $120 billion to $200 billion.

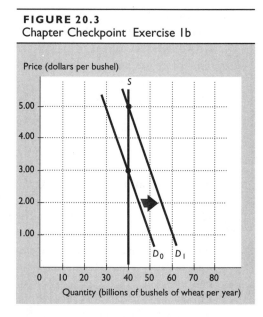

FIGURE 20.3
Chapter Checkpoint Exercise 1b

2. The main sources of falling farm prices are increases in technology that allow farmers to use capital more intensively, hire fewer workers, and increase their supply of farm products. Increases in productivity (for instance, improved seeds that are drought and pest resistant as well as improved fertilizers) allow more output per acre. Falling prices have brought exit

from farming. There are fewer farmers, but larger farms. Greater capital intensity has required farms to be larger in order to spread increased fixed costs across a larger output.

3a. In a normal year a price support system would not affect incomes, prices, production, consumer surplus, or taxes. There would be no deadweight loss created. Basically, the price support system would have no effect.

3b. In a year with a bumper harvest, the price support system has an effect. The equilibrium price with a bumper harvest is below the supported price. As a result, the price equals the higher, support price. Compared to the situation without the support price, farmers' incomes are higher, production is higher, consumer surplus is lower, taxes are higher, and a deadweight loss is created with a price support. (Production likely will be higher because farmers know at least some time before harvesting their crop if a year will have a bumper harvest and, in the absence of the higher price support, some farmers would decide that the expected low price warrants harvesting only part or none of their crop. With the support price, all the crop will be harvested.)

3c. In a year with a poor harvest, the market price increases compared to a normal year. As a result, a price support system has no effect because its price is less than the equilibrium price. Hence there is no effect on farmers' incomes, prices, production, consumer surplus, taxes. There is no deadweight loss created.

4a. Trade in tomatoes is not totally free, but barriers are small and being removed. With NAFTA, some tariff barriers to Mexican tomatoes were removed by 1998, and the remaining barriers are scheduled to be removed by 2003. Mexican tomatoes are subject to a minimum price that must be charged. Canadian barriers are currently zero, but until 2008 there is the chance they might recur depending on the amount of tomatoes imported from Canada. Cherry tomatoes have no barriers.

4b. The United States imports tomatoes from Mexico (83 percent of imports), Canada (9 percent of imports), and the Netherlands (3 percent of imports).

4c. As more tomatoes have been imported into the United States, the price of tomatoes has fallen from what it otherwise would have been. If U.S. growers had a price support, the government would either need to purchase more U.S. tomatoes in order to keep the price of U.S. tomatoes at the support price or else would need to lower the price support.

5a. The U.S. Sugar Beet Web's page asserts: "According to a report by Landell Mills Commodities Studies, Oxford, England, sugar producers in the United States are among the most efficient in the world. Out of 96 sugar-producing countries, the United States ranks 18th lowest cost in overall sugar production. When corn sweeteners are added and the U.S. gets half of its nutritive sweetener from corn the United States ranks an impressive 12th lowest cost out of 112 producing countries." The problem with this analysis is that it does not mean that the United States has the most efficient industry. Indeed, it indicates that the United States does *not* have the most efficient industry because, insofar as one takes the report commissioned by the sugar industry at face value, there are at least 11 nations with lower costs of sugar production than the United States.

5b. According to "The Waste Basket's" Web page, taxpayers will need to "fork out more than $1 billion to prop up a wasteful and failing U.S. sugar program." In the middle of 2000, the USDA estimated that it would spend $140 million in 2000 to "bail out the sugar industry."

5c. If sugar producers were supported using flexible production contracts, the U.S. price of sugar would be substantially lower because, presumably, the United States would allow imports of sugar. The sugar market would move closer to efficiency.

6a. The thrusts of the article is that urban "sprawl" is occurring at a much lower rate than typically believed, that such suburbanization is not harmful, and is what people desire. A further thrust of the article is that government planning to limit suburbanization is not the solution to any problem that might exist.

6b. Whether the student agrees or disagrees depends on the student. One point that likely should be made is the general tenor of the article is in line with the model of the equilibrium size of the city developed in the chapter. The other point that might be made is that the author sees very few, if any, externalities from growth in city size.

6c. If urban sprawl is a problem because of external costs, the first step in the solution is to precisely define the costs. Determine if the externalities can be eliminated by assigning property rights. If not, can user fees be instituted so that the creator of the external cost bears the entire cost of his or her action?

7a. Singapore has developed an extensive system of public transportation. But it has also limited private ownership of vehicles by establishing very high taxes and tariffs on cars and also requiring that drivers purchase expensive "certificates of entitlement" in order to own a car. Singapore cuts the costs of car ownership for drivers who drive only on weekends and in the evenings. Hence the demand for roads during peak congestion hours is reduced. For very high-demand areas, namely the central business districts, Singapore requires that the driver have a license to enter the area (the "Area Licensing Scheme" or ALS). Currently, Singapore is pricing other congested areas (such as expressways). Some of the older methods used licenses, such as the ALS. However, electronic road pricing (ERP) is coming into use. With ERP, a driver will have essentially a debit card displayed on the window and when the driver approaches an area controlled by ERP, the system will automatically detect the card and then deduct the price of driving in the area.

7b. Whether the student thinks the ideas are good or not as well as whether they are needed in the United States is the student's opinion. I suspect most people would have doubts that extremely high taxes on cars are politically viable in the United States. The ERP program might prove more acceptable.

8. HOT lanes (High-Occupancy Toll) are lanes that allow drivers to pay a toll to bypass congested freeways. These are sometimes called "Lexus lanes"

because of the (somewhat unfounded) belief that only the rich will use these lanes. The tolls charged for the HOT lanes can vary according to the time of day.

ADDITIONAL EXERCISES FOR ASSIGNMENT

■ Questions

1. Some sugar producers argue that if price supports were eliminated sugar prices would increase, not decrease, in the long run. They assert that without price supports, in the short run the price would temporarily fall but the lower price would lead sugar farms to shut down. As a result of the decrease in supply, the price rises and so in the long run the price of sugar is higher without the supports. This argument is flawed—expose the flaw.

■ Answers

1. The elimination of price supports would mean a sharp drop in sugar prices received by farmers. Many farmers would see prices fall below their cost of production. As this occurred, some farmers would go out of business, which would lead to a decrease in the supply of sugar. The decrease in supply will, indeed, drive up the price from the depths encountered immediately after the price supports are removed. But it will not drive up the price so much that the price exceeds the support price. At the support price, sugar producers are earning large profits. If the price (somehow) reached this level, new producers would quickly enter the market to earn some of the high profit and would thereby push the price downward to its new equilibrium level, which must lie below the support price. The price cannot rise so much that in the long run it is above the support price. Consumers will gain from a lower price in both the short run and the long run.

ANSWERS TO ECONOMICS IN THE NEWS

■ End Sugar Subsidies

1. The U.S. government protects U.S. sugar producers by severely limiting the amount of sugar that may be imported into the United States. In addition, the United States also guarantees loans to sugar producers that effectively serve as a price support for the price of sugar because if the producer decides not to repay the loan in money, the producer can repay the loan by giving the government sugar at a pre-set price per pound of sugar.

2. The EU has strict import limitations and export subsidies. The EU also has price supports that require the European governments to purchase massive amounts of sugar that are then dumped on the world market. The price of sugar in the EU is between two to three times higher than the world price.

3. Sugar consumers in both the United States and the EU must pay much higher prices for sugar than would otherwise be the case. Sugar growers in other countries face two problems: First, they are not allowed to sell much sugar in the United States and the EU. Second, the EU will dump sugar—sell at a price much lower than the cost of production—into their countries. Sugar consumers in other countries benefit, particularly when the EU dumps sugar because they receive the benefit of much lower prices.

USING EYE ON THE U.S ECONOMY

■ The Fluctuating Price of Wheat

The story provides a good example of the price of wheat decreasing over the last 30 years. You can draw supply and demand curves for the wheat market and have students discuss shifts in the curves. You can list the factors that impact the market (technology, productivity, income, and population) and then ask students how the curves will be impacted. Make sure to distinguish between changes in demand (or supply) versus changes in quantity demanded (or supplied). Also make sure your market shows an increase in output and a decrease in price as a result of the shifts!

■ The Changing Farm Economy

This story provides an excellent introduction to the section in the book on "Down on the Farm." Farm prices have decreased as a result of increases in technology and productivity. Highlight the features of changes in fixed costs (shown in Figure 20.4) that "require" farms to be larger. You can have students use the Internet or library to see how the number of people employed on farms has changed over the past 30 years.

■ Farm Subsidies

The data in this article should be extremely interesting to your students. One experiment you can do is make an overhead or handout of the chart with the data. Then, before you reveal it to your students, list a few products—say, sugar, milk, wheat, beef, poultry, and eggs—and ask your class which of these products receives the most support from the government. Try to have you class vote for which product receives the most and which receives the second most as well as which receives the least. Unless you have a classroom full of agricultural experts, it is highly unlikely that your students have any idea that sugar and milk are so heavily subsidized while eggs receive virtually nothing. If you want to expand upon this discussion, you can ask your students why some products receive huge amounts of support and others receive little at all. Although there is probably no definitive answer, the right answer likely looks at the political pressure the different producers can wield.

USING EYE ON THE GLOBAL ECONOMY

■ Farm Subsidies Around the World

This is an interesting story because, similar to the Eye on the U.S. Economy "Farm Subsidies," you can use this story to ask students why they think the subsidies vary so much. Why are subsidies higher in Korea and Switzerland than in New Zealand and Australia? Tell your students that there are probably a variety of reasons, but try to guide them away from thinking of a reason for every country. It is much better to have a theory that applies to many countries rather than just one! Probably a couple of factors that matter are the size of the farming community—too large and the subsidies cost too much and it is too difficult to organize a lobbying group, or too small and no politician cares about the lobby—and the nation's ability to compete on the world food market without a subsidy—nations that find it difficult to compete, say Switzerland, Iceland, and Norway, have more subsidies than nations that find it easy to compete, say New Zealand and Australia.

International Financial Markets

Chapter

21

CHAPTER ROADMAP

■ Where We Are
This chapter is the last in the book. It studies international finance. The concentration is on the balance of payments accounts and the foreign exchange rate.

■ Where We've Been
This chapter primarily uses the supply and demand model, developed in Chapter 4, in an application to the foreign exchange market.

IN THE CLASSROOM

■ Class Time Needed
If you have little or no class discussion, you can cover the material in this chapter in one to one and one half class periods.

An estimate of the time per checklist topic is:

• 21.1 Financing International Trade—20 to 35 minutes

• 21.2 The Exchange Rate—30 to 40 minutes

■ Extended Lecture Outline

21.1 Financing International Trade
A. Balance of Payments Accounts

The **balance of payments accounts** are the accounts in which a nation records its international trading, borrowing, and lending. The balance of payments accounts are the:
1. **Current account,** the record of international receipts and payments for primarily exports and imports. The current account balance equals exports minus imports plus net interest plus net transfers
2. **Capital account,** the record of foreign investment in the United States minus U.S. investment abroad.
3. **Official settlements account,** the record of the change in U.S. official reserves.

B. Borrowers and Lenders, Debtors and Creditors
1. **Net borrower** is a country that is borrowing more from the rest of the world than it is lending to the rest of the world.
2. **Net lender** is a country that is lending more to the rest of the world than the rest of the world is lending to it.
3. **Debtor nation** is a country that during its entire history has borrowed more from the rest of the world than it has lent to the rest of the world and so has a stock of debt it owes to the rest of the world.
4. **Creditor nation** is a country that during its entire history has lent more to the rest of the world than it has borrowed from the rest of the world.

21.2 The Exchange Rate

A. The **foreign exchange market** is where foreign currencies are traded.

  1. The **foreign exchange rate** is the price at which one currency trades for another.

  2. **Currency depreciation** is the fall in the value of one currency in terms of another currency.

  3. **Currency appreciation** is the rise in the value of one currency in terms of another currency.

B. Demand in the Foreign Exchange Market

  Demand depends on the exchange rate, interest rates in the United States and other countries, and the expected future exchange rate.

C. The Law of Demand for Foreign Exchange

  The higher the exchange rate, the smaller the quantity of U.S. dollars demanded. The law of demand is the result of the:

  1. Exports Effect

    The lower the value of the exchange rate, the larger the value of U.S. exports, and so the larger the quantity of dollars demanded on the foreign exchange market.

  2. Expected Profit Effect

    The lower the exchange rate, the larger the expected profit from holding dollars, and so the greater the quantity of dollars demanded on the foreign exchange market.

D. Changes in the Demand for Dollars

  1. Interest Rates in the United States and Other Countries

    The larger the **interest rate differential,** which is the U.S. interest rate minus the foreign interest rate, the more U.S. assets demanded, and hence the greater the demand for U.S. dollars.

  2. The Expected Future Exchange Rate

    Other things remaining the same, the higher the expected future exchange rate, the greater the demand for dollars.

E. Supply in the Foreign Exchange Market

  Supply depends on the exchange rate, interest rates in the United States and other countries, and the expected future exchange rate.

F. The Law of Supply for Foreign Exchange

  The higher the exchange rate, the larger the quantity of U.S. dollars supplied. The law of supply is the result of the:

  1. Imports Effect

    The higher the exchange rate, the larger the value of U.S. imports, and so the larger is the quantity of foreign currency demanded to pay for these imports. And when people buy foreign currency, they supply dollars.

  2. Expected Profit Effect

    The higher the exchange rate, the larger the expected profit from holding a foreign currency, the greater is the quantity of that currency demanded and so the greater is the quantity of dollars supplied in the foreign exchange market.

G. Changes in the Supply of Dollars

  1. Interest Rates in the United States and Other Countries

    The larger the U.S. interest rate differential, the smaller is the demand for foreign assets, and the smaller is the supply of dollars on the foreign exchange market.

  2. The Expected Future Exchange Rate

    The higher the expected future exchange rate, the smaller is the supply of dollars today.

H. Market Equilibrium

Market equilibrium occurs at the (equilibrium) exchange rate such that the quantity of dollars demanded equals the quantity supplied and there is neither a shortage nor a surplus.

I. Changes in the Exchange Rate

The exchange rate changes when either the supply and/or demand for dollars changes.

1. Why the Exchange Rate Is Volatile

Supply and demand are not independent of each other in the foreign exchange market. For example, a change in the expected future exchange rate or a change in the U.S. interest rate differential changes both demand and supply and in opposite directions.

2. A Depreciating Dollar: 1994–1995

During 1994, traders expected the U.S. dollar to depreciate against the yen. They expected a lower exchange rate. As a result, the demand for dollars decreased and the supply of dollars increased.

3. An Appreciating Dollar: 1995–1998

The dollar appreciated against the yen. Interest rates in Japan fell and the yen was expected to depreciate. The demand for yen decreased and the demand for dollars increased, and the supply of dollars decreased.

J. Exchange Rate Expectations

1. Purchasing Power Parity

Purchasing power parity is the situation in which money buys the same amount of goods and services in different currencies.

2. Interest Rate Parity

Interest rate parity is the situation in which the interest rates in one currency equals the interest rate in another currency when exchange rate changes are taken into account.

K. The Fed in the Foreign Exchange Market

1. If the Fed buys dollars (sells foreign currency), the exchange rate appreciates.

2. If the Fed sells dollars (buys foreign currency), the exchange rate depreciates.

3. The Fed cannot indefinitely buy or sell dollars because it either runs out of foreign currency or it accumulates too much foreign currency.

■ Lecture Launchers

1. Sometimes economics teachers are afraid to make analogies to personal finance when it comes to discussing the finance of international trade. The argument is that governments are very different entities than households. That's a good argument. However, there are some similarities that merit examination and facilitate the discussion of international finance. For instance, ask your class what is going on when a household consumes more than its income. They will respond that it is going into debt.

Immediately move to the national level. If a country is importing more than it exports, this is the equivalent of saying that the country is going into debt because exports are the nation's "income" from the rest of the world and imports are the nation's "spending" to the rest of the world. Thus just as a family goes into debt if its consumption exceeds its income, so too does a nation go into debt if its imports exceed its exports. This simple analogy is "safe" and quite helpful to the students!

2. Students generally are interested in the whole topic of exchange rates. They hear of fantastic stories of private individuals making a fortune from the foreign exchange markets. They might read in the news that the president of Malaysia accused George Soros of single-handedly devaluating his country's currency. They might have been invited by someone, either on the Internet or via mail solicitation, to open up a trading account in the foreign exchange market. The allure of riches is quite enticing indeed.

    These facts can provide you with the opportunity to warn your class that although the basics of supply and demand operate in the foreign exchange markets just as they do in any other market, there is a pitfall to avoid. Return to a basic supply and demand scenario, say the market for personal computers. Who does the supplying? Firms. Who does the demanding? Consumers. In other words, suppliers and demanders are different entities.

    Explain that this is *not* the case in the foreign exchange market. Suppose that you plan a trip to Mexico and know in advance that you plan to spend 30,000 pesos on gifts, meals, hotels, taxi fares, and entertainment. You are explicitly demonstrating a demand for 30,000 pesos. If the exchange rate before you leave is 10 pesos to the dollar that means that you will need $3,000 dollars to purchase these pesos. You are a supplier of dollars. Perhaps you are not conscious of this fact but it is nevertheless true. What a strange situation. You are both a demander and a supplier simultaneously! In many ways this makes the analysis simple because it means that we do not have to really worry about two separate foreign exchange markets. Once we speak of a demand for pesos, we know that implies a supply of dollars. Likewise those who bring forth the pesos for your trip to Mexico are not only suppliers of pesos but are also demanders of U.S. dollars. Why else would they give you pesos for dollars unless they intended to use the dollars for some purpose of their own? However, it also complicates the analysis because factors that change the demand for a currency also change its supply. Tell the students to be alert to this fact because it is for this reason that the exchange rate is so volatile.

■ Land Mines

1. It never fails that when I mention the fact that depreciation makes domestic goods and services more attractive to foreigners, at least a handful of students will be excited by this prospect. In fact, the ones that are most excited are generally those from foreign countries. So every now and then a student from one of these countries will propose to me the following: If depreciation is such a good thing (of course, I never said that it was) then why don't governments simply depreciate their own currencies to make their goods and services more competitive on world markets? This question deserves to be taken seriously, even though there are flaws in the argument. Ask the student if a 10 percent depreciation is good enough to get the job done. Honestly, it is difficult to answer this question without actual data. But pursue the line of reason anyway by asking if a 20 percent depreciation would be better than a 10 percent depreciation. The student probably will respond in the affirmative. But then ask, what about a 30 percent, 40 percent or 50

percent depreciation? The student will get the point: You will have eventually depreciated your currency to the point of making it worthless. What's more, now that it is virtually worthless, foreign goods are prohibitively expensive for the domestic consumers! Remind your students that the whole point of exporting goods in the first place is so that a country can earn the foreign exchange necessary to purchase imports. No country makes itself better off by simply exporting. The moral of the story: You can't "export" yourself into prosperity through devaluation.

A good practical example will solidify the argument if your students are still not convinced. A few years ago China considered this very strategy, that is, depreciation. It backed off when it realized that many of the goods and services that it assembles for export (toys, games, and textiles) depend on raw materials purchased from the very countries to which China exports. In other words, a depreciation of China's currency would have meant that China would have had to pay more for its imported raw materials. It didn't take leaders long to put two and two together to realize that this was a recipe for disaster!

ANSWERS TO CHECKPOINT EXERCISES

■ CHECKPOINT 21.1 Financing International Trade

a. The current account balance plus the capital account balance plus the official settlements balance equal zero. The capital account balance is given in the exercise as $600 billion and the official settlements balance is the negative of the change in official reserves, so it equals $10 billion. Therefore the balance of payments formula gives 0 = current account balance + $600 billion + $10 billion, so the current account balance is –$610 billion.
   The official settlements balance was calculated above as $10 billion.
   Finally, to calculate imports, use the definition that the current account balance equals net exports plus net interest income plus net transfers. Net interest income is –$200 billion and net transfers is –$50 billion. The current account balance equals –$610 billion, so the definition gives –$610 billion = net exports + (–$200 billion) + (–$50 billion) so that net exports equals –$360 billion. Net exports are defined as exports minus imports, so with net exports of –$360 and exports of $1,800 billion, imports must be $2,160 billion.
b. The United States has become a larger debtor nation.
c. If imports increased by $100 billion, net exports would equal –$460 billion so the current account balance would become –$710 billion. The balance of payments formula, current account balance plus the capital account balance plus the official settlements balance equal zero, means that 0 = –$710 + capital account balance + $10 billion, so the capital account balance surplus increases by $100 billion to $700 billion.

■ CHECKPOINT 21.2 The Exchange Rate

a. Yesterday a Canadian dollar purchased 75 U.S. cents; today a Canadian dollar buys only 70 U.S. cents. The Canadian dollar buys fewer U.S. cents and so the Canadian dollar has depreciated. The U.S. dollar has appreciated.

b. The main events that might have caused the appreciation of the U.S. dollar and the depreciation of the Canadian dollar are an increase in the U.S. interest rate, a decrease in the Canadian interest rate, or concern that the Canadian dollar will depreciate (the U.S. dollar will appreciate) even more in the future.

c. As pointed out in the second Lecture Launcher, the foreign exchange market is unlike "typical" markets because the factors that affect the supply also affect the demand. Hence the factors listed in part (b) all affected both the demand for Canadian dollars as well as the supply of Canadian dollars. All the factors listed decreased the demand for Canadian dollars and increased the supply.

d. To stabilize the value of the Canadian dollar at 75 U.S. cents, the Bank of Canada would have needed to decrease the supply of Canadian dollars. Hence the Bank of Canada would have needed to buy Canadian dollars.

e. When the Bank of Canada buys Canadian dollars, it decreases Canadian official reserves.

ANSWERS TO CHAPTER CHECKPOINT EXERCISES

1a. Use the definition that $CAB = NX$ + Net interest income + net transfers. Thus $CAB = -\$100$ billion + $(-\$10$ billion$)$ + $\$35$ billion = $-\$85$ billion.

1b. The capital account balance equals foreign investment in Antarctica minus Antarctica's investment abroad, or $\$125$ billion – $\$55$ billion = $\$70$ billion

1c. Use the definition that (current account) + (capital account) + (official settlements account) = 0. So, $(-\$85$ billion$)$ + $(\$70$ billion$)$ + (official settlements account) = 0 means that official settlements account is $\$15$ billion. Thus Antarctica's official reserves decreased by $\$15$ billion.

2a. All of the answers to this question will depend on when you assign the problem so be alert to changes that occur after this book is printed. Unless the U.S. balance of payments position undergoes a large change and a surplus emerges, the last time the United States had a current account surplus was in the second quarter of 1991.

2b. Unless some major change occurs, the United States has a deficit in trade in goods.

2c. Unless some major change occurs, the United States has a surplus in trade in services.

2d. Unless some major change occurs, on net foreigners have invested in the United States over the last decade.

2e. The only issue that might concern the students is the fact that the United States is now a debtor nation. But, as the text points out, U.S. borrowing has gone toward increasing the U.S. capital stock, so the fact that the United States is a debtor nation should be of little concern.

3a. Your students' answers will depend on the nations they select and when you assign the exercise. The key point to look for in the answers is that when explaining why the exchange rate changed, the factors discussed in the book (which is what the students should focus upon!) shifted *both* the demand and supply curves. So, be sure that both the supply and demand curves have been shifted in your students' answers.

3b. Once again, your students answers will vary. A point to note about the answer is that it should be aligned with the answer to part (a). In other words, if in part (a) the student responded that the expected future exchange rate rose and that change increased the current exchange, be certain that in the answer to this part that the student continues to use an increase in the expected future exchange rate.

3c. The exchange rate might have been limited in its change if the central bank of either nation intervened in the foreign exchange market.

3d. In order to determine if the central bank intervened to affect the exchange rate, data on either the sales or purchases of the central bank in the foreign exchange market would precisely answer the question. Absent those data, data on the government's holding of foreign reserves can also be used to indicate the answer.

4a. If the Fed intervenes in the foreign exchange market by selling dollars, it increases the supply of dollars and *depreciates* the exchange rate rather than appreciates it.

4b. If people expect the dollar to appreciate, the demand for dollars immediately increases and the supply immediately decreases, which leads to an immediate appreciation of the U.S. dollar exchange rate.

4c. If the U.S. interest rate differential narrows, the demand for U.S. dollars decreases and the supply increases, which brings about a depreciation of the U.S. dollar exchange rate, not an appreciation.

4d. If the U.S. current account goes into deficit, the value of imports increases relative to the value of exports. In order to import goods and services into the United States, importers supply U.S. dollars so that they can buy foreign exchange. The supply of dollars increases, which depreciates the U.S. exchange rate rather than appreciating it.

ADDITIONAL EXERCISES FOR ASSIGNMENT

■ Questions

1. Explain the major difference between the supply and demand analysis that is used to evaluate foreign exchange markets versus how it is used to evaluate product markets, such as the market for pizza.

■ Answers

1. The major difference in the supply and demand analysis when it is used to examine the foreign exchange market is that the influences that affect supply are not independent of the influences that affect demand. This is not true when applied to product markets. In product markets, factors that affect supply and demand are independent.

ANSWERS TO ECONOMICS IN THE NEWS

■ The Euro Sags

1. The euro is the European currency. It was issued in January, 1999 when European nations had agreed to use a common currency, the Euro.
2. The euro has generally depreciated against the yen.
3. The story suggests that the euro fell because foreign exchange market participants thought that European interest rates would be lowered in the near future. If European interest rates were lowered, the demand for the euro would decrease and so the price of the euro would fall. Hence holding euros would lock in a loss, a situation that traders wanted to avoid. So they sold euros in advance of the decision on the interest rate.
4. With the concern that the price of a euro would be lower in the future, the demand for euros decreased and the supply of euros increased. Thus the demand curve for euros shifted leftward and the supply curve shifted rightward.
5. The ECB (European Central Bank) can raise interest rates in Europe in order to increase the demand for (and decrease the supply of) Euros. So doing would appreciate the Euro. But it would seem at least somewhat foolhardy to raise interest rates and have major domestic effects simply to raise the value of the Euro.

USING EYE ON THE PAST

■ The U.S. Balance of Payments

One good way to start a discussion of this chart is to focus on the last ten years. You can ask your students why the current account deficit for the United States rose in spite of the fact that the economy was quite strong and booming in this period. For some students, this apparent incongruity is difficult to reconcile. One explanation is that with a booming economy, domestic consumers not only increased their consumption of domestically produced goods but foreign-produced goods as well. As long as the increase in imports is moving at a faster clip than an increase in exports, the current account deficit will grow. By the way, the current account narrowed so much in 1990 as a result of the Gulf War because the Allies repaid the U.S. government for many expenses of the Gulf War.

■ The Dollar and the Yen Since 1980

Ask your students what monetary policies the Bank of Japan pursued that might have caused the dollar to appreciate against the yen after 1995. The one that is noteworthy is the zero interest rate policy brought about by expansionary efforts of Japan's central bank. Short-term nominal interest rates in Japan are near zero percent. This fact caused some degree of capital flight as investors sought greater returns elsewhere. The decline in the demand for the yen led to its depreciation against the dollar (the dollar's appreciation).

USING EYE ON THE GLOBAL ECONOMY

■ Current Account Balances Around the World

While it is true that no other country has a current account deficit remotely similar to that of the United States, it is also true that no other country, with the exception of Japan, has an economy the size of the United States. You might want to ask your students to look up the latest real GDP figures for some of the nations listed in the categories so that they can see for themselves the disparities in sheer size of economies. The Web site for the CIA would be a good place to look up this information (www.cia.gov).

■ Purchasing Power Parity

Ask your class why central bank intervention is unwise if purchasing power parity holds in the long run. The answer is that if purchasing power parity holds, currencies that are overvalued will eventually depreciate and currencies that are undervalued will eventually appreciate.

A popular (and fun!) measure of purchasing power parity is the "McDonald's Index." This index, created by *The Economist* magazine, tracks the price of a Big Mac in over 25 nations. Although there are drawbacks to this index (contrary to *The Economist*, a Big Mac is not identical in different nations) but it is still interesting. To get the latest version of the Big Mac index, go to www.economist.com and search for "McDonald's" in *The Economist*.

■ The Sliding Euro

This represents a good opportunity to take a look at the mechanics of how central bank intervention affects the value of a currency. Ask one of your students to trace out how the European Central Bank's efforts unfolded in the last half of 2000. You should get an answer similar to the following. By increasing interest rates on euro-denominated government debt relative to interest rates in other nations, the ECB attracted foreign investors to buy these securities. To do so investors must purchase them using euros. The increased demand for the euro caused it to appreciate.